D1283863

Beyond Training and Development

Enhancing Human Performance through a Measurable Focus on Business Impact

Third Edition

William J. Rothwell

HRD Press, Inc. • Amherst • Massachusetts

Copyright © 2015 by William Rothwell

All rights reserved. No part of this publication may be reproduced or transmitted in any form or by any means, electronic or mechanical, including photocopying, recording, or by information storage and retrieval system, without written permission from the publisher.

Published by: HRD Press, Inc.
22 Amherst Road
Amherst, MA 01002
413-253-3488
800-822-2801 (U.S. and Canada)
413-253-3490 (fax)
www.hrdpress.com

ISBN 978-1-61014-395-0

Editorial services by Sally Farnham
Production services by Jean Miller
Cover design by Eileen Klockars

Dedication

This book is dedicated to my loving and patient wife, Marcelina V. Rothwell, and to my fun-loving daughter, Candice S. Rothwell. They *are* my inspiration.

Contents

List of Exhibits

Preface to the Third Edition

In a bid to please everyone, training and development practitioners too often go along with their customers' ill-advised expectations that they will confine their efforts to providing courses, entertaining employees, making people feel good, and fixing isolated problems. This focus, however, minimizes the importance of integrating training with organizational strategy, assessing learning needs, ensuring the transfer of training from instructional to work settings, evaluating training results, and (most important) achieving performance gains and productivity improvement. It creates a conspiracy of failure in many organizations. Rothwell's *Theory of Visible Activity* states that customers of training think that high-profile activity automatically means results and, therefore, that offering a lot of training automatically improves employee performance. Of course, such a view is mistaken.

Although many training departments have historically been *activity-oriented*, a focus on enhancing human performance is implicitly *results-oriented*. Intensifying that focus *is* a need for training to be offered faster, geared to the quickly changing needs of performers, offered in convenient locales (and online), and prepared in ways intended to harness the advantage of new and even emerging instructional technologies.

The time has come to move beyond training as a quick fix (or fix-all) and to focus instead on applying a wide range of human performance enhancement (HPE) strategies. It is also time to emphasize the strategic and long-term role of HPE efforts and to transform training and development professionals into HPE practitioners. This book is a manual for doing just that.

Sources of Information

As I began writing this book, I decided to explore HPE practices. In this process I consulted several major sources of information:

- **The literature.** I conducted a literature review on HPE, examining particularly what has been written on the subject since 2005 when the second edition of this book was published. I also looked for case study descriptions of what organizations have been doing to apply human performance enhancement.
- **Presentations.** I have presented my views on reinventing the training function at numerous locations around the world. I have done presentations in Singapore, Hong Kong, Beijing, London, Accra, Johannesburg, and many other locations. In the process I fire-tested my views on the subject with live—and highly critical—audiences of training and development professionals and operating managers.
- **Experience.** As a former training director in the public and the private sectors, I draw on my own experiences in this book. I also make use of the experience I have gained while serving as an external consultant to organizations while working as a professor who teaches courses on human performance enhancement, training, and organization development.

My aim in using these sources has been to ensure that this book provides a comprehensive, up-to-date treatment of typical *and* best-in-class HPE (and related) practices.

The Scheme of This Book

Beyond Training and Development, Third Edition is written for those wishing to revolutionize, reengineer, reinvent, or revitalize the training function in their organizations. This book is thus an action manual for change. It should be read by professionals in training and development, organization development, human resources management, human performance enhancement, human performance improvement, and human performance technology. It should also be read by chief executive officers, chief operating officers, general managers, university faculty members who teach in academic training and development programs, operating managers, managers of total quality, team leaders working on process reengineering efforts, and others participating in training or learning activities. In short, this book offers something valuable to just about everybody.

The book is organized in five parts. Part One sets the stage. Consisting of Chapters 1, 2 and 3, it explains the need for trainers—and others—to move beyond training.

Chapter 1 offers a critical view of training as an isolated HPE strategy. The chapter opens with vignettes illustrating typical—and a few atypical—human performance problems. It implies what roles HPE practitioners should play in enhancing human performance. The chapter also lists key problems with traditional training in organizations, reviews trends affecting organizations, and summarizes research on traditional training and development roles and competencies.

Chapter 2 surveys the landscape of HPE. It opens with a case study describing how one major company reinvented training to focus on HPE. The chapter also defines *training, performance,* and *human performance enhancement,* reviews the most widely used methods for analyzing human performance, presents an HPE model, and introduces a competency model to guide HPE professionals. Taken together, the HPE model and the HPE competency model are the key organizing devices for this book. Chapters 4 through 14 are loosely organized around the HPE model and the competencies listed in this chapter.

Chapter 3 offers advice to training and development professionals setting out to transform the training or human resource development (HRD) department or function in their organizations into an HPE department or function. A key point of the chapter is that such a transformation demands a deliberate strategy undertaken to yield long-term impact. Steps in making the transition covered in the chapter include the following:

- making the case for change with trainers and stakeholders
- building awareness of the possibilities
- assessing and building support for change
- creating a flexible road map for change
- building competencies keyed to the change effort

Readers are introduced to the chapter with a warm-up activity to rate how much support exists in their organizations to make such a transformation.

Part Two is titled "Troubleshooting Human Performance Problems and Analyzing Human Performance Improvement Opportunities." Using the new HPE model introduced in Chapter 2, the chapters in this part examine the approaches that HPE professionals may use to answer two key questions about human performance:

1. What is happening?
2. What should be happening?

Chapter 4 examines how HPE professionals analyze present conditions. The chapter opens by explaining what it means to identify *what is happening*. HPE practitioners are also advised to consider what prompted the investigation, how to gather and document facts and perceptions, and how to analyze present conditions.

Chapter 5 explains what it means to assess *what should be happening*. It offers advice about choosing sources of information and methods to answer that question. A key point of the chapter is that, to enhance human performance, trainers and their stakeholders must clearly envision what results they want before they undertake a change effort. Therefore, visioning is critical to identifying what should be happening.

Part Three shows how to discover opportunities for enhancing human performance. Comprising Chapters 6, 7, and 8, the part examines how to clarify gaps in human performance, how to assess their relative importance, how to distinguish symptoms from causes, and how to determine underlying causes of performance gaps.

Chapter 6 describes how to find performance gaps between *what is* (actual) and *what should be* (ideal). The chapter defines the meaning of *performance gap*, explains the possible roles of HPE practitioners in identifying those gaps, and offers some approaches to identifying performance gaps.

Chapter 7 explains how HPE practitioners, working with others in their organizations, can discover the importance of performance gaps. This chapter defines *importance,* explains how to assess consequences, provides some guidance about who should determine importance, and offers some ideas about how to assess present importance and forecast future importance.

Chapter 8 treats a critically important but difficult topic: how to detect the underlying cause(s) of human performance gaps. It is important because no HPE strategy can successfully solve a human performance problem or take advantage of a human performance improvement opportunity unless the underlying cause of the performance gap has been determined. However, it is tricky because performance gaps are usually evidenced more by *symptoms* (noticeable consequences of a problem) than by underlying *root causes* (the reason for the gap's existence). This chapter defines *cause,* explains how to distinguish a cause from a symptom, suggests who should determine the cause(s) of human performance gaps, offers advice about when the cause of a performance gap should be identified, summarizes some approaches to identifying the underlying causes of performance gaps, and explains how—and why—the causes of performance gaps may change over time.

Part Four is entitled "Selecting and Implementing HPE Strategies: Intervening for Change." It comprises Chapters 9 through 13. The chapters in this part explain how to choose and use HPE strategies directed at the four performance quadrants described earlier in the book. Those quadrants are, of course:

1. The organizational environment (the world outside the organization)
2. The work environment (the world inside the organization)
3. The work (how results are achieved)
4. The worker (the individuals doing the work and achieving the results)

Chapter 9 provides a framework for other chapters in Part Four. It offers rules of thumb for selecting one—or several—HPE strategies to solve human performance problems or to seize human performance improvement opportunities. The chapter defines *HPE strategy,* articulates assumptions guiding the selection of HPE strategy, and summarizes a range of possible HPE strategies.

Chapter 10 takes up where Chapter 9 leaves off. It helps HPE practitioners identify the most important external stakeholders of their organizations. The logic of starting HPE by looking outside the organization is simply that, if quality is defined by the customer, then human performance must be defined by the customer as well. The chapter also engages readers in analyzing how well the organization is interacting with external stakeholders, identifying what HPE strategies can improve the organization's interactions with external stakeholders, and considering how HPE strategies should be planned and carried out.

Chapter 11 examines HPE strategies geared to improving the work environment—that is, the world inside the organization. Although many such HPE strategies are possible, the chapter emphasizes only two:

1. Enhancing organizational policies and procedures
2. Enhancing organizational design

Chapter 12 examines HPE strategies geared to improving the work. Here, too, many such HPE strategies are possible. However, I have chosen to direct attention to such well-known and important HPE strategies as

- redesigning jobs or job tasks;
- improving information flow about work-related issues;
- improving feedback to performers;
- using structured practice;
- improving on-the-job and off-the-job training;
- improving the use of equipment and tools;
- using job or performance aids;
- improving reward systems.

Each can be used alone or in combination with other HPE strategies to improve human performance or address underlying cause(s) of human performance problems stemming from the work.

Chapter 13 examines HPE strategies geared to workers—that is, groups or individuals who do the work. Although a conceptual overlap exists between Chapters 12 and 13 in that some methods treated in Chapter 12 can also improve individual performance, I have chosen to concentrate on three HPE strategies in Chapter 13:

1. Identifying and building worker competencies
2. Improving employee selection methods
3. Applying progressive discipline

Part Five consists of only one chapter. Chapter 14 reviews approaches to evaluating HPE strategies. The chapter defines *evaluation*, explains how HPE strategy evaluation methods resemble training evaluation methods, explains how HPE strategy evaluation methods differ from training evaluation methods, and offers three step-by-step models to guide approaches to HPE strategy evaluation before, during, and after HPE implementation.

The book ends with several appendices. They provide various tools for applying information found in the book. Appendix I summarizes competencies for Human Performance Enhancement (HPE) Practitioners; Appendix II gives readers a chance to assess themselves against the competencies listed in Appendix I; Appendix III provides worksheets for analyzing and enhancing human performance; and Appendix IV gives readers a tool for preparing proposals to conduct HPE interventions.

In summation, this book is an action manual for reinventing the training department (or other departments) by placing a new emphasis on the myriad ways by which human performance may be enhanced in organizational settings.

Acknowledgments

Writing a book can be an ordeal. During the process, an author makes new discoveries, reviews (and often discards) old assumptions, and undergoes many bouts of depression about the number of excellent ideas that must be left out of a book to keep its length manageable. Completing the process also requires an author to engage in lively debate with many people.

This section is my opportunity to thank those who engaged me in that lively debate and helped me survive the ordeal. I would therefore like to extend my sincere appreciation to my talented graduate research assistant, Jong Gyu Park, for scouting out for me obscure references on human performance enhancement and related topics and for helping me to secure copyright permissions when needed.

Everyone I have talked to has provided me with valuable advice, information, and encouragement on the rough draft of the book. Though I must shoulder ultimate responsibility for the quality of the final product, they helped me survive the ordeal of writing this book.

Last, I would like to express my appreciation to my publisher, Bob Carkhuff, Jr., who patiently accepted my pleas for extra time despite his eagerness to have the manuscript, and graciously offered ideas to improve the book.

About the Author

William J. Rothwell, Ph.D., SPHR, CPLP Fellow is president of Rothwell & Associates, Inc. and Rothwell & Associates, LLC (see www.rothwellandassociates.com). He is also a professor in the Workforce Education and Development program, Department of Learning and Performance Systems, at The Pennsylvania State University, University Park campus. He has authored, co-authored, edited, and co-edited 300 books, book chapters, and articles—including 87 books.

Before arriving at Penn State in 1993, he had 20 years of work experience as a training director and HR professional in government and in business. He has also worked as a consultant for more than 40 multinational corporations—including Motorola China, General Motors, Ford, and many others. In 2012 he earned ASTD's prestigious Distinguished Contribution to Workplace Learning and Performance Award, and in 2013 ASTD honored him by naming him as a Certified Professional in Learning and Performance (CPLP) Fellow. In 2014, he was given an International Personality Brandlaureate Award for Asia-Pacific (see http://www.thebrandlaureate.com/awards/ibp_bpa.php). His recent books include the following:

- *Organization Development Fundamentals: Managing Strategic Change.* (ATD Press)
- *The Competency Toolkit,* 2 vols., 2nd ed. With J. Graber, D. Dubois, A. Zabellero, C. Haynes, A. Alkhalaf, & S. Sager. (HRD Press, 2014)
- *Creating Engaged Employees: It's Worth the Investment.* With R. Alzhahmi, C. Baumgardner, O. Buchko, W. Kim, J. Myers, & N. Sherwani. (ASTD Press, 2014)
- *Performance Consulting* (Wiley, 2014)
- *Optimizing Talent in the Federal Workforce* (Management Concepts, 2014)
- *ASTD Competency Study: The Training and Development Profession Redefined* (ASTD, 2013)
- *Becoming an Effective Mentoring Leader: Proven Strategies for Building Excellence in Your Organization* (McGraw-Hill, 2013)
- *Talent Management: A Step-by-Step Action-Oriented Approach Based on Best Practice* (HRD Press, 2012)
- The edited three-volume *Encyclopedia of Human Resource Management* (Wiley/Pfeiffer, 2012)
- *Lean but Agile: Rethink Workforce Planning and Gain a True Competitive Advantage* (Amacom, 2012)
- *Invaluable Knowledge: Securing Your Company's Technical Expertise-Recruiting and Retaining Top Talent, Transferring Technical Knowledge, Engaging High Performers* (Amacom, 2011)
- *Competency-Based Training Basics* (ASTD Press, 2010)

- *Effective Succession Planning: Ensuring Leadership Continuity and Building Talent from Within*, 4th ed. (Amacom, 2010)
- *Practicing Organization Development*, 3rd ed. (Pfeiffer, 2009)
- *The Manager's Guide to Maximizing Employee Potential: Quick and Easy Ways to Build Talent Every Day* (Amacom, 2009)
- *Basics of Adult Learning* (ASTD, 2009)
- *HR Transformation* (Davies-Black, 2008)
- *Working Longer* (Amacom, 2008)
- *Cases in Government Succession Planning: Action-Oriented Strategies for Public-Sector Human Capital Management, Workforce Planning, Succession Planning, and Talent Management* (HRD Press, 2008)

William Rothwell can be reached by email at wjr9@psu.edu and by phone at 814-863-2581. He is located at 310B Keller Building, University Park, PA 16803.

Advance Organizer for This Book

Complete the following assessment before you read this book. Use it to help you assess the need for human performance enhancement (HPE) in your organization. You may also use it as a quick reference to topics in the book that are of special importance to you now.

Directions: For each activity listed in the left column below, rate how well your organization performs the activity in the center column. Think of HPE in your organization as you believe it is and not as you think it should be. Use this scale:

0 = Not applicable to my organization
1 = Performed not at all well in my organization
2 = Performed adequately in my organization
3 = Performed well in my organization
4 = Performed very well in my organization

When you finish, score and interpret the results using the instructions appearing at the end of this Advance Organizer. Then be prepared to share your responses with others in your organization as a starting point for planning. If you would like to learn more about one of the items, refer to the number in the far right column to find the chapter in this book in which the subject is discussed.

Activities Related to Human Performance Enhancement						
How well does your organization apply the principles of human performance enhancement routinely to...	**Scoring of Your Organization**					**Chapter**
1. Analyzing what is happening when human performance *does* match expectations or other requirements?	0	1	2	3	4	4
2. Envisioning what should be happening when human performance *does not* match expectations or other requirements?	0	1	2	3	4	5
3. Clarifying present and future performance gaps?	0	1	2	3	4	6
4. Determining the importance of performance gaps?	0	1	2	3	4	7
5. Identifying the underlying causes of performance gaps?	0	1	2	3	4	8
6. Selecting human performance enhancement strategies?	0	1	2	3	4	9

Advance Organizer (concluded)

Activities Related to Human Performance Enhancement	Scoring of Your Organization					Chapter
7. Implementing human performance enhancement strategies to address organizational environment problems/opportunities?	0	1	2	3	4	10
8. Implementing human performance enhancement strategies to address *work* problems/ opportunities?	0	1	2	3	4	11
9. Implementing human performance enhancement strategies to address work environment problems/opportunities?	0	1	2	3	4	12
10. Implementing human performance enhancement strategies to address *worker* problems/ opportunities?	0	1	2	3	4	13
11. Evaluating human performance enhancement strategies?	0	1	2	3	4	14
12. Preparing for the future of human performance environment in your organization?	0	1	2	3	4	Epilogue
TOTAL: (Add all columns to the right and place the sum in the box at right)						

SCORING

48–37 Your organization is using human performance enhancement already.

36–25 While your organization is using some principles of human performance enhancement, improvement can be made. Consider an action plan for improvement.

24–13 Your organization is not really using many principles of human performance enhancement. Consider developing a plan to do so.

12–0 Your organization is not using any principles of human performance enhancement. Develop an improvement plan.

Part One: The Need to Move beyond Training

CHAPTER 1: Why Training Is Not Enough

CHAPTER 2: What Is Human Performance Enhancement (HPE)?

CHAPTER 3: Transforming a Training Department into a Human Performance Enhancement (HPE) Department

CHAPTER 4: Analyzing *What Is* Happening

CHAPTER 5: Envisioning *What Should Be* Happening

CHAPTER 6: Clarifying Present and Future Performance Gaps

CHAPTER 7: Determining the Importance of Performance Gaps

CHAPTER 8: Identifying the Underlying Causes of Performance Gaps

CHAPTER 9: Selecting Human Performance Enhancement (HPE) Strategies

CHAPTER 10: Implementing Human Performance Enhancement (HPE) Strategies to Address Organizational Environment Problems or Opportunities

CHAPTER 11: Implementing Human Performance Enhancement (HPE) Strategies to Address Work Problems or Opportunities

CHAPTER 12: Implementing Human Performance Enhancement (HPE) Strategies to Address Work Environment Problems or Opportunities

CHAPTER 13: Implementing Human Performance Enhancement (HPE) Strategies to Address Worker Problems or Opportunities

CHAPTER 14: Evaluating Human Performance Enhancement (HPE) Strategies

Chapter 1
Why Training Is Not Enough

How does your organization manage employee training? Read the following vignettes and, on a separate sheet of paper, record how your organization would solve the problem presented in each. If you can offer an effective solution to all the vignettes, then your company may already be effectively managing training; otherwise, it may have an urgent need to take a fresh look at reinventing training practices to emphasize human performance enhancement (HPE).

Introductory Vignettes

1. Chief executive officer (CEO) Landers Meriwether calls Mary Johnson, the corporate director of training and development. Here is a brief transcript of the phone conversation:

   Meriwether: We have just hired consulting firm X to help us install a customer service improvement effort in the company. We need to offer training as a first step to make everyone aware of the importance of high-quality customer service. Can you make that happen?

   Johnson: Yes. How many people do we want to train, and how quickly do they need to be trained?

   Meriwether: We need everybody in the organization trained as soon as possible.

   Johnson: No problem.

2. Training director Juanita Adams receives a request from business manager Landa Henderson to conduct training on appropriate ways to dress for work for all employees in the organization. The reason: That morning, when Henderson arrived at work, she found a customer service representative standing at the customer service desk wearing a shirt emblazoned with the inscription *Things Just Happen*. Henderson feels that the inscription sends the wrong message to customers and that refresher training on what to wear to work should be delivered to all employees. Thrilled to receive a request, Adams agrees that training is warranted in the situation. She also agrees to develop a proposal to bring in an image consultant to design and deliver training on appropriate ways to dress.

3. Mary Landers is the training director for a large company that recently downsized. She was just asked by George Rawlings, vice president of human resources and Mary's supervisor, to conduct training on a new performance management system for all executives, middle managers, and supervisors. Aware of how difficult it may be to get voluntary attendance at this training, Mary proposes making attendance at the training sessions mandatory. George agrees and assures her that he will obtain the chief executive officer's support to make sure everyone attends.

4. Morton Adams earned a graduate degree in training and development. He also has extensive work experience in training. He was recently hired as a training and development professional in a medium-size organization. A believer in taking charge of his own new employee orientation, he decides to ask his supervisor, Harriet Harper, a few questions about the company's training and development practices. Here are his questions:

    - How does the training and development department contribute to achieving the organization's strategic objectives? To meeting or exceeding customer requirements?
    - How does training and development conduct training needs assessment?
    - How does training and development prove the return on training investments?
    - How are problems that should be solved by training distinguished from problems that should be solved by management action?
    - How do operating managers hold employees accountable on their jobs for what they learn in training?

    To his surprise, Morton learns that the training and development department has made no effort to link what it does to the organization's strategic objectives or show how it contributes to meeting or exceeding customer requirements. Further, the training and development department does not assess training needs systematically, does not try to demonstrate a financial return on training investments, and does not distinguish training from management problems. Line managers are not asked to hold employees accountable on their jobs for what they learned in training, and the training and development department makes no effort to furnish line managers with tools or techniques enabling them to do that.

5. Marina Vostop is the general manager of a large plant in the northeastern United States. Like many managers, she is working hard to improve business processes, enhance customer service, and upgrade product quality. She believes that she can achieve breakthrough productivity improvements by introducing team-based management to her plant. She has read many articles and a few books about teams, visited plants in the industry to see how they installed employee teams, and discussed approaches to team installations with production and human resources staff members in the plant and at corporate headquarters.

Marina asks the corporate training and development department to help in this effort. She is told by representatives of that department that "we can do nothing unless we can first prove that it will yield a measurable financial return on the investment." She is asked to supply figures to show what financial returns in productivity improvements will be realized by introducing teams to her plant. Marina explains that she cannot prove productivity improvement for a change that has yet to be made. She is then told to "try piloting some teams, get some financial figures we can use to justify the training effort, and call us back."

Marina is stunned. Like many managers, she believes that training and development departments should show financial returns from their efforts. However, she also thinks there must be ways to do that that allow partnering with line management on innovative efforts designed to improve human performance.

Problems with Traditional Approaches to Training

As these vignettes illustrate, traditional approaches to training can be fraught with problems in today's organizations. These problems can usually be classified into four general categories. First, training often lacks focus. Second, it lacks management support. Third, it is not always planned and conducted systematically in ways consistent with what have long been known to be effective approaches to training design. Fourth and last, it is not effectively linked to other organizational initiatives. Each problem warrants additional attention because each may dramatize the need to move beyond traditional training—and training as a standalone change strategy—to focus on more holistic approaches to enhancing human performance.

Training Lacks Focus

What should training be called? This question has larger implications than may be immediately apparent. The issue amounts to much more than a question about semantics or definitions; rather, it goes to the heart of what training and development professionals should be doing. Confusion over the name of the training field underscores training's lack of focus.

The training field has been called by many different names, including the following:

- training
- education
- development
- training and development
- employee education
- staff development
- personnel development
- in-service education
- human resource development

- human performance technology
- human performance improvement
- organization development
- human performance enhancement
- workplace learning and performance
- learning and performance

Job titles have also reflected these differences in terminology.

The point is that what training and development professionals are called affects the roles they are expected to play. Those roles are not always clear—and frequently lack focus. They may even be inappropriate.

If you do not believe that, ask a group of line managers to do a word association activity with each term in the list in Exhibit 1-1. Alternatively, try that activity yourself and then ask some peers in your organization or in other organizations to do likewise (see Exhibit 1-1). Then summarize the individual associations for each term and feed them back to the participants. Ask them which associations do—and do not—match up to what they believe should be the role of training and development professionals in today's organizations. The odds are great that *training* is a limiting term that does not do justice to the broad and challenging range of roles that training and development professionals play today to enhance human performance in their organizations.

Exhibit 1-1. A Word Association Activity

Directions: Ask a group of line managers or training and development professionals to do a word association activity. For each word listed in the left column, ask participants to give the first word or phrase that enters their minds when they hear the word. When they finish, ask participants to call out the words/phrases they identified for each word. Write their responses on a flipchart. Then compare them to see if common themes emerge. If so, ask participants whether they believe these associations match up to the role that the training function should be playing in the organization.

Word or Phrase	Associations (Words or Phrases)
Training	
Education	
Development	
Training and development	
Employee education	
Staff development	
Personnel development	
In-service education	
Human resource development	
Human performance technology	
Human performance improvement	
Organization development	
Human performance enhancement	

Training Lacks Management Support

Ask any group of training and development professionals to list the biggest problems they face on their jobs, putting the greatest single problem they face at the top of the list. There is a good chance that "lack of management support" will rank high—if not highest—on the list (see Exhibit 1-2).

Exhibit 1-2. What Are the Biggest Problems of Trainers?

Directions: Ask a group of training and development professionals to list the biggest problems they encounter on their jobs. Prioritize the list, with the most important problem appearing as number 1 on the list. When you finish, compare the participants' individual responses. If you wish, write their responses on a flipchart. Then compare them to see if common themes and priorities emerge. If so, ask participants why they believe such problems exist—and what should be done to solve them.

Priority Number	Problem Description
1	
2	
3	
4	
5	
6	
7	

Why does training so frequently lack management support? There are many reasons. For one thing, training may not be perceived as

- important;
- an effective strategy for introducing or consolidating change;
- worth the time it may require;
- well designed;
- credible;
- work- or job-related;
- quick enough in response time;
- effective, considering the results typically realized from it.

Building management support is a time-consuming effort. Often it must begin with the managers rather than with a sales effort by training and development professionals. Managers must value human contributions to organizational productivity. They must also value efforts to improve human performance and feel that such efforts are just as important as undertakings intended to improve the organization's financial, marketing, and production/service delivery performance. From that point, training and development professionals can take additional steps to build management support by proving that specific training projects can pay off. Customers of training efforts should be involved in many, if not all, steps in the training process so that they have shared ownership in the results eventually achieved.

On the other hand, if managers do not value human contributions and do not believe that investments in them can yield measurable productivity improvement, then the problem resides not with training and development professionals but with themselves. They may miss opportunities for achieving dramatic breakthroughs in productivity improvement. Little can be done to convince some hard-eyed skeptics, so training and development professionals should work with those who are more supportive of human performance enhancement and who are willing to champion such efforts.

Training Is Not Conducted Systematically

Over the years, systematic models for instructional design and development have been devised that, if properly applied, will achieve demonstrable results. Many such models exist, but they all have certain features in common.[1] Each step in training or instructional design should be systematically linked to other steps.[2]

As a first step, training and development professionals should always analyze human performance problems or improvement opportunities to distinguish those that lend themselves to training solutions from those that do not. Training will solve only problems resulting from an individual's lack of knowledge, skill, or appropriate attitude; training will *not* solve problems stemming from poor management practices such as lack of adequate planning, lack of communication of job performance standards or work expectations, lack of feedback, or lack of supervision.

As a second step, training and development professionals should analyze who will receive training, what working conditions will exist when learners try to apply on their jobs what they learned, and how work expectations will be measured to provide the basis for judging work performance.

Third, training and development professionals should assess training needs to clarify gaps between what performers should know, do, or feel and what they already know, do, or feel. From this gap, training and development professionals should take the fourth step, clarifying instructional objectives to articulate exactly what learners should know, do, or feel when they complete training. The fifth step is establishing measurement criteria by which to assess success in training and sequencing instructional objectives for presentation to learners. Sixth, training and development professionals should decide whether to make, buy, or buy and modify instructional materials to achieve the instructional objectives. The seventh step is testing the instructional materials to ensure that they work and revising them to make them more effective with the targeted learners. The eighth step is delivering the training to learners. The ninth and last step is evaluating results and feeding the results back into step 1. These steps are depicted in Exhibit 1-3.

Unfortunately, training and development professionals do not always follow these steps. Some or all are often omitted, sometimes because training and development professionals have not been trained themselves on effective approaches to designing and delivering instruction. (Many trainers are promoted from within, and their immediate organizational superiors are unaware that they should receive instruction on training.) Sometimes training and development professionals are told to deliver training in such short time spans that they have no time to carry out instructional design rigorously and systematically, thus sacrificing effectiveness for speed; sometimes they are judged by participant reactions only or by visible activities, such as number of students who attend training classes, rather than by more effective, deliberative measures of how well results are achieved.

Whatever the causes, training is frequently designed and delivered in ways that do not match what is known about effective approaches to training. Few organizations conduct systematic evaluation of training.

Exhibit 1-3. A Model of Instructional Systems Design (ISD)

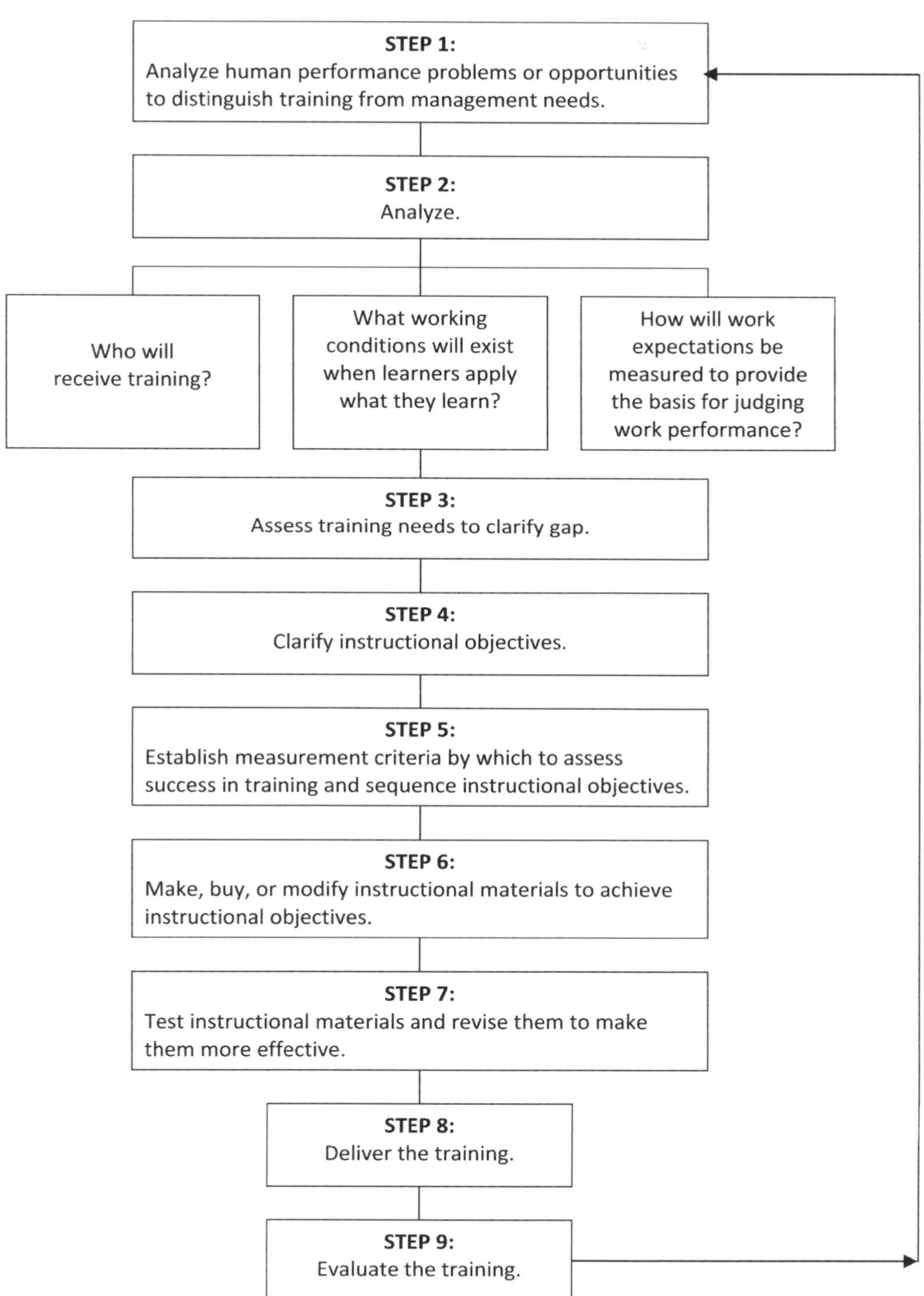
STEP 1:
Analyze human performance problems or opportunities to distinguish training from management needs.
STEP 2:
Analyze.
Who will receive training?
What working conditions will exist when learners apply what they learn?
How will work expectations be measured to provide the basis for judging work performance?
STEP 3:
Assess training needs to clarify gap.
STEP 4:
Clarify instructional objectives.
STEP 5:
Establish measurement criteria by which to assess success in training and sequence instructional objectives.
STEP 6:
Make, buy, or modify instructional materials to achieve instructional objectives.
STEP 7:
Test instructional materials and revise them to make them more effective.
STEP 8:
Deliver the training.
STEP 9:
Evaluate the training.

Training Is Not Linked to Other Organizational Initiatives

Training is sometimes approached as an isolated effort that is not linked to, or integrated with, other organizational initiatives, such as corporate strategy, policy, rewards, or promotions. The frequently disappointing results are sometimes blamed on the training—or, worse, on the training and development professionals spearheading the effort.

Perhaps the best examples of this problem are so-called *sheep dip training* experiences in which the same training is delivered to everyone indiscriminately to build awareness. Almost every experienced training and development professional has had the misfortune of conducting at least some sheep dip training, though few are proud to admit it. The reason: sheep dip training is rarely effective.

Take, for instance, training designed to inform employees, supervisors, and managers about a law, such as the Affordable Care Act. Such training is often designed around explaining the provisions of the new law or regulation. Training and development professionals may not effectively translate what the new law or regulation means to the learners in their work-related activities. When that happens, the training is not linked to or supported by other organizational initiatives. The result is little or no change in what people do.

In contrast, effective training is built using the steps described in Exhibit 1-3. It is also systematically and deliberately tied to other organizational initiatives, such as employees' job descriptions, performance appraisals, selection decisions, transfer decisions, promotion decisions, succession planning efforts, and compensation or reward decisions.

Trends Affecting Organizations

Organizations, and their training programs, have been affected by many trends in recent years.[3] Each trend has created the need for training professionals to take a new look at what they do and has created an impetus for moving beyond training as a solitary change strategy and instead focusing on more holistic approaches to enhancing human performance.

Four trends have exerted perhaps the most profound influence on organizations. First, they are being challenged to keep pace with rapid external environmental change. Second, efforts are under way to establish high-performance work environments that are optimally conducive to human productivity. Third, work activities are increasingly being organized in innovative ways, centering on teams or contingent or temporary workers or relying on outsourcing. Fourth, employees themselves are finding that they must prepare themselves for continually upgrading their competencies in real time. Each trend is a driving force behind holistic approaches to improving human performance. Of course, other trends are important as well.

Trend 1: Keeping Pace with Rapid External Environmental Change. "There is no prescription which says it outright," writes Tom Peters in *Thriving on Chaos,* "yet it lurks on every page. It is the true revolution to which the title refers. The world has not just `turned upside down.' It is turning every which way at an accelerating pace."[4] Peters' central point is that increasingly rapid external environmental change has become commonplace. Evidence can be seen in dynamically changing customer needs and expectations, strategies for coping with those changes, and innovative organizational structures.

Everything has turned topsy-turvy. There is no time for slow, inflexible approaches to coping with or anticipating change. Indeed, an organization's ability to respond quickly to change has become a competitive advantage.[5] That means that organizations must find faster ways to innovate, take advantage of innovation, adapt to changing competitive landscapes, and adapt to (or even anticipate) the human changes linked to competitive, technological, and social change.

Traditional training approaches rarely work anymore as the only effective tool for helping people meet the competitive challenges they face. One reason is that traditional training approaches—and even well-designed online approaches to training—are slow and require too much time to design and deliver. Worse yet, productive employees have to be taken off line to participate in traditional training experiences or else sacrifice diminishing personal time off-the-job to do it. That is particularly problematic in downsized organizations in which managers cannot easily justify pulling stressed-out people away from their overwhelming workloads to attend corporate schoolhouses.

Training and development professionals must find better ways to design and deliver training, ways that permit training to occur just in time for it to be applied.[6] Moreover, a more complete toolbox of change strategies—including but not limited to training—must be found to help people adapt to, or anticipate, change. One way is to encourage planned on-the-job training;[7] another is to encourage learners to take charge more assertively of their own self-directed on-the-job learning.[8]

Trend 2: Establishing High-Performance Work Environments. As total quality guru W. Edwards Deming wrote in his classic book *Out of the Crisis,* "The supposition is prevalent the world over that there would be no problems in production or service if only our production workers would do their jobs in the way that they were taught. Pleasant dreams. The workers are handicapped by the system, and the system belongs to management."[9] As little as 20 percent of all human performance problems is attributable to individual employees; as much as 80 percent of all such problems is attributable to the work environments or systems in which employees work. Effective human performance enhancement methods should therefore begin by examining the strengths and weaknesses of work environments rather than individual deficiencies or proficiencies.

Efforts to establish effective work environments have led to continuing interest in *high-performance workplaces* (HPW).[10] Although defined in various ways, an HPW is usually typified by flexibility, organizational practices that support prompt decision making, and few layers of command. In an HPW, employees are empowered to meet or exceed customer needs and are supplied with the right resources at precisely the right times to perform optimally. The HPW should be of interest to trainers and HPE practitioners alike for the simple reason that, if workers are performing in an HPW, they are less likely to experience any performance problems created by the organizational context.

The U.S. Department of Labor (DOL) conducted a classic multiyear research study of high-performance workplaces and identified criteria by which such workplaces may be identified (the criteria are listed in Exhibit 1-4).[11] Note in the exhibit that the criteria are organized into four major categories:

I. Skills and information

II. Participation, organization, and partnership

III. Compensation, security, and work environment

IV. Putting it all together

Exhibit 1-4. U.S. Department of Labor High Performance Workplace Criteria

I. Skills and Information			
I.1	**Training and continuous learning**	I.1.1	Investments in training and employee development constitute a higher proportion of payroll than they do for competitors.
		I.1.2	There are programs to support continuous learning (e.g., job rotation and cross-functional team training).
		I.1.3a	Training program effectiveness is measured.
		I.1.3b	Training programs are effective.
I.2	**Information sharing**	I.2.1	All workers receive information on operating results, financial goals, and organizational performance.
		I.2.2	Employees are appropriately trained to apply information on the organization's operating results, financial goals, and organizational performance.
		I.2.3	There are multiple mechanisms by which internal communication occurs so that information flows up, down, and across the organization.

Exhibit 1-4 (continued)

II. Participation, Organization, and Partnership			
II.1	**Employee participation**	II.1.1	Workers are actively involved in continuously improving their work process(es) and redefining their jobs.
		II.1.2	Workers can rapidly modify their work processes to correct quality, safety, or other problems.
		II.1.3	Workers are actively involved in problem solving, selecting new technology, modifying the product or service, and meeting with customers.
		II.1.4	When individuals or teams make suggestions, they always receive feedback about their suggestions.
II.2	**Organization structure**	II.2.1	The organization has recently made one or more efforts to reduce layers of management.
		II.2.2	Most workers are organized into work teams with substantial autonomy.
		II.2.3	There are cross-functional teams or other mechanisms to share innovative ideas across organizational boundaries.
II.3	**Worker management partnerships**	II.3.1	Workers and their representatives are partners in decision making on a range of issues traditionally decided solely by managers (e.g., new technology, quality, and safety).
		II.3.2a	If the organization is unionized, the union-management relationship has moved toward joint participation and decision making.
		II.3.2b	If the organization is unionized, collective bargaining is based on interest-based techniques and cooperative problem solving.
		II.3.3	If the organization is unionized, the company and the union have engaged in innovative collective bargaining arrangements.

Exhibit 1-4 (continued)

III. Compensation, Security, and Work Environment			
III.1	**Compensation linked to performance and skills**	III.1.1	The organization's incentive system incorporates new ways of rewarding workers.
		III.1.2	Individual workers or work teams receive financial rewards when they improve the product or work process or make other improvements.
		III.1.3	Individual compensation is tied to both individual and corporate performance.
		III.1.4	Executive pay is tied to corporate (or business unit) performance.
III.2	**Employment security**	III.2.1	Comprehensive organization employment planning strategies and policies exist in order to minimize or avoid worker layoffs.
		III.2.2	If layoffs have occurred in recent years, the organization has actively helped laid-off workers find new jobs.
		III.2.3	The organization has a stated policy that workers will not suffer adverse effects from suggestions that result in productivity gains.
III.3	**Supportive work environment**	III.3.1	The company attracts and retains a talented workforce. (**Issue to consider:** Why do people leave?)
		III.3.2	There are policies and programs in place to encourage better employee morale and greater workforce commitments. (**Issue to consider:** What practices are in place to ensure that all morale problems are promptly and systematically addressed?)
		III.3.3	Employees are actively involved in designing and implementing health and safety policies and programs.
		III.3.4	Accident rates in this organization are below the industry average.
		III.3.5	Family-supportive policies are in place (e.g., flexible work schedules, child care, and/or elder care).
		III.3.6	The organization actively hires, trains, retrains, and promotes a diverse workforce.

Exhibit 1-4 (concluded)

	IV. Putting It All Together
IV.1	The company fully integrates its human resources policies and workplace practices with other essential business strategies.
IV.2	Quality and continuous improvement efforts are meshed with training, work organization, employee involvement, and alternative compensation programs.
IV.3a	Workers are involved in the design and purchase of new technologies.
IV.3b	Workers have the opportunity to modify the technologies they use.
IV.3c	Employees receive adequate training to use new technologies effectively.

Source: *The Road to High Performance Workplaces* (Washington, DC: Office of the American Workplace, U.S. Department of Labor, 1995).

The criteria are further subdivided into 13 second-level and 31 third-level categories.

By focusing on creating workplaces that are conducive to optimum employee performance, employers can maximize organizational productivity while minimizing finger pointing for lower-than-expected production levels or quality measures.[12]

As interest in HPW grows, training and development professionals may find that they need competencies beyond those they have traditionally needed to carry out their jobs effectively. Installing and maintaining HPWs requires training and development professionals to acquire competencies associated with facilitating group-oriented rather than individually oriented change efforts. Generally speaking, the competencies needed to work effectively with group change efforts have historically been associated with organization development (OD).[13] After all, OD focuses on changing groups or organizations.

Trend 3: Organizing Work Activities in Innovative Ways. Organizations are revolutionizing the way they structure work, shifting from narrowly defined jobs to teams responsible for entire work processes. One aim in doing that is to give workers more control over the work process from start to finish in order to build their pride in excellence.

Another aim is to streamline processing time so that fewer steps are needed during production or service delivery. Innovative work design approaches include developing teams in which all members are cross-trained so that they function interdependently and interchangeably, outsourcing work so that the organization can focus on only those core processes that it can do most cost effectively, and employing flexible staffing that relies on temporary workers and external consultants who are brought into organizations on a short-term basis.

Against the backdrop of these trends, traditional training approaches focused on changing individuals are becoming less appropriate. Planned learning now works best when it is organized around team-related issues and cross-training for team work activities. Training for outsourced work is minimal, though it may be necessary to train some suppliers. Training for temporary workers poses a special challenge, since it must be performed just in time to maximize the productivity of people whose stay in the work setting is typically brief. Since companies wish to reduce their investment in developing people not employed by them on a permanent basis, some place most or all of the burden for training temporary workers on the vendors that supply those workers.

Trend 4: Upgrading Employee Competencies in Real Time. Given the continuing trend toward downsizing organizations to increase productivity and profits and to improve communication, individuals are finding that they must assume a proactive role in their own development. No longer can they safely assume a passive role, depending on their employers to supply infrequent training experiences or direct their career goals. Instead, they must shoulder responsibility for their own self-directed learning. Otherwise, they will be ill equipped for the marketplace should they find themselves suddenly thrust into it by an unexpected forced layoff.

Traditional training approaches have tended to minimize or marginalize the learner's role in every step of designing, delivering, and evaluating instruction.[14] Rarely are learners involved in analyzing human performance problems or improvement opportunities; clarifying who should receive training; crafting the training so that it will dovetail with the working conditions in which performers must apply what they have learned on their jobs; clarifying the work expectations that will be the foundation for judging learner job performance; assessing training needs; formulating instructional objectives; establishing measurement criteria by which to assess success in training; sequencing instructional objectives for presentation to learners; making, buying or modifying instructional materials to achieve instructional objectives; testing training materials to ensure that they work; revising training materials to make them more effective; delivering training; or evaluating results. However, learners must be involved in training design and empowered to learn on their own in the future.

Against this backdrop, the traditional role of training and development professionals and managers must change. They must facilitate, rather than direct, planned learning. Building learner competence in learning how to learn is thus becoming more important.[15] So is the use of approaches such as action learning in which learners are involved in designing and delivering instruction.[16]

What Have Training and Development Professionals Historically Done?

Before turning to a possible new role for training and development professionals, let us consider what training professionals have traditionally been expected to do in organizational settings. One way to do that is to review the competencies of training and development (T & D) professionals. (It is worth noting that, just as HPE professionals are variously called performance consultants, human performance technologists, and human performance improvement practitioners, so too are training and development professionals variously called by such other names as trainers, human resource development (HRD) practitioners, workplace learning and performance professionals, learning and development professionals, and learning and performance practitioners.)

A brief summary of some important studies follows.

Models for HRD Practice

In 1989, the American Society for Training and Development published *Models for HRD Practice.*[17] The study was led by Patricia McLagan and focused attention on human resources development (HRD) in addition to training. According to McLagan's landmark research, HRD was defined by the study as "the integrated use of training and development, organization development, and career development to improve individual, group, and organizational effectiveness."[18]

The 1989 study identified the following 11 roles carried out by HRD professionals:[19]

- researcher
- marketer
- organization change agent
- needs analyst
- program designer
- HRD materials developer
- instructor/facilitator
- individual career development adviser
- administrator
- evaluator
- HRD manager

The study identified 35 core competencies necessary for HRD work: (1) adult learning understanding, (2) career development theories and techniques understanding, (3) competency identification skill, (4) computer competence, (5) electronic systems skill, (6) facilities skill, (7) objectives preparation skill, (8) performance observation skill, (9) subject matter understanding, (10) training and development theories and techniques understanding, (11) research skill, (12) business understanding, (13) cost-benefit analysis skill, (14) delegation skill, (15) industry understanding, (16) organization behavior understanding, (17) organization development theories and techniques understanding,

(18) organization understanding, (19) project management skill, (20) records management skill, (21) coaching skill, (22) feedback skill, (23) group process skill, (24) negotiation skill, (25) presentation skill, (26) questioning skill, (27) relationship building skill, (28) writing skill, (29) data reduction skill, (30) information search skill, (31) intellectual versatility, (32) model building skill, (33) observing skill, (34) self-knowledge, and (35) visioning skill.[20]

ASTD Models for Human Performance Improvement

ASTD Models for Human Performance Improvement was a research-based study. One important feature of this study is that the human performance improvement (HPI) process can be carried out by many people—HRD professionals, operating managers, and others who care about improving human performance. It was thus not a competency study limited to HRD or workplace learning and performance (WLP) professionals alone. Its implications are broader: anyone can play the role of a performance improvement practitioner.

The study defined *human performance improvement* (HPI) as "the systematic process of discovering and analyzing important human performance gaps, planning for future improvements in human performance, designing and developing cost-effective and ethically justifiable interventions to close performance gaps, implementing the interventions, and evaluating the financial and nonfinancial results."[21] The *HPI process model*, introduced in this study, was defined as "a six-step model that describes key steps in conducting human performance improvement work."[22] The steps in the HPI process model included the following:[23]

- **Step 1 – Performance Analysis:** The first step involves "identifying and describing past, present, and future human performance gaps."
- **Step 2 – Cause analysis:** "The root causes of a past, present, or future performance gap are identified."
- **Step 3 – Selection of Appropriate Interventions:** "Here people who do human performance work consider possible ways to close past, present, or possible future performance gaps by addressing their root cause(s)."
- **Step 4 – Implementation:** In this step, "people who human performance improvement work help the organization prepare to install an intervention."
- **Step 5 – Change Management:** "During this step, people who do human performance improvement work should monitor the intervention as it is being implemented."
- **Step 6 – Evaluation and Measurement:** "At this point, those conducting human performance improvement work take stock of the results achieved by the intervention."

Four roles are identified in the study:[24] (1) *analyst*: "conducts troubleshooting to isolate the cause(s) of human performance gaps and identifies areas in which human performance can be improved"; (2) *intervention specialist*: "selects appropriate interventions to address the root cause(s) of performance gaps"; (3) *change manager*: "ensures that interventions are implemented in ways consistent with desired results and that they help individuals and groups achieve results"; and (4) *evaluator*: "assesses the impact of interventions and follows up on changes made, actions taken, and results achieved in order to provide participants and stakeholders with information about how well interventions are being implemented. The study also listed 38 competencies and 95 terminal and enabling outputs linked to the work of HPI practitioners. A casebook was subsequently published that demonstrated how the HPI process is being used in organizational settings.[25]

ASTD Models for Learning Technologies

ASTD Models for Learning Technologies was a research-based study that directed attention to the impact of changing technology on the roles of HRD professionals.[26] Its focus was thus narrower than its predecessors. Its purpose was not to examine all the roles, competencies and outputs of training and development (T & D) or human resource development (HRD). Instead, it examined how traditional roles, competencies, and outputs are influenced by new, emerging, and cutting-edge technologies.

ASTD Models for Workplace Learning and Performance

ASTD Models for Workplace Learning and Performance introduced the role of workplace learning and performance (WLP).[27] Rothwell, Sanders, and Soper defined it as "the integrated use of learning and other interventions for the purpose of improving individual and organizational performance. It uses a systematic process of analyzing performance and responding to individual, group, and organizational needs. WLP creates positive, progressive change within organizations by balancing human, ethical, technological, and operational considerations."[28] It lists seven roles of WLP professionals:[29]

- A *manager* plans, organizes, schedules, monitors, and leads the work of individuals and groups to attain desired results; facilitates the strategic plan; ensures that WLP is aligned with organizational needs and plans; and ensures accomplishment of the administrative requirements of the function.
- An *analyst* troubleshoots to isolate the causes of human performance gaps or identifies areas for improving human performance.
- An *intervention selector* chooses appropriate interventions to address root causes of human performance gaps.
- An *intervention designer and developer* creates learning and other interventions that help to address the specific root causes of human performance gaps. Some examples of the work of the intervention designer and developer include serving

as instructional designer, media specialist, materials developer, process engineer, ergonomics engineer, instructional writer, and compensation analyst.

- An *intervention implementor* ensures the appropriate and effective implementation of desired interventions that address the specific root causes of human performance gaps. Some examples of the work of the intervention implementor include serving as administrator, instructor, organization development practitioner, career development specialist, process re-design consultant, workspace designer, compensation specialist, and facilitator.
- A *change leader* inspires the workforce to embrace the change, creates a direction for the change effort, helps the organization's workforce to adapt to the change, and ensures that interventions are continuously monitored and guided in ways consistent with stakeholders' desired results.
- An *evaluator* assesses the impact of interventions and provides participants and stakeholders with information about the effectiveness of the intervention implementation.

The study also identified 52 competencies of WLP practitioners. Of course, the competencies essential to succeed are continually under review.[30]

ASTD 2004 Competency Study: Mapping the Future: New Workplace Learning and Performance Competencies

In 2004, the American Society for Training and Development published *Mapping the Future*.[31] The study was conducted by a team consisting of Paul R. Bernthal, Karen Colteryahn, Patty Davis (of DDI), William J. Rothwell, and Jennifer Naughton (of ASTD). This study, the basis for ASTD's Certified Professional in Learning and Performance (CPLP), began with a literature review, expert interviews with more than 100 subject experts, and onsite interviews at the 2003 ASTD International Conference and Exposition. The results of this foundation provided the basis for a draft summary report. That report, in turn, led to expert focus group interviews and a validation survey with more than 2,000 WLP professionals rating 269 individual key actions.

The 2004 study identified the following four roles carried out by WLP professionals:[32]

- learning strategist
- business partner
- project manager
- professional specialist

The study also identified nine major Areas of Expertise (AOEs). These were: (1) designing learning; (2) improving human performance; (3) delivering training; (4) measuring and evaluating; (5) facilitating organizational change; (6) managing the learning function; (7) coaching; (8) managing organizational knowledge; and (9) career planning and talent management.[33] To carry out those AOEs, practitioners would require three areas of foundational competencies: (1) interpersonal; (2) business/ management; and (3) personal.[34]

ASTD Competency Study: The Training and Development Profession Redefined

The most recent competency study conducted by ASTD was published in 2013.[35] Conducted by a team consisting of Justin Arneson (CPP, Inc.), William J. Rothwell, and Jennifer Naughton (ASTD), the complex study involved a literature review, a study of trends, an update of the 2004 study described above, and a study of products that could support application of the model. A detailed survey was conducted with 188 participants.

Several major findings resulted from the study. First, "roles" were abolished. What remained were six foundational competency areas and 10 areas of expertise. The foundational competencies were business skills, interpersonal skills, global mindset, personal skills, industry knowledge, and technology literacy.[36] The areas of expertise consisted of performance improvement, instructional design, training delivery, learning technologies, evaluating learning impact, managing learning programs, integrated talent management, coaching, knowledge management, and change management.[37]

Other Studies

There have been other studies that are relevant to HPE, of course, and many websites that are relevant to the competencies of HPE. Learning HPE can be situated in the job context.[38] It is fraught with emotional issues associated with emotional intelligence.[39] Recent research has also helped to shed important light on current issues associated with competence in the field.[40]

Chapter 2
What Is Human Performance Enhancement (HPE)?

How can training and development professionals move beyond training in their organizations? This chapter addresses that important question. It defines key terms, describes key principles governing human performance enhancement (HPE), reviews some important models for troubleshooting human performance problems, introduces a model to guide HPE, and reviews competencies for HPE.

Performance Breakthroughs Are the Results of Human Choices, Not Technological Wizardry: A Case Study*

A New Model for Performance Improvement

Once you understand that organizations and the work systems they contain are systems whose performance is significantly determined by human choice, you begin to understand why theories based on technical or rational scientific factors alone cannot account for or engender the extra effort and energy that come from human commitment. The performance breakthroughs that are required, particularly in difficult times like these, require leadership that understands the importance of surfacing all doubts and concerns and working authentically to resolve them through choice rather than attempting to overwhelm them with rational solutions. This story demonstrates the power of the convergence of individualism, teamwork, leadership, and commitment.

There are three main players in this story:

1. Individual interests
2. Team (peer group) interests
3. Organizational interests

All of these were seen as legitimate and honored by the process used, which was designed to build on and integrate the strengths of individualism, teamwork, and leadership. These, I believe, are the three primary forces operating in all organizations at all times whether we acknowledge them or not.

---

*__Source:__ Larry Davis. "Performance Breakthroughs Are the Results of Human Choices, Not Technological Wizardry: A Case Study," *The Journal of Quality and Participation, 24*(2001), No. 3, 42–47. Used with permission.

The Manufacturing Problem

The problem began seven years before the improvement work described here took place. The company contracted with a European vendor to adapt a large multi-station piece of manufacturing equipment to the manufacturing requirements for one of their highest volume hospital products. Management and engineering at the corporate and plant levels were involved in the decision.

During acceptance testing at the vendor's plant in Europe the initial machine performed below expectations. The lure of a significant potential cost reduction for the product was so great, and competitive pressures were so fierce, that the company decided to ship the equipment to the company's plant where clean room conditions would provide far more controlled test conditions. The equipment did perform better at the plant, but still not up to the expected standard. Several engineering changes made at that time were showing promise and with the continued lure of the substantial cost savings, the company ordered two more machines and had them installed.

Over the next seven years, all three machines performed at levels far below expectations. Many improvements were tried, including major engineering modifications, but only incremental gains were achieved. The entire effort became a source of frustration for all involved. There was considerable anger and finger-pointing and several careers were damaged. It was at this point when a new kind of intervention was attempted—the one described below.

The Conflicting Interests

The following quotes are from initial interviews I had with some of those involved. They capture the flavor of the conflict and conflicting interests surrounding this problem.

"Those machines are pieces of JUNK," one mechanic said. "Nah," another said, "that ain't fair, you don't flush junk down the toilet." "Manufacturing management is playing musical chairs by rotating the equipment operators. One of those self-directed team ideas. Variety makes life more interesting, or something like that. Nobody knows how to run the equipment. It's a people problem. Some days we operate at standard. That's at least some indication that the machines can do it," said an engineer. "Every mechanic has his own way of adjusting the machines. Sometimes something works, but then another mechanic adjusts something else and the whole thing goes to pot. It's worse odds than a crap shoot," the operator added. "Our expert engineers can't agree on anything. One corporate engineer strongly believes it's an RF problem. The plant engineers think that the mechanical design of one of the feeders is wrong. The vendor's engineers are clueless. We can't agree on the core cause. We can't even agree on a priority list of problems to attack. Can you help us out here?" the corporate engineering manager asked me.

Every function had its own favorite core cause and there were many competing individual ideas about what fix was necessary. After years of failure, all camps were armed with their own data and their own proof. When we began the new improvement process, those involved could not even agree on relevant objective criteria for studying the problem. To attempt to get a consensus list of priority actions would have been a joke. Management could have imposed one (as they had done in the past), but management was also divided and frustrated by past efforts to solve the problem.

To make matters worse, several careers had stalled, a few people received negative performance evaluations, and some of the early players even lost their jobs. Everyone felt like a scapegoat or a whipping boy and after interviewing all involved, I tended to agree.

What was the core cause of the problem? My somewhat startling conclusion reached after touring the equipment on separate occasions with a representative from each of the functions was that everyone's diagnosis was correct. Each had part of the puzzle and consequently, each had part of the solution. There was no likely core cause, and the approach we eventually used was based on an assumption of multi-causation.

The following is a brief description of the competing and conflicting interests and the effect they had on how people viewed the problem.

Individual Interests

The Engineers. The corporate engineer assigned to the project replaced the original engineer who was one of the early scapegoats. He took over the project just before the acceptance decision was made on the initial machine. While he had little to do with that decision, he was inclined to view the problem primarily as one of poor maintenance and unskilled (musical chairs) operators. Still, he knew that his career potential was tied to solving the problem and merit increases had not been forthcoming. In addition, as an engineer, he also passionately wanted to solve it—he hated to see machinery operating badly. He had a few ideas for reengineering that he advocated. He was almost violent in his disagreement with those ideas advocated by the plant engineer, his technician, and several of the mechanics. They were barely able to talk to one another, and they did not help implement each other's improvement efforts.

The plant engineer was involved early in the project. He voiced many reservations about the equipment, but signed off on its acceptance. He received poor performance evaluations based on his attitude, not on his engineering performance. Managers said he tended to get into conflicts with others. He believed that his career was at a dead end. Still, the engineer in him also had strong opinions about how to fix the problem and a passionate desire to do so. He and his technician believed that a particular feeder was the main culprit and they devised a relatively simple engineering solution. He displayed contempt for the corporate engineer and the corporate engineer's manager.

The Mechanics. Work life for the mechanics was a catch-22 situation—there was no way to achieve success:

- There were seven interrelated operations performed by the equipment simultaneously. A problem at one of the seven stations shut down everything.
- It was a three-shift, around the clock operation.

- Preventive maintenance was a joke. It took hours (of nonproduction) to do the basics. Then because of the intricate interrelations of the equipment's mechanics, heat sealing, RF sealing, sensors, and software, small deviations anywhere sent waves of deviation throughout the system.
- The strategy adopted by most mechanics was making small adjustments on the fly, knowing that a vicious circle of deviation was constantly evolving with no way to bring anything back to standard or baseline. To make matters worse, each of the three machines had its idiosyncrasies. As a result, each of the mechanics had favorite fixes and the only goal was to get through the shift with as little downtime as possible. Quality problems simply had to be weeded out farther down the line.

The mechanics on each shift blamed the previous shift for making changes that caused problems. Or they blamed the operators, who often improvised fixes on their own. The mechanics also blamed management and corporate engineering for buying equipment that was hopelessly over-engineered. None of the mechanics could get a raise or promotion. They jumped at every opportunity to transfer out and this made it difficult for management to keep even skeleton crews working.

The Operators. As part of the cost-reduction plan for this equipment, the position of lead operator was eliminated. In return, the operators had been empowered to be self-directing. Since they had little chance of individual gain such as promotion or bonuses, their best strategy was to minimize pain. This resulted in a frequent rotation of stations so no one would be sentenced to a problem station for too long. They only got praise for keeping the equipment running. Blame for quality problems was diffused by the rotation scheme. The operators also looked for transfer opportunities. They were perhaps the most cynical about yet another intervention to fix things.

The Managers. The corporate (divisional) manager for manufacturing engineering was not in that position when the equipment was accepted, installed, and certified, but he was given a key performance objective to make it work. His career possibly depended on it. He was equal in rank to the plant manager who was not an engineer. He realized he would need to work as a peer with the engineering manager at the plant to achieve any results. He was frustrated by the lack of agreement among the engineers about the problem and its solution. He viewed the plant engineer's attitude as a major factor in not being able to reach agreement. He was ready to try something new to see if addressing the people problems might lead to a solution.

The plant engineering manager was not in his role when the machines were selected and was strongly motivated to help solve the problem. He was in agreement with the corporate engineering manager that solving the people problem was probably the place to begin. He also managed the mechanics and felt some tension about the conflicting views. He was committed to supporting the plant manager in achieving bottom-line results and needed to maintain good relations with the plant production manager.

The plant production manager was mainly concerned about quality production rates. He had a manual backup system for the production line in question and could achieve results without the problems being fixed. But he was also committed to the plant manager for bottom-line results and felt that bringing down cost would enhance his career prospects. He was skeptical about the new intervention, but was willing to cooperate.

The plant manager and the corporate manufacturing engineering manager both reported to the same corporate divisional manager. He wanted results, but completely delegated the decision about means to the managers below him. The plant manager was hands-off but was willing to be supportive where needed.

Team (Peer Group) Interests

Operators and mechanics versus engineers versus managers. Each of the three major functional groups tended to see the source of the problem as one or both of the other groups. There was peer pressure in these groups to close ranks. Initially, this made it difficult to get divergent opinions that could serve as the basis for a consensus action plan. Each of the groups perceived that it had something to lose in seeking a solution and little to gain.

Worker versus management. Even though this was a nonunion plant, there was the typical line and management difference in interests.

The operators and mechanics shared the view that management was unlikely to reward them in any monetary way for improvements, so any motivation would come from a potential reduction in pain. Pride in the job had long since eroded.

Plant versus corporate. There was the usual norm to be loyal to the local group, which tended to block agreement with anyone from the other side, even if they were thought to be right. This initially made consensus very difficult.

Leadership Interests

Management was committed to participation and used it extensively but had not extended it to full participation in the bottom-line math. Management was aligned around the goal of cost-reduction as the only viable bottom-line strategy. They needed this equipment to work. This consideration weighed more heavily than the interests of workers. They believed workers would not be interested in the abstract detail involved and probably suspected that workers would only be self-interested and not collaborate on plans that might be best for the company but would cost them something.

The Convergent Process

The project (seven months) had four phases:

1. Preparation
2. Diagnosis and treatment

3. Reengineering
4. Optimization

Total project time could not be determined in advance since the time needed for engineering changes would not be known until the diagnosis was complete.

The process involved a typical mixture of project steps:

- briefing sessions
- interviews
- one-on-one mediations
- equipment inspections with functional representatives
- hard data reviews
- a three-day meeting of cross-functional representatives and managers to reopen communication
- a larger two-day meeting including more mechanics and operators for priority setting and developing commitment/action plans for immediate improvements
- statistical and engineering studies
- frequent meetings of a steering group

There was little unique about the steps in the process; the company had done things like this before. The difference was in the convergent principles that shaped each event.

Ten Principles for Convergence

The 10 principles of convergence that I used to make this round of improvement efforts different from those tried before at this company were:

1. **Develop management understanding of the conflict → convergence → commitment process. Gain management commitment to a more comprehensive analysis of causality.** The managers involved were believers in broad participation and versed in the practices of brainstorming. However, when evaluating ideas, they had established a norm that gave little attention to individual or group interests. They gave their attention to measurable data and usually focused only on the performance of the machinery or on measurable data about the product. This biased solutions to favor the interests of the company often at the expense of those doing the work. Solutions that involved individual and team interests seldom received priority treatment, and if individuals continued to raise them, they were often labeled as complainers. When the managers became more deeply aware of the human commitment process and its huge impact on performance, it was then possible to gain their commitment to a much more comprehensive analysis of causality.

2. **Expand data collection and legitimize the interests and perceptions of all.** With the commitment to the interests of people established, it was then possible to gain credibility when briefing the employees about the project and the process

to use. These briefings were conducted in functional group meetings with the plant manager, the corporate engineering manager, the plant engineering manager, and the production manager present to answer questions. As a result, the interviews were extremely candid. All observations were given credence and separate inspections of the manufacturing line led by representatives of each function built even more trust in the process. Copies of all statistical and engineering studies were available to all groups with the opportunity to validate or dispute the conclusions.

3. **Establish climate for fuller communication and develop tentative trust agreements.** Representatives from each function, plant, and corporate engineers and technicians, and the four managers directly involved attended a three-day meeting that began with a discussion of norms for the meeting:

   - It was agreed that all perspectives of the company history with the equipment would be heard with respect and not debated.
   - It was also agreed to avoid personal critiques.

   This allowed for a great deal of venting, but it had the more important benefit of giving everyone a much fuller picture of the issues involved. The basis for cooperating with tentative trust was in place. This enabled participants to reach full agreement on a number of the next steps.

4. **Foster understanding and develop commitment to the interests and perspectives of all involved.** In a second two-day meeting with expanded participation of mechanics and operators, the findings of the first meeting were shared and discussed. Each person publicly committed to work for solutions that served the interests of all to the greatest degree possible.

5. **Explore solutions that incorporate the interests and recommendations of all (a 100 percent solution) and lead to a convergence of interests and commitment. This often requires getting outside the box of 80/20 thinking and the core cause machine paradigm.** At the second two-day meeting, participants formed small cross-functional groups that included representatives from both corporate and plant and a mixture of managers, supervisors, and workers. Few people were in the same group with their boss (this reduced the chain-of-command tendency toward collusion).

   Each group took a different part of the problems for deeper discussion and the development of proposed solutions. These were reported to the full group and discussed. We agreed that while priorities were important, it was also important to work in the direction of solutions to all the problems and concerns that were voiced. This is what I call a 100 percent solution. Even though managers believed this would be too expensive, since it was now clear that such a solution was more likely to gain the full, willing commitment of all, everyone agreed to a time-limited trial. This agreement released the commitment energy needed to replace a seven-year climate of despair and anger with one of hope and excitement.

6. **Work the numbers together.** We used the small groups at this same meeting to develop budgets while another special group worked on bottom line numbers factoring in both cost and expected payoffs. This exercise resulted in many ideas for less expensive ways to achieve the same ends. Most of these ideas came from rank-and-file workers, which surprised a number of managers. It demonstrated that most employees make good business partners if they are involved in the considerations of finance. The priorities and action plans were revised and the climate now included a spirit of determination.
7. **Seek total commitment to plans.** The meeting ended with an individual statement of commitment to the plan and a description of what each person would do about it beginning the next day. One of the operators said this sounded like signing the Declaration of Independence. Following that comment, arrangements were made for the group to reconvene briefly in a few days at the plant to have a signing ceremony for the transcribed action plan. Copies of the document were then posted on plant bulletin boards.
8. **Establish cross-functional reengineering teams.** Rather than simply hand off the reengineering work to the engineers, to preserve the convergent commitment, cross-functional teams were formed to work with the engineers at every step. Additionally, plant and corporate engineers worked together. Telecommunications were used extensively to reduce travel and time away from production.
9. **Establish linked accountability implementation.** During implementation, the functions and shifts typically do their parts separately. In this case, they collaborated in establishing very visible, linked accountability handoffs. Problems were addressed immediately and the data communicated to all. Production rates shot up within two weeks.
10. **Analyze results frequently and fine-tune.** The large group created an ongoing cross-functional, multilevel steering committee to monitor results and fine-tune all aspects of a project. These meetings quickly became celebration. Membership was rotated so everyone could participate in the fun.

The Payoffs

Production rates increased by 67 percent within a month and quality problems dropped to near zero. The equipment now exceeded the original standards. At last check, this was maintained for more than two years with no further improvements needed.

The final costs of improvements were less than expected and were recovered within a short time. The overall desired manufacturing cost reduction was achieved, translating to lower, more competitive product pricing.

Workers received bonuses, engineers received raises and promotions, and the managers involved also got promotions. For both manufacturing and equipment maintenance employees, working on this line became the most coveted assignment in the plant.

The time for convergent leadership and processes is now. Convergent improvement projects or convergent management practices have yielded similar results in other industries. In one software development company, a similar process achieved a 30 percent gain in delivery time. At the Texas Rehabilitation Commission, local units achieved gains of 30 percent to 60 percent in successful rehabilitation and job placement. At the Post Ranch Inn, a boutique resort in California, convergent management practices have produced one of the highest levels of service in the world with a year-round occupancy rate that is the envy of the industry.

Since the fall of dot-com businesses and the more generalized slow down, leadership practices seem to be rapidly returning to the days of downsizing and attempting to serve the interests of investors at the expense of nearly everyone else.

The damage to employee commitment and innovation is evident across the global economy. Today's global economy is so intricately networked and interdependent that these old paradigms will not serve. Convergent leadership and processes, on the other hand, can get us on the move again.

Defining Key Terms

As Chapter 1 explained and as the preceding case focusing on convergent problem-solving dramatizes, organizations must go beyond training if they are to be fully successful in unleashing worker creativity, improving productivity, maintaining their competitive edge, and ensuring orderly succession. To understand this approach, readers must understand certain important terms clearly. Therefore, it is worthwhile to devote some time to defining *training, performance,* and *human performance enhancement* (HPE).

What Is Training?

Training is the field of activity that, in a still-relevant definition, "focuses on identifying, assuring, and helping develop, through planned learning, the key competencies that enable individuals to perform current or future jobs. Training's primary emphasis is on individuals in their work roles. The primary training intervention is planned individual learning."[1] Training is thus directed to improving how well individuals perform and is based on what they need to know or do to perform competently.

Of course, people need more than information, skills, or appropriate attitudes to work competently and thereby achieve results. There are major differences between approaching human performance enhancement from a traditional training-oriented view and approaching it from a new, performance-oriented view. These differences are contrasted in Exhibit 2-1.

Exhibit 2-1. Comparing Traditional Training and Human Performance Enhancement

Issue	Traditional Training Approach	New Human Performance Enhancement Approach
Sample mission statement of the training and development department	To provide all types of training support services to all employees	To assist in increasing the effectiveness and efficiency of all individuals in the organization
Measures of success	• Hours of training • Persons trained • Classes delivered • Media produced • Instructional objectives accomplished • Course catalogs	• Job behaviors • Job performance • Problems solved • Cost savings to organization • Product quantity • Product quality • Lower absenteeism • Lower turnover • Some measures in the traditional approach
Origin of performance problems	Problems are brought to the training and development department. Staff then responds according to time available and the perceived importance of the person bringing the problem. Less time for problem solving, as much time is devoted to delivering courses from a training catalog (for example, "Introduction to Supervision").	Problems are brought to the training and development department, or the training and development department anticipates problems on the basis of independent analysis of projected personnel needs using forecasting methods. More time exists for problem solving since fewer training courses are delivered on a scheduled basis.
Audiences served	All audiences of the organization are served, though distinctions are made for administrative reasons to separate training and development departments for technical skills training, supervisory training, and management development.	All audiences of the organization are served; fewer distinctions are made to separate audiences served in recognition of the interrelatedness of performance problems.
Relationship with organizational goals	Training and development is a support function often referred to as a cost center as opposed to a profit center. Little relationship exists between the department's activities and organizational goals.	Training and development is a proactive function, generating profits to the organization by documenting savings related to reduction in waste, turnover, defects, and down-time. A high relationship exists with organizational goals.

Exhibit 2-1 (concluded)

Issue	Traditional Training Approach	New Human Performance Enhancement Approach
Perception of others	Training and development is the department that provides training programs and schedules, organizes special programs, and reviews the appropriateness of vendor programs.	Training and development is the department that helps other departments analyze their problems and solve them using training and non-training solutions. Provides special programs if they are consistent with goals.
Staff skills required	• Delivering training • Creating lesson plans • Media production • Department budgeting • Course scheduling • Coordinating events • Developing surveys, questionnaires	• Consulting • Needs assessment • Needs analysis • Data collection • Systems design • Long-range planning • Cost-benefit analysis • Evaluation • Research • Most traditional training approach skills
Potential for survival in difficult times	Training and development department is one of the first to be eliminated. Training and development is considered "nice to have" for the benefit of employees.	Training and development department may be eliminated, but its chances of survival are generally as good as the organization as a whole. Training and development is considered essential to maintaining market competitiveness.

Source: Ron Jacobs. *Human Performance Technology: A Systems-Based Field for the Training and Development Profession.* (Columbus, Ohio: Center on Education and Training (formerly NCRVI), The Ohio State University). Copyright © 1967. Used with permission.

What Is Performance?

Understanding the meaning of performance is essential to transforming traditional training into human performance enhancement. Performance is synonymous with outcomes, results, or accomplishments. It should not be confused with behaviors, work activities, duties, responsibilities, or competencies. A *behavior* is an observable action taken to achieve results. A *work activity* is a task or series of tasks taken to achieve results. Any work activity has a definite beginning, middle, and end. A *duty* is a moral obligation to perform, and a *responsibility* is an action or a result for which one is accountable. A *competency* is "an area of knowledge or skill that is critical for producing key outputs. A competency is an internal capability that people bring to their jobs, a capability that may be expressed in a broad, even infinite array of on-the-job behaviors."[2] Studying competencies typically means identifying the underlying characteristics shared by successful performers.[3]

What Is Human Performance Enhancement (HPE)?

Human performance enhancement is the field focused on systematically and holistically improving present and future work results achieved by people in organizational settings. HPE, synonymous in this book with *human performance technology* (HPT) and *human performance improvement* (HPI), is a "systematic approach to improving productivity and competence."[4] As William A. Deterline and Marc J. Rosenberg explain, HPE "is a set of methods and procedures, and a strategy for solving problems, or realizing opportunities related to the performance of people. It can be applied to individuals, small groups, and large organizations."[5]

Others have attempted to define human performance technology (HPT), human performance improvement (HPI), or human performance enhancement (HPE) as well. Here are a few more carefully chosen definitions from classic sources:

- Performance technology is about "outcome signification—discovering valid, useful performance objectives and stating them in terms that are easily understood."[6]
- HPT "is concerned with measurable performance and the structuring of elements within the system to improve performance."[7]
- HPT "is, therefore, a field of endeavor that seeks to bring about changes to a system in such a way that the system is improved in terms of the achievements it values."[8]

Unlike traditional training, which frequently limits change efforts to individuals only, HPE takes a broader view that change must be holistically focused and that any change effort must accommodate the systemic issues associated with people.[9] To be carried out effectively, any change must be driven by threats or opportunities from the external environment within which the organization operates. If change is to be successful, it must in turn be aligned with the organization's mission, strategy, and goals and carried out with due attention to comparisons between desired and actual performance. HPE focuses on solving human performance problems and seizing human performance improvement opportunities.

Important Propositions of HPE

A performance mindset requires attention to three key principles:[10] (1) it uses a results-based, systematic approach; (2) it begins by focusing on accomplishments and not behavior; and (3) it regards organizations as systems. The performance mindset has a long history.[11]

Ron Jacobs, in an earlier but classic treatment, identified 11 important propositions that underlie HPE:[12]

1. **"Human performance and human behavior are different, and knowledge of the differences is important for achieving the goal of the field."**[13] It is easy for training and development professionals and managers to lose sight of the fundamental difference between *what people do* and *what results they achieve.* It bears emphasizing that the focus of HPE efforts is consistently on results. Of course, behavior warrants attention because it influences performance.
2. **"Any statement about human performance is at least about organizational performance as well."**[14] Human performance is critical to organizational performance. Conversely, organizational conditions are critical to human performance, as advocates of the high-performance workplace have so eloquently pointed out. Therefore, any statement about the future goals, strategies, or results of the organization applies to individual performance expectations as well.
3. **"Costs of improving performance should be regarded as investments in human capital, yielding returns in terms of increased performance potential."**[15] Training, as well as other human performance enhancement efforts, should not be regarded as a frivolous expense; it is an important investment if planned and executed properly. Like all investments, however, investments in HPE should be weighed cautiously and managed properly. Those who stand to benefit from improvements, such as managers and employees, should be involved in forecasting the return on investments made in HPE.
4. **"Organizational goals as well as individual goals must be considered to define worthy performance."**[16] Individual performance is tied to organizational performance. Hence, organizational goals are tied inextricably to individual goals.
5. **"The domain of human performance technology consists of management functions, development functions, and systems components."**[17] All performance in organizations is affected by what management does, what individuals do, and what the organization does. *Management functions* have to do with management's role in guiding and controlling the system and the people; *development functions* have to with cultivating individuals to improve their abilities and capabilities; *systems components* are work environment variables that affect organizational and individual performance.
6. **"Knowing how to engineer human performance and the conditions that affect it is as important as explaining why the behavior occurred."**[18] Explaining why people do what they do is important. But knowing how to change results is (at least) equally important. Engineering human performance implies that improvements can (and should) be planned.

7. **"To diagnose problems, one should analyze the present system and then examine the differences between it and an ideal system. To avoid anticipated problems, one should analyze the planned system and modify it to approximate an ideal system."**[19] Problem analysis is present-oriented; planning is future-oriented. HPE requires troubleshooting present human performance problems, planning for future human performance improvements, and finding ways to leverage talent.[20]

8. **"Exemplary performance provides the most logical referent for determining job performance standards."**[21] An *exemplar* is a top-performing individual. Exemplars can achieve results superior to others having the same job title; differences in outputs (productivity) among individuals having the same job title may vary dramatically. Hence, exemplars warrant study because what they do, how they do it, and what results they achieve can provide concrete and compelling evidence of human performance enhancement opportunities. To estimate the value of human performance enhancement, one can subtract the actual output of every performer from the output of the highest performer, place financial value on these differences, and then sum the differences. The result is called *performance improvement potential* (PIP).[22]

9. **"Human performance problems can have different root causes, and these causes are generally classified as either originating from the person, from something in the person's environment, or both."**[23] This proposition is fundamentally important to HPE. All problems stem from individuals, the work environment, or both. The source of a problem suggests where corrective action should be taken.

10. **"The performance of one subsystem affects the performance of other subsystems in somewhat predictable ways, requiring that problem causes be analyzed at more than one level of the organization."**[24] Organizations are *open systems* that are absolutely dependent for success on their external environments.[25] Open systems receive inputs from the environment, process them, and release outputs into the environment. *Inputs* include raw materials, orders placed, people, capital, and information. *Processes* are the work methods applied to the inputs. *Outputs* are the results of processes, such as finished goods or services. *Feedback* is provided by customers, suppliers, or distributors on the basis of their experiences with the organization. For any organization to remain in existence, some advantage must be gained from these transactions. Profit is such an advantage.

Each part of an organization contributes to the organization's mission. Each part of an organization is a *subsystem* (part of the organizational system) interacting with a *suprasystem* (the environment external to the organization). Actions taken to affect one subsystem affect others.

Efforts to improve human performance should allow for the environments within which performance occurs. These environments may be called by different names. For simplicity's sake, we shall label them as follows:

- The *organizational environment* is synonymous with the suprasystem. It is everything outside the organization—the *external environment.*
- The *work environment* is everything inside the organization—the *internal environment.*
- The *work* consists of processes used to transform inputs into *outputs.*
- The *worker* is the individual who performs work and *achieves results.*

An excellent way to understand the interdependence of these environments is to think of four concentric circles (see Exhibit 2-2). As the concentric circles imply, performance at each level affects performance closer to the center of the circles. The organizational environment exerts the most profound influence, affecting all other levels of performance.

Exhibit 2-2. The Environments of Human Performance

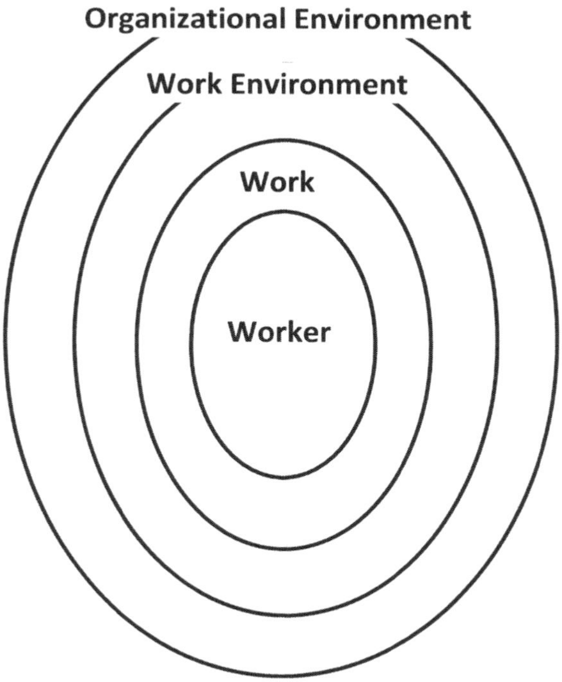

11. **"Many different solutions may be used to improve human performance. Selection of any one solution is dependent upon the cause and the nature of the performance problem, and the criteria used to evaluate a solution must include its potential to make a measurable difference in the performance system."**[26] Many solutions—what are called *human performance enhancement strategies*—are possible to solve human performance problems or to take advantage of improvement opportunities. Such strategies are not limited to training; they should be chosen on the basis of the human performance problems they are to solve or the human performance improvement opportunities they are to cultivate.

Key Models Governing HPE

Many models have been introduced to guide thinking about performance in organizational settings. Two are particularly important.[27] One is holistic; the second is situational. The *holistic model* provides a broad perspective, a big-picture view of performance. A *situational model*, on the other hand, should be used to troubleshoot specific incidents or events or occasions and to distinguish training from management needs. Both models are important tools for HPE practitioners to remember and apply.

A Holistic Model for Human Performance Enhancement

A classic holistic model for human performance technology was introduced by Thomas Gilbert in his important (and classic) book *Human Competence: Engineering Worthy Performance.* Gilbert, one of the great pioneers in human performance enhancement, believed that performance is a function of *behavior* (processes or what can be observed as an activity) and *accomplishment* (what you see after people stop working).

For Gilbert, any performance system can be analyzed from six vantage points:

1. **The philosophical level**—the beliefs within which the organization functions
2. **The cultural level**—the larger environment within which the organization operates
3. **The policy level**—the missions that define the organization's purpose
4. **The strategic level**—the plans the organization has established to accomplish its mission
5. **The tactical level**—specific duties carried out to realize plans
6. **The logistical level**—all support activities that help performers conduct their duties[28]

Gilbert believed that HPE practitioners should begin their efforts by deciding what accomplishments they—or others—desire. They should measure opportunities for improvements and then select performance enhancement techniques.

Gilbert developed several important models to describe his ideas. One, called the ACORN model, was intended to bring clarity to the mission level. ACORN is an acronym based on the first letters of the following words:

Accomplishment	Is the stated accomplishment a result, not a behavior?
Control	Does the performer possess the necessary authority to carry out the accomplishment?
Overall Objective	Does the accomplishment represent the real reason for the job's existence, or is it merely one of several tasks?
Reconcilable	Is this accomplishment reconciled with, or congruent with, the mission of the organization and the goals for carrying it out, or is it inconsistent?
Numbers	Can the accomplishment be measured to determine practicality and cost-effectiveness?[29] On a practical level, the ACORN model can be immensely helpful in identifying problems stemming from job design—that is, the way the organization has established individual accountabilities and responsibilities.

Even more important is Gilbert's Behavior Engineering Model (BEM).[30] The BEM is a holistic performance enhancement model, intended to bring a comprehensive perspective to troubleshooting existing human performance problems or identifying possible human performance improvement opportunities (see Exhibit 2-3). The model distinguishes between two dimensions (the individual performer and the work environment) and among three components (stimuli, response, and consequences). When examining performance, HPE practitioners should assess what the performer and the environment contribute to results. *Stimuli* prompt action; *response* represents behaviors; *consequences* are the results of behaviors.

Exhibit 2-3. The Behavior Engineering Model

STIMULI	RESPONSE	CONSEQUENCES
THE WORK ENVIRONMENT		
Cell 1-E Information	**Cell 2-E Resources**	**Cell 3-E Incentives**
• Description of what is expected of performance • Clear and relevant guides on how to do the job • Relevant and frequent feedback about the adequacy of performance	• Tools, resources, time, and materials designed to achieve performance needs • Access to leaders • Organized work processes	• Adequate financial incentives made contingent upon performance • Nonmonetary incentives • Career development opportunities • Clear consequences for poor performance
THE INDIVIDUAL PERFORMER		
Cell 4-1 Knowledge	**Cell 5-1 Capacity**	**Cell 6-1 Motives**
• Systematically designed training that matches requirements of exemplary performers • Opportunity for training	• Match between people and positions • Good selection processes • Flexible scheduling of performance to match peak capacity of workers • Prostheses or visual aids to augment capacity	• Recognition of workers' willingness to work for available incentives • Assessment of workers' motivation • Recruitment of workers to match realities of work conditions

Source: T. F. Gilbert. *Human Competence: Engineering Worthy Performance.* (New York: McGraw-Hill, 1978), p. 18. Used by permission of Mrs. T. F. Gilbert.

Although Gilbert's BEM model is an excellent tool, it can be extremely difficult to explain. A better approach is to pose questions about performance based on the BEM model, such as those listed in Exhibit 2-4. Those questions can yield comprehensive information about the environment in which people perform.

Exhibit 2-4. PROBE Questions

Questions about the behavioral environment:

A. Directional Data

1. Are there sufficient, readily accessible data (or signals) to direct an experienced person to perform well?
2. Are they accurate?
3. Are they free of confusion—"stimulus competition"—that slows performance and invites error?
4. Are directions free of "data glut"—stripped down to the simplest form and not buried in a lot of extraneous data?
5. Are they up-to-date and timely?
6. Are good models of behavior available?
7. Are clear and measurable performance standards communicated so that people know how well they are supposed to perform?
8. Do they accept the standards are reasonable?

B. Confirmation

1. Is feedback provided that this is "work-related"—describing results consistent with the standards and not just behavior?
2. Is it immediate and frequent enough to help employees remember what they did?
3. Is it selective and specific—limited to a few matters of importance and free of data glut and vague generalities?
4. Is it educational—positive and constructive so that people learn something from it?

C. Tools and Equipment

1. Are the necessary implements usually on hand for doing the job?
2. Are they reliable and efficient?
3. Are they safe?

Exhibit 2-4 (continued)

D. Procedures

1. Are procedures efficient and designed to avoid unnecessary steps and wasted motion?
2. Are they based on sound methods rather than on historical happenstance?
3. Are they appropriate to the job and skill level?
4. Are they free of boring and tiresome repetition?

E. Resources

1. Are adequate materials, supplies, assistance, etc., usually available to do the job well?
2. Are they efficiently tailored to the job?
3. Do ambient conditions provide comfort and prevent unnecessary interference?

F. Incentives

1. Is the pay for the job competitive?
2. Are there significant bonuses or raises based on good performance?
3. Does good performance have any relationship to career advancement?
4. Are there meaningful non-pay incentives (e.g., recognition) for good performance (based on results and not on behavior)?
5. Are they scheduled well, or so frequent as to lose meaning, or so infrequent as to be useless?
6. Is there an absence of punishment for performing well?
7. Is there an absence of hidden incentives to perform poorly?

Questions about the behavioral repertoires:

G. Knowledge and Training

1. Do people understand the consequences of both good and poor performance?
2. Do they grasp the essentials of performance—do they get the "big picture"?
3. Do they have the technical concepts to perform well?
4. Do they have sufficient basic skills (e.g., reading)?

Exhibit 2-4 (concluded)

5. Do they have sufficient specialized skills?
6. Do they always have the skills after initial training?
7. Are good aids available?

H. Capacity

1. Do the incumbents have the basic capacity to learn the necessary perceptual discriminations with accuracy and speed?
2. Are they free of emotional limitations that would interfere with performance?
3. Do they have sufficient strength and dexterity to learn to do the job well?

I. Motives

1. Do incumbents seem to have the desire to perform when they enter the job?
2. Do their motives endure (e.g., is the turnover low)?

Source: Thomas F. Gilbert. "A Question of Performance Part I: The PROBE Model," *Training and Development Journal* (September 1982); Thomas F. Gilbert. "Applying the PROBE Model," *Training and Development Journal* (October 1982). Used by permission of The American Society for Training and Development and Mrs. T. F. Gilbert. All rights reserved.

The Situational Model for Human Performance Enhancement

A situational model was first described by Robert F. Mager and Peter Pipe in their classic book *Analyzing Performance Problems or You Really Oughta Wanna.*[31] The classic model is most effective for troubleshooting a discrepancy between *what is* and *what should be* happening. Examples of such troubleshooting situations include requests for training or requests for other HPE strategies. Consider the following examples:

- Managers request training on "telephone usage" for all employees.
- A manager feels that her 30-year veteran employees should be required to attend the company's new employee orientation program "as a refresher."
- A manager in a downsized organization cannot figure out why employee production is decreasing, and she asks for help.
- A supervisor is trying to decide how to deal with one employee who is not performing up to measurable job performance standards despite having received rigorously planned on-the-job training.

Each of these situations represents an opportunity to apply Mager and Pipe's classic model. The classic model, since revised and modified in 1997, begins with three steps:

1. **Describe a performance discrepancy**—the difference between actual and desired results. Such a discrepancy may surface as difference between actual and desired production outputs or in quality measures, scrap rates, or customer service measures. These discrepancies are cause for concern, since accepted variations are rarely the basis for taking corrective actions.
2. **Determine the importance of the discrepancy.** If it is not important, then no further action is warranted, and managers, employees, and HPE practitioners should turn their attention to more important discrepancies.
3. **Determine the cause of the discrepancy.** Does it stem from a skill deficiency by an individual (or group), or does it stem from another deficiency? If it is caused by a skill deficiency, then HPE practitioners should ask additional questions:
    - *Are employees used to performing?* If the answer is no, then the problem may be solved by arranging formal (planned) training. If the answer is yes, then the discrepancy does not result from lack of knowledge, and the troubleshooter should continue diagnosing the problem.
    - *Are employees used to performing often?* If the answer is no, then the problem may be solved by arranging practice. If the answer is yes, then the discrepancy is not caused by lack of practice, and the troubleshooter should arrange feedback.

Once these questions have been considered, additional questions may be asked about performance discrepancies that appear to stem from a skill deficiency:

- *Is there a simpler way to address the skill deficiency?* Alternatives to consider may include changing the job (job redesign) or arranging on-the-job training (OJT).
- *Does the performer have the potential to perform?* If the answer is no, then action should be taken with the performer, such as transferring the performer to work for which he or she is better suited or terminating the performer.

If the performance discrepancy is not caused by a skill deficiency, then HPE practitioners should ask four related questions:

1. *Does performance lead to punishment?* Are employees somehow punished for performing? If the answer is yes, then the deficiency can be rectified by removing the punishment; if the answer is no, then another cause should be considered.
2. *Is the nonperformance rewarded?* Are employees somehow benefiting by not performing properly? If the answer is yes, then the deficiency can be rectified by arranging positive consequences. In other words, employees should be given

appropriate incentives or rewards for performing as they are expected or desired to perform.

3. *Does performance matter?* Do performers understand what consequences stem from what they do? (Do they, for instance, appreciate how the results of their labors fit into the big picture, help other people in the organization do their jobs, or benefit customers?) If the answer is no, then the problem may be rectified by arranging consequences or improving the feedback that performers receive about their work results.
4. *Do obstacles stand in the way of performance?* An obstacle is anything that prevents people from performing. If the answer to this question is yes, then the obstacles must be removed. (That is, admittedly, often easier said than done.) If the answer is no, then the performance discrepancy must stem from a different cause.

Both sides of the flowchart lead to two final steps: (1) *selecting best solution(s)*, and (2) *implementing the solution(s).* One or more strategies may be selected and implemented.

Enhancements and Critiques of the Classic Holistic and Situational Models

Both the holistic and the situational models provide excellent foundations on which to plan HPE strategies. Taken together—and combined with the propositions of human performance enhancement described in the preceding part of this chapter—they suggest new, important roles for training and development professionals as HPE practitioners.

However, no model is perfect. These classic models, while excellent starting points, do have drawbacks. Both can be too reductive, making complex problems or situations appear simpler than they really are. The chief failing of Gilbert's BEM model is that it is difficult to explain to managers—and to some training and development professionals. Indeed, some training and development professionals just do not understand how to classify performance elements into cells of the BEM model.

Applying Mager and Pipe's classic model can lead to what logicians call the *either/or fallacy,* meaning that, if examined strictly, it appears to divide the complex world of organizational performance into *skill deficiencies* (which may require training solutions) and *other deficiencies* (which may require management solutions). Rarely is the world that simple, however. More often than not, training and development professionals—and managers and employees in today's organizations—confront wicked problems that defy quick and dirty solutions and call for combination solution strategies. Unintended side effects and many new problems may result if they are approached simplistically, as has been pointed out in a classic work on strategic planning.[32]

Recent thinking on performance improvement has tended to focus on positives (individual and organizational strengths) rather than negatives (gaps).[33] That is very much in keeping with notions of so-called *appreciative inquiry*,[34] which focuses on questions having to do with what gives strength, and organizational core competencies,[35] which focus on what makes an organization better and different from its competitors.

Introducing an HPE Model

What is needed is a model for HPE that can be applied both situationally (like Mager and Pipe's classic model) and comprehensively (like Gilbert's classic model). Such a model should focus attention both outside the organization (from customers, suppliers, distributors, and other stakeholders) and inside, thus giving due consideration to the four environments that affect human performance as depicted in Exhibit 2-2. The model could, in turn, become the basis for identifying core competencies required for success by HPE practitioners and become the basis for selecting, training, developing, appraising, and rewarding HPE practitioners.

Exhibit 2-5 depicts a new HPE model. It calls for the HPE specialist, working with the full collaboration of stakeholders, to do the following:

1. Analyze what is happening.
2. Envision what should be happening.
3. Clarify present and future gaps.
4. Determine the present and future importance of the gaps.
5. Identify the underlying cause(s) of the gap(s).
6. Select human performance enhancement strategies, individually or collectively, that close the gaps by addressing their root cause(s).
7. Assess the likely outcomes of implementation to minimize negative side effects and maximize positive results.
8. Establish an action plan for implementation of the human performance enhancement strategies.
9. Implement HPE strategies.
10. Evaluate results during and after implementation, feeding information back into Step 1 to prompt continuous improvement and organizational learning.

Exhibit 2-5. A Model for Human Performance Enhancement

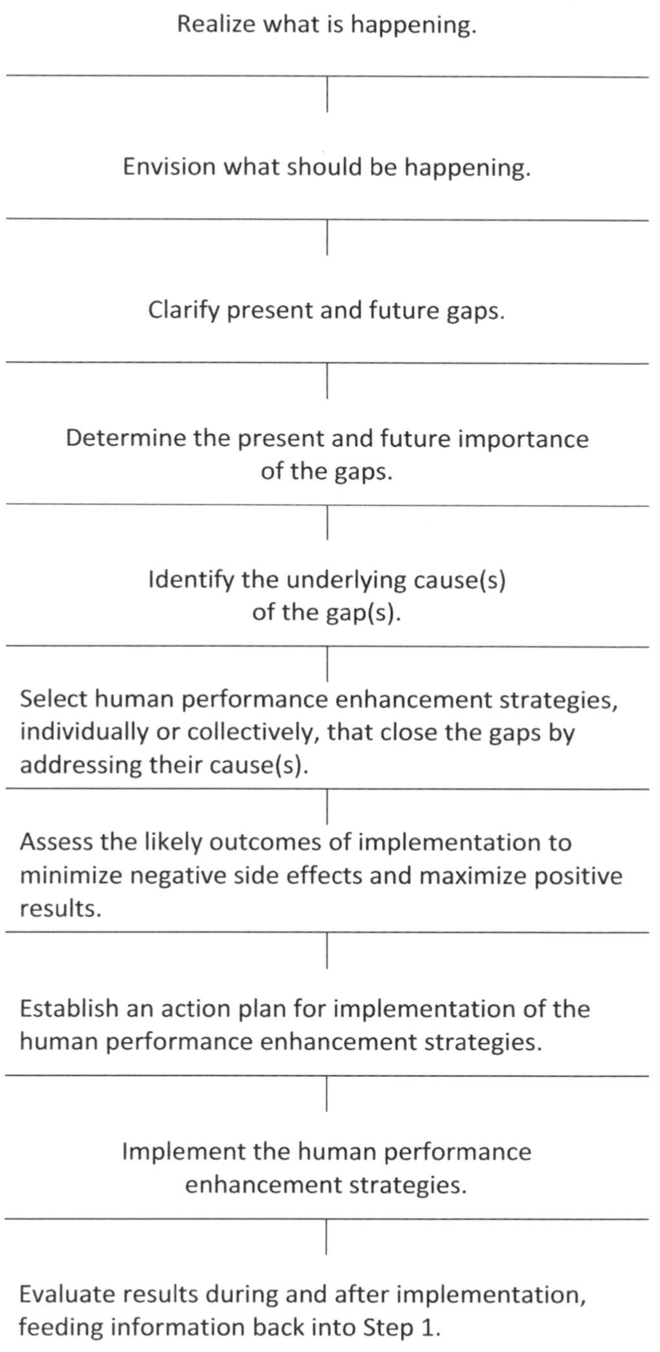
Realize what is happening.
Envision what should be happening.
Clarify present and future gaps.
Determine the present and future importance of the gaps.
Identify the underlying cause(s) of the gap(s).
Select human performance enhancement strategies, individually or collectively, that close the gaps by addressing their cause(s).
Assess the likely outcomes of implementation to minimize negative side effects and maximize positive results.
Establish an action plan for implementation of the human performance enhancement strategies.
Implement the human performance enhancement strategies.
Evaluate results during and after implementation, feeding information back into Step 1.

This model integrates the classic elements found in Mager and Pipe's and Gilbert's models. It is a systematic approach to identifying or anticipating human performance problems and human performance improvement opportunities. This model is the basis for the remainder of this book—and for the competency model for HPE practitioners described later in this chapter.

What Do Human Performance Enhancement Professionals Do?

Models are worthwhile only if they can be applied. One way to make them easier to apply is to use them as the basis for group and individual expectations. Models can become the basis for a competency model that clarifies what results should be achieved by exemplary performers and what they need to know to achieve those results.

Jacobs's Competency Model for HPE

Only a few systematic efforts have been made to identify the competencies necessary for success in HPE. However, Ron Jacobs has offered the following classic list of competencies for training and development professionals who set their sights on becoming HPE practitioners. HPE practitioners should do the following:

1. Identify organizational needs.
2. Analyze indicators, causes, and costs of human error.
3. Conduct job and task analyses.
4. Specify job performance standards.
5. Select appropriate training and development solutions.
6. Design instructional methods and media.
7. Construct non-training job performance aids.
8. Specify and implement appropriate motivational, job redesign, and environmental solutions.
9. Control and ensure the quality of training and development projects.
10. Assess the effectiveness of performance systems.
11. Maintain credible and collaborative consulting relationships.
12. Consider themselves members of a helping profession.
13. Understand/perform research related to the improvement of professional practices in training and development.
14. Engage in professional and self-development activities.
15. Promote the understanding/use of models and practices related to the improvement of human and organizational performance.[36]

Jacobs's competency model provides an excellent starting point for additional research.

Stolovich, Keeps, and Rodrigue's Competency Model

Harold Stolovich, Erica Keeps, and Daniel Rodrigue offered a classic and comprehensive competency model for HPE (see Exhibit 2-6).[37] Like Jacobs's model, it represents a useful starting point for transforming training and development professionals into HPE practitioners and can, if necessary, be modified to meet the needs of a unique corporate culture.

Exhibit 2-6. Human Performance Technology (HPT) Skills

Basic Skill Groups	Human Performance Technology Skill/Competency Requirements
Analysis and observation	1. Determine projects appropriate for human performance technology. a. Analyze information regarding a situation and decide if it is a human performance problem. b. Determine if the situation is suitable for human performance technology analysis and intervention.
Analysis	2. Conduct needs assessment/front-end analysis. a. Develop needs assessment/front-end analysis including selection of procedures and instruments. b. Conduct needs assessment/front-end analysis and interpret results to suggest appropriate actions or interventions. c. Determine the appropriateness, completeness, and accuracy of given needs assessment/front-end analysis plans and results.
Analysis and observation	3. Assess performer characteristics. a. Discriminate and select among entry skills assessment, prerequisite assessment, and aptitude assessment. b. Discriminate exemplary performer from average performer. c. Observe exemplary performer to determine the activities, job steps, procedures he/she does that the average performer does not do. Note the relevant expert characteristics and methods of working thinking. d. Determine the appropriateness, comprehensiveness, and adequacy of a given assessment of worker/job situation characteristics.
Analysis	4. Analyze the structural characteristics of jobs, tasks, and content. a. Select and apply a procedure for analyzing the structural characteristics of a job, task, or content that is appropriate to that job, task, or content. b. State a rationale for the selection.

Exhibit 2-6 (continued)

Basic Skill Groups	Human Performance Technology Skill/Competency Requirements
Analysis and communication	5. Write statements of human performance technology intervention outcomes. a. Discriminate objectives stated in performance behavioral terms from human performance technology intervention goals, instructional goals, organizational goals, learner/worker activities, instructional/other people activities, and objectives written in other styles. b. State outcomes in performance terms that convey the intent of the human performance technology intervention. c. Evaluate the accuracy, comprehensiveness, and appropriateness of statements of worker outcomes in terms of the job, task, or content analysis and judgment/opinion of the client, subject matter expert, or other relevant stakeholder.
Analysis and observation	6. Analyze the characteristics of a setting (learning/working environment). a. Analyze setting characteristics to determine relevant sources and constraints. b. Evaluate the accuracy, comprehensiveness, and appropriateness of a setting analysis.
Design	7. Sequence performance intervention outcomes. a. Select a procedure for sequencing performance outcomes appropriate to a given situation. b. Sequence the outcomes and state a rationale for the sequence.
Design	8. Specify performance improvement strategies. a. Select a strategy that is appropriate to the setting, the performance gap to be addressed, the average performer's characteristics, resources, and constraints, desired outcomes, and other relevant information. b. State a rationale for the selection.
Design	9. Sequence performance improvement activities. a. Specify a sequence of performance improvement activities appropriate to the achievement of specified outcomes. b. State a rationale for the selection.

Exhibit 2-6 (continued)

Basic Skill Groups	Human Performance Technology Skill/Competency Requirements
Design and management	10. Determine the resources (e.g., media, money, people) appropriate to the performance improvement activities and create all components. a. Develop resource specifications for each specified human performance technology intervention strategy and performance outcome. b. Evaluate existing human performance technology interventions to determine appropriateness with respect to specified performance outcomes. c. Adapt existing HP interventions. d. Prepare specifications for the production of materials where required (e.g., storyboards, job aids, procedure manuals). e. Organize, supervise, and monitor development and production of materials. f. Create interventions ready for testing.
Analysis and communication	11. Evaluate human performance technology intervention. a. Plan a formative evaluation (trials with subjects, expert review, analysis of implementation consideration). b. Develop a range of information-gathering techniques (questionnaires, interviews, tests, simulations, observations). c. Conduct trials. d. Analyze data. e. Generate specifications for revision based on evaluation feedback. f. Evaluate the appropriateness, comprehensiveness, and adequacy of formative evaluation plans, information-gathering techniques, and revision specifications.
Design	12. Create human performance technology intervention, implementation, monitoring, and maintenance plan. a. Determine the components of each HP intervention. b. State the rationale for each HP intervention. c. Evaluate the appropriateness, comprehensiveness, and adequacy of each HP intervention. d. Create an implementation plan for each human performance technology intervention as well as for the entire human performance technology intervention system. e. Design means for evaluating human performance technology intervention once implemented. f. Design means for monitoring and maintaining the effects of human performance technology interventions.

Exhibit 2-6 (concluded)

Basic Skill Groups	Human Performance Technology Skill/Competency Requirements
Management	13. Plan, manage, and monitor human performance technology projects. a. Create a human performance technology project plan (including timelines, budgets, staffing) appropriate to the nature of the project and the setting. b. Manage and monitor a human performance technology project.
Communication	14. Communicate effectively in visual, oral, and written form. a. Create error-free communications that result in specified performance improvement. b. Create reports that are meaningful and informative to the client organization. c. Create audit trails that document all aspects of a human performance technology project. d. Create communications that are free of bias.
Communication	15. Demonstrate appropriate interpersonal, group process, and consulting behaviors. a. Demonstrate appropriate interpersonal behaviors with individuals and groups, and state a rationale for selecting the behaviors for each situation. b. Demonstrate appropriate group process behaviors with individuals and groups, and state a rationale for selecting the behaviors for each situation. c. Demonstrate appropriate consulting behaviors with individuals and groups, and state a rationale for selecting the behaviors for each situation. d. Evaluate the appropriateness of interpersonal, group process, and consulting behaviors in given situations.
Communication	16. Promote human performance technology as a major approach to achieve desired human performance results in organizations. a. Select appropriate strategies for promoting human performance technology for specific organizational settings. b. State a rationale for selecting each strategy. c. Create opportunities for promoting human performance technology. d. Implement appropriate promotion strategies for each opportunity.

Source: Harold D. Stolovich, Erica A. Keeps, and Daniel Rodrigue, "Skills Sets for the Human Performance Technologist," *Performance Improvement Quarterly, 8,* no. 2 (1995): 46–47. Used by permission of the Learning Systems Institute, Florida State University.

What Are the Essential Competencies of HPE Professionals and Clients of HPE?

Although the HPE model provides the basis for viewing performance enhancement problems and opportunities, it does not provide sufficient guidance to training and development professionals who wish to transform themselves into HPE practitioners. To that end, a competency model for HPE is necessary. That model transcends the roles, competencies, and work outputs described in previous competency studies of training and HRD as described in Chapter 1.

Using the model of HPE as a starting point, a competency model for HPE practitioners is delineated in Appendix I. The steps in the HPE model are incorporated into the competency model, and each step becomes the basis for a role. (A *role* should not be confused with a *job title*. It is merely a way to show the parts played by HPE practitioners.) In each step, subsequent competencies are focused around the four environments within which human performance is enacted. Since all organizational and human performance is ultimately dependent on successful reception by the external (organizational) environment, that is the starting point for HPE competencies. Subsequent competencies are focused around the work environment, work, and workers. Additional competencies may have to be added to reflect unique requirements in one corporate culture, and to reflect feelings, attitudes, and values.

Clients, however, must also have characteristics that dovetail with, and support, those of HPE practitioners. Perhaps most important of client competencies are these:

- willingness to take the time to determine root causes of human performance problems and/or to permit the HPE specialist to do so
- willingness to provide access to HPE practitioners to sources of information about human performance problems
- willingness to listen, with an open mind, to the data collected (that is, the evidence gathered) from HPE practitioners about the root causes of performance problems
- willingness to consider one or more possible causes of human performance problems
- willingness to consider one or more possible interventions to address root causes
- a dissatisfaction with the status quo—and a sense of urgency to get results

In short, clients should take responsibility to work with HPE practitioners to solve problems rather than to seek quick fixes or band-aid solutions.

The competency model for HPE practitioners, paired with the model of HPE that we have proposed, is a secondary organizing scheme for this book. Each of the following chapters in this book is designed to build HPE competencies for training and development professionals who aspire to become HPE practitioners. Appendix II contains an assessment instrument based on the competency model that may be used by training and development professionals as the basis for self-assessments and for 360-degree assessment that includes the ratings of customers, distributors, suppliers, organizational superiors, peers, and organizational subordinates.

Research on HPE

More research is needed on HPE.[38] How much pressure do training and development professionals feel to focus on solving human performance problems or seizing human performance improvement opportunities instead of fulfilling their traditional roles of offering training? It is worth emphasizing that training and development professionals are feeling increased pressure to assume a broader role.

Cross-Cultural Issues in HPE

It is worth emphasizing that HPE efforts must be grounded in the cultures in which they are enacted.[39] Many of the same principles affecting other forms of cross-cultural work also affect HPE. Consequently, HPE professionals are well-advised to find what cross-cultural informants they can and seek advice for what they do—before they do it. Of special value is finding more than one informant and identifying, and planning for, shared concerns raised as common threads across them.

The increasing nature of global work means that the challenge of learning how to carry out HPE in other cultures is actually becoming more critical. Of special importance is the relative openness of people in other cultures to speak their minds about their views of performance problems and their relative importance. Not all cultures encourage the same kind of openness that is often taken for granted in Western cultures. Hence, it is important to check whether there might be culturally based reasons for individuals in other cultures to remain silent when asked for their views—or else to speak only what they believe the socially desirable responses might be that their supervisors would prefer to have noted.

Ethical Issues in HPE

HPE professionals must be as sensitive—and perhaps more sensitive—to ethics than other professionals. Since unique issues affect the professional practice of HPE, a unique professional code of conduct is warranted.[40]

But perhaps the biggest ethical dilemmas affecting HPE professionals center on four key issues:[41] (1) Should HPE professionals just do what they believe is necessary and tell the client later? (2) Should HPE professionals agree to interventions but condition their willingness to undertake it on an upfront investigation? (3) Should HPE professionals agree to an intervention but turn it toward performance improvement? and (4) Should HPE professionals agree to do what their clients ask but ensure that other interventions are added, when needed, to ensure that the performance gap is closed? These four questions essentially boil down to how much HPE practitioners should substitute their own judgment for that of their clients and/or fail to be open with clients about the symptoms, root causes, and interventions with which the HPE practitioners work. If all other things are equal, of course, the best course of action is to be open about what are the symptoms of human performance problems, what are their root causes, and what interventions are essential to get results. HPE practitioners should not secretly substitute their judgment for the client's.

Common Fallacies about HPE

There are common fallacies about human performance enhancement. Consider that HPE is more than

- Tom Gilbert's model;
- focusing on how to solve daily, individual people problems;
- a bag of tricks, tools, or techniques;
- a fad.

Some people associate HPE—variously named as Human Performance Improvement, Human Performance Technology, or Performance Consulting—with Thomas Gilbert's classic work as outlined in *Human Competence*. While Gilbert's work is foundational, it is not the only thinking of value in HPE. Confusing Gilbert's well-known Behavioral Engineering Model with HPE is like confusing the planet Jupiter with the entire solar system.

Some people also mistakenly associate HPE with the process of troubleshooting isolated performance problems of individuals. While analyzing why individuals do not do their jobs or achieve results desired from them is important, it is also too limiting for what HPE is. HPE can analyze more than individuals—such as teams, work groups, departments, divisions, organizations, industries, communities, nations, and even relations among nations.

Nor should HPE be regarded as merely a bag of tricks, tools, or techniques. While various models, tools, or techniques can be helpful in carrying out HPE, they do not encompass the field itself. To do that is to confuse aids with the field on which those aids are based. It would be much like confusing the field of medicine with a stethoscope or other medical tool.

Finally, HPE is not the latest fad. It is not a flavor of the month. While there probably have been people who expected a quick payoff from HPE without investing the time, money, and effort necessary for success, such thinking is not typical but is rather atypical. Most HPE practitioners realize that a systematic approach to analyzing problems or opportunities with human beings is not something that is prone to going out of style. It just makes good business sense.

Chapter 3
Transforming a Training Department into a Human Performance Enhancement (HPE) Department

Reinventing a training department does not happen overnight. It is not a painless process; it is, instead, a deliberate strategy undertaken to yield long-term payoffs to the organization. It requires attention to key success factors. Although the way the transformation is made may differ across organizations because of differences in corporate cultures, felt needs, and available resources, key steps in the process may include

- making the case for change to training and development professionals and stakeholders
- building awareness of the need for change;
- assessing and building support for change;
- creating a flexible road map for change;
- building competencies keyed to change.

Rarely are these steps short-circuited. Making the change takes time—and adequate preparation. This chapter focuses on these key steps.

As a warm-up to this chapter, complete the activity in Exhibit 3-1 to assess how much support for this transformation already exists in your organization.

Exhibit 3-1. Assessing Support for Transforming the Training/HRD Department to a Human Performance Enhancement Department

Directions: Your perceptions are important. They can give you valuable insights about conditions in your organization that may or may not support the process of transforming a training or HR department into a human performance enhancement department. Use this activity to help you assess conditions in your organization. Circle a code at the right for each statement in the left column. There are no right or wrong answers. Use the following rating scale:

5 = Strongly agree
4 = Agree
3 = Neutral
2 = Disagree
1 = Strongly disagree

Total the scores for each section by adding up the circled numbers. When you finish this activity, refer to the scoring section at the end.

Exhibit 3-1 (continued)

Making the Case for Change	Strongly Agree				Strongly Disagree
1. There are compelling reasons, stemming from organizational problems or opportunities, for transforming the training department into a human performance enhancement department.	5	4	3	2	1
2. Training and development professionals can see the need for changing the focus of the training department from training to enhancing human performance.	5	4	3	2	1
3. Top managers, middle managers, supervisors, and employees feel a need to move from traditional training to human performance enhancement.	5	4	3	2	1
Making the Case for Change Score: (Total the scores for items 1–3 and place the score in the box at right. Then continue to the next section.)					☐

Building Awareness of the Possibilities	Strongly Agree				Strongly Disagree
1. Training and development professionals in the organization are willing to listen to information about human performance enhancement.	5	4	3	2	1
2. Methods exist to circulate articles, conduct staff meetings, and generally provide training and development professionals with information about human performance enhancement.	5	4	3	2	1
3. Management and non-management employees are willing to listen to information about human performance enhancement.	5	4	3	2	1
4. Methods exist to circulate articles and generally provide managers and non-management employees with information about human performance enhancement.	5	4	3	2	1
Building Awareness of the Possibilities: (Total the scores for items 1–4 and place the score in the box at right. Then continue to the next section.)					☐

Exhibit 3-1 (continued)

Assessing and Building Support for Change	Strongly Agree				Strongly Disagree
1. Someone in the training department is willing to assess the support available to move beyond training to human performance enhancement.	5	4	3	2	1
2. Someone outside the training department is willing to help assess (and investigate) the need for moving beyond training to HPE.	5	4	3	2	1
3. Someone in the training department is willing to build support for change from training to HPE.	5	4	3	2	1
4. Someone outside the training department is willing to help build support for changing the role of the training department to focus on HPE.	5	4	3	2	1
Assessing and Building Support for Change: (Total the scores for items 1–4 and place the score in the box at right. Then continue to the next section.)					☐

Creating a Road Map for Change that Involves Key Decisionmakers and Stakeholders	Strongly Agree				Strongly Disagree
1. Training and development professionals are willing to create a road map for change to transform their department into a human performance enhancement department.	5	4	3	2	1
2. Training and development professionals are involved in the process of developing the change road map.	5	4	3	2	1
3. Training and development professionals are willing to involve others from inside and outside the organization in developing a change road map.	5	4	3	2	1
4. Training and development professionals have benchmarked human performance enhancement efforts in other organizations.	5	4	3	2	1
Creating a Road Map for Change: (Total the scores for items 1–4 and place the score in the box at right. Then continue to the next section.)					☐

Exhibit 3-1 (concluded)

Building Competencies Keyed to the Change Effort	Strongly Agree				Strongly Disagree
1. The organization is willing to invest in helping traditional training and development professionals receive the retraining they need to function effectively as internal consultants on human performance enhancement.	5	4	3	2	1
2. The organization is willing to train managers on approaches to enhancing human performance.	5	4	3	2	1
3. The organization is willing to train employees on approaches to enhancing human performance for themselves and their coworkers.	5	4	3	2	1
Building Competencies Keyed to the Change Effort: (Total the scores for items 1–3 and place the score in the box at right. Then continue to the next section.)					☐

Scoring:

Use the preceding activity to help you assess the readiness of your organization to move beyond training to enhancing human performance. Generally speaking, the lower the score in each of the five parts of the activity, the greater the need to concentrate your attention on that issue in building support for action.

A score between 3 and 6 in the **making the case for change** section of the activity indicates significant barriers to action in that area. If your score is in that range, devote your initial efforts to making the case for change.

A score between 4 and 8 in the **building awareness** section of the activity indicates significant barriers to action in that area. If your score is in that range, devote your initial efforts to building awareness.

A score between 4 and 8 in the **assessing and building support for change** section of the activity indicates significant barriers to action in that area. If your score is in that range, devote your initial efforts to assessing and building support for change.

A score between 4 and 8 in the **creating a road map for change** section of the activity indicates significant barriers to action in that area. If your score is in that range, devote your initial efforts to creating a road map for change.

A score between 3 and 6 in the **building competencies keyed to the change effort** section of the activity indicates significant barriers to action in that area. If your score is in that range, devote your initial efforts to building knowledge, skills, and abilities to the change effort.

If you scored differently, then give initial priority to the area in which you scored lowest. If you wish, administer the activity to all members of the training department, compile the individual scores, feed the results back to the participants, and use it as a basis for joint problem solving and action planning.

How Should Organizations Support HPE: Key Success Factors

Numerous success factors contribute to the successful implementation of HPE, according to previous work on the topic.[1] Apart from what will be discussed in the following sections of this chapter, success in implementing HPE hinges on a willingness to identify root causes, a willingness of HPE consultants to partner with clients, an aversion to overly quick rushes to select and implement interventions, and avoidance of the rigid adherence to models. Success is particularly dependent on five principles:[2] (1) following strategy; (2) devising and implementing a communication plan; (3) selecting and using a tracking technology to identify and provide feedback on successes; (4) educating people about HPE; and (5) providing people with recognition and rewards for participating. Of particular importance is that, to the extent that training and development professionals are involved and are slated to become HPE professionals, they undergo a change of mindset to focus on results rather than on the activity of training.[3] Of particular importance for trainers is learning to say "no" when asked for the wrong interventions by their customers.[4] A particular useful approach is to begin with "I don't know" and ask many questions to clarify the situation—perhaps even in the client's mind.[5]

Making the Case for Change

Making the case for change to training and development professionals and stakeholders simply means convincing people that change is needed. Every change effort, if it is to be successful, should begin with this step, simply because people are unwilling to change unless they see worthwhile reasons for doing so.

When making the case for change, someone or some group will need to be convinced early. That person or group, the *change agent* or catalyst for change, should begin by collecting evidence of a compelling need for change.

Finding a Change Agent

Change of any kind usually begins with dissatisfaction with the way things are. The change agent can be the individual or group that is most dissatisfied. Driven by dissatisfaction, change agents seek innovative solutions to tough problems or creative improvement strategies to take advantage of opportunities they see.

Change agents can surface from inside or outside an organization. Rarely is it necessary for someone to find them, because they usually find themselves. They may read an article, listen to a presentation, or have a discussion that prompts dissatisfaction with the status quo and then set about seeking innovations to relieve their dissatisfaction.

The same process occurs at the outset of an effort to transform a training department into an HPE department. Change agents must become dissatisfied with traditional approaches and thinking about training. They then seek evidence of a need for change and possible approaches to making that change.

Seeking Evidence of the Need for Change

Dissatisfaction is not enough to create a foundation for change. A new vision of the way things ought to be should also exist. But such a vision rarely comes into existence spontaneously. Typically it is necessary to begin by conducting an open-ended search for evidence that others also believe that change is needed.

Methods of seeking such evidence are limited only by the creativity of change agents. However, here are some possible strategies:

- **Collect benchmarking information from "best-in-class" organizations.** Many well-known organizations have made the switch from focusing on training as a standalone effort to a broader focus on enhancing performance. Change agents should obtain the names of individuals at those organizations, phone or write them, ask them what business reasons or business issues prompted the change, and ask them how they approach solving human performance problems or seizing human performance enhancement opportunities.
- **Collect benchmarking information from within the industry or locally.** Sometimes "best-in-class" organizations are threatening to others precisely because their approaches are cutting-edge. For that reason, some change agents may prefer to discuss the need for moving beyond training with others in the same industry or with training and development professionals employed by other organizations located in the same geographical area. A good approach is to ask them how they ensure that human performance enhancement occurs *before* and *after* training. Listen carefully to any strategies they use, because they may suggest innovative approaches to enhancing human performance.
- **Examine the organization's strategic plan.** How might the organization's strategic plan provide evidence that a need exists to improve human performance? Can a convincing case be made that the strategy implies the need for a training department to assume a new, expanded role in enhancing human performance? If so, in what specific ways?
- **Focus on customer or stakeholder needs.** Change agents can solicit evidence from customers and other stakeholders that a change is warranted. How might recent problems with customers provide compelling evidence that a need exists to move beyond traditional training and to focus on enhancing human performance?
- **Collect testimonial evidence from the organization.** Have there been recent cases when training, carried out as a solitary change effort, failed to facilitate a change in the organization? If so, can change agents collect evidence about the failure as a starting point for making the case for change?

- **Identify underlying causes of recent crises.** Related to testimonial evidence is information about the underlying causes of recent crises in the organization. Could any have been averted by applying a more holistic approach to enhancing human performance? Can such evidence be found, and can the differences in approaches be described?
- **Identify existing problems.** What are the most pressing problems confronting the organization? How might traditional training approach those problems? How might a more holistic approach to enhancing human performance contrast with a traditional training approach? Can such a difference be dramatically described and illustrated?
- **Build from the values of decision makers.** What have top managers and other leaders in the organizations identified as high priorities? Could a human performance enhancement approach yield more useful ideas than training about effective approaches to achieve desired goals?

Building Awareness of the Need for Change

Change agents may be convinced of the need for change, and they may be able to marshal evidence to show that it is needed. But to build an impetus for transforming a traditional training function into a human performance enhancement function, change agents will also need to find a change champion, present their evidence of the need for change, build awareness of possible directions for change, and broaden the scope of the change effort.

Finding a Change Champion

Change agents are early advocates for transforming a training department into an HPE department. However, they rarely have complete authority to make their wishes turn into realities. For that purpose they require a *change champion* whose role is to provide credibility for the effort and garner the resources to help make it happen.[6] The change champion is usually a key customer of the training department from inside or outside the organization, often a top manager or key operating manager; however, the change champion may be an entire work team, department, or division. With the change champion's support, the transformation from a training to a human performance enhancement department commands the attention of the training staff; the champion lends credibility to the effort and locates resources.

To find a change champion, change agents should look to longtime supporters of traditional training efforts. Change agents should then use the evidence they have accumulated from other sources to show that training can be transformed to focus on HPE. Change agents usually have to make their case for change through personal selling (such as meetings with the customers) or by circulating books and articles about HPE to change champions and others affected by the change.

Presenting Evidence of the Need for Change

Who is the target of the effort to move beyond traditional training? Is it a centralized training department or function, decentralized training departments or functions, or key operating managers? In most cases, it is all of them—and in the order indicated—unless the organization is lacking one or more of these groups.

The most frequent target of efforts to win support for the change is the centralized training department. After all, training and development professionals must see and feel a need for change before they can support it. Effective ways to begin with the training department include the following:

- Present evidence accumulated externally and internally that supports the need to transform the training department into an HPE department.
- Provide information about differences between traditional training and HPE.
- Address key objections raised by those affected by the change.
- Broaden the base of change agents, enlisting training and development professionals to collect evidence of the need for change, possible directions for that change, and possible strategies by which to make the change.
- Develop strategies for involving training and development professionals' customers in the process.

Change agents may begin by presenting evidence they have already accumulated. They can also draw on the change champion to support the change effort, provide the business reasons to justify it, and lend credibility to it. That is accomplished by making presentations at meetings of training and development department staff, writing and circulating concept papers that explains the need for change and what it means, or circulating books and articles showing that such change is warranted.

Building Awareness of Possible Directions for Change

Change agents can continue building awareness by focusing staff meeting discussions around the need for change, circulating articles or books that describe possible approaches to enhancing human performance, inviting training and development professionals to take field trips to "best-in-class" organizations that have successfully transformed their training departments into human performance enhancement departments, or asking training and development professionals to complete a questionnaire to dramatize differences between the activities of traditional training or HRP departments and human performance enhancement departments.

Change agents must be prepared to address objections raised about the change by training and development professionals, line managers, and external stakeholders. Some major barriers to moving beyond training, which usually surface as objections, are presented in Exhibit 3-2. Examine the barriers listed in the exhibit and formulate possible responses to them before they arise.

Exhibit 3-2. Barriers to Transforming the Training Department into a Human Performance Enhancement Department

Directions: For each barrier (possible objection) to transforming a training department listed in the left column below, write your notes about ways of overcoming these barriers (or answering these objections) in the space to the right. Involve training and development professionals in this activity, if possible.

Barrier/Objection	Possible Strategies for Overcoming the Barrier and Answering the Objection
Lack of knowledge about human performance enhancement	
Lack of time to focus attention on holistic human performance improvement instead of traditional training	
Lack of resources (time, money, equipment, staff)	
Lack of training and development professionals' support	
Lack of management support	
Rivalry across (or within) departments	
Lack of observable success	
Lack of consistent buy-in	
Poor incentives	
Other (list your own barriers):	

Source: The barriers listed in the left column are adapted from Peter Dean, "Examining the Practice of Human Performance Technology." *Performance Improvement Quarterly, 8,* no. 2 (1995): 85. They are used by permission of the Learning Systems Institute, Florida State University.

Broadening the Scope of the Change Effort

At this point the change agent or change champion should seek to include others in the change effort. That may mean forming an *ad hoc* team composed of training and development professionals and the change champion to collect evidence of the need to move beyond traditional training. For purposes of credibility, such a team should be handpicked to include the most credible members of the training department, the training director, his or her organizational superior (such as the vice president for human resources), and a key operating manager or top manager. Such a team, which can become the basis for later efforts to identify HPE needs and to establish HPE strategies to meet them, should operate according to the principles of *action learning* (see Exhibit 3-3).

Exhibit 3-3. A Model of Action Learning

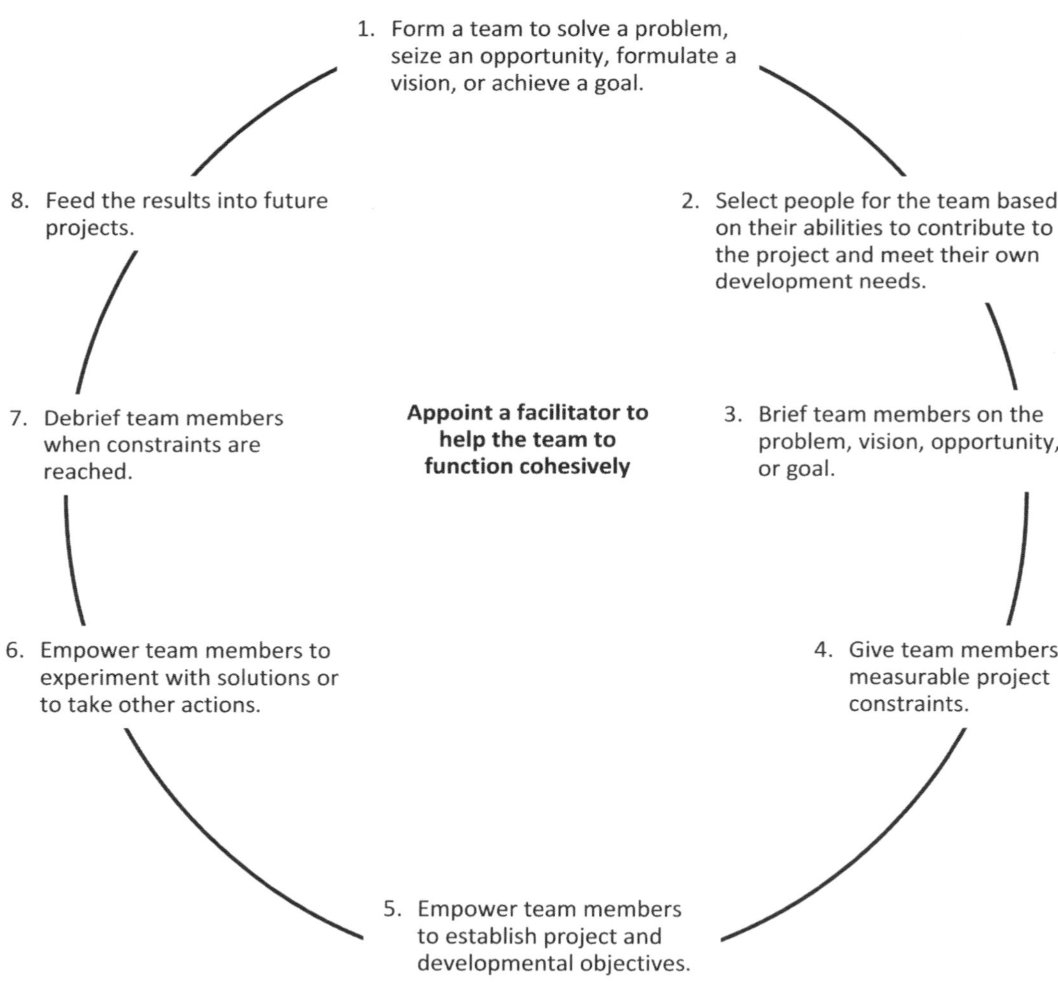

1. Form a team to solve a problem, seize an opportunity, formulate a vision, or achieve a goal.
2. Select people for the team based on their abilities to contribute to the project and meet their own development needs.
3. Brief team members on the problem, vision, opportunity, or goal.
4. Give team members measurable project constraints.
5. Empower team members to establish project and developmental objectives.
6. Empower team members to experiment with solutions or to take other actions.
7. Debrief team members when constraints are reached.
8. Feed the results into future projects.
Appoint a facilitator to help the team to function cohesively

The team should be

- formed with a specific mandate to collect more evidence, develop strategies for introducing change into the training department, craft strategies for expressing the need for the change and what it will mean to key stakeholders, and formulate strategies for introducing the change;
- composed of credible people who are carefully chosen for the competencies they bring to the project and for their own development needs;
- briefed on what they are to investigate and on possible methods of carrying out the investigation;
- given measurable project constraints expressed in time, money, and staff;
- given broad latitude to establish project objectives and individual developmental objectives;
- facilitated by someone who has the ability to help the group function cohesively (perhaps the change agent);
- empowered to collect evidence, creatively present it to peers (and others), and prepare an action plan for moving a traditional training department from "where it is" to "where it should be" as an HPE department;
- debriefed upon project completion—and there should be a "sunset time"—for what was learned collectively by team, what was learned individually by members, how the same approach could be applied to future efforts (such as similar teams formed cross-functionally with operating departments), what developmental needs emerged for the team over the project's life, and what individual team member needs emerged over the project's life.

This approach resembles the approach used in forming and conducting process improvement teams. That is not an accident, because teams charged with collecting evidence in support of "reinventing" the training or HRD department or function and formulating ideas about how to do that are functioning as process management teams. When the first team has completed its work, other teams should be formed to disseminate the evidence and strategies to other parts of the organization, thereby giving employees and management an involvement in the process and tailoring efforts to the unique perspectives of different organizational functions and geographical locations.

Assessing and Building Support for Change

Once change agents have made a convincing case for moving beyond traditional training and have set in motion methods of building awareness about what that will mean to training and development professionals, they should then focus on assessing and building organizational support for the change. No change has a chance of success if key customers reject it.

But what is support? How can it be assessed? How can it be built?

What Is Support?

Support means *readiness for change backed by the resources necessary for acting appropriately.* It also connotes the willingness of others to cooperate with change. Support may be viewed as a continuum (see Exhibit 3-4), ranging from lack of support to full support backed by a personal commitment to garner the resources necessary for realizing the desired change.

Exhibit 3-4. A Continuum of Support for Change

Level 1 No Support	Level 2	Level 3 Partial Support	Level 4	Level 5 Full Support
Nobody sees the need for change, and nobody is willing to support it.	A small number of people see a need for change, are willing to support it, and will take personal risks to see that the change is adopted.	A larger number of people see a need for change but are unsure of what to do.	People support change but pay it lip service or are unwilling to make a personal commitment or provide resources.	Almost everyone sees a need for change, is willing to provide resources to implement it, and is willing to be personally involved in making it happen.

Support can vary on the continuum among different groups. For full support to be achieved, everyone involved in transforming the training department into an HPE department should be positioned on the far right of the continuum.

How Can Support Be Assessed?

Assessing support is a political activity. To carry it out successfully, change agents and/or training and development professionals should identify key decision makers who are likely to back or to back away from a proposed change. Consider at least five key questions when assessing support for making the transformation from a training to an HPE effort:

1. How well satisfied are decision makers and other stakeholders with the training department's products and services?
2. How much are decision makers and other stakeholders aware of alternatives to traditional training?
3. How well has the organization traditionally supported training?
4. How well does the corporate culture support the change?
5. What has been the track record of the training department in delivering what it has promised?

If everyone is satisfied with the job that the training department is doing, the pressure for change will not be great. Change agents will have to mount a forceful, persuasive campaign to build awareness of a new, expanded role for the training department.

If decision makers and other stakeholders are not aware that they can ask more than training of a training department, they will not do so. It is for this reason that many training departments, as an early step in moving beyond training, go through appropriate channels to change their names to "performance enhancement," "performance improvement," or "performance technology." The new title signals a new mission, shows that it is organizationally supported, and advertises a new role.

If the organization has not traditionally supported training—that is, if support for training is on level 1, 2, 3, or 4 in Exhibit 3-4—then it will be exceedingly difficult to move beyond training. Efforts must first be made to establish support at level 5. From there a move beyond training should be possible.

Corporate culture also provides a yardstick for measuring support. Understood to mean the *"basic assumptions* and *beliefs* that are shared by members of an organization, that operate unconsciously, and that define in a basic 'taken-for-granted' fashion an organization's view of itself and its environment,"[7] culture is important because "people are animals suspended in webs of significance they themselves have spun, and culture can be understood to be those webs."[8] Culture may pose a barrier to change. Assess how supportive of change the organization's culture will be by asking experienced training and development professionals—and other seasoned veterans of the organization—about efforts by the training department to take innovative action in the past. Stories are often the best indicators of culture, and seeking information about past efforts to introduce innovation may provide valuable clues about what to do—and what to avoid—when transforming a training department into a human performance enhancement department. Soliciting stories may provide a means to conduct a culture audit.[9]

The training department's track record may also provide valuable clues about how easy—or how difficult—it will be to move beyond training. If the department has a history of promising more than it could deliver—or of being set up for failure by ill-conceived management schemes—then the department and its members will lack credibility. That will impede the transformation process, making it more difficult to convince others that training and development professionals can handle an expanded role.

How Can Support Be Built?

Several strategies may be used to build support for broadening the training department's role to include HPE.

One strategy is for the training department to create a sterling track record of accomplishment in its traditional role. Training and development professionals focus attention on problems that are the most pressing to the organization, marshal considerable efforts to solve the problems, and then use the enhanced credibility stemming from these successful efforts to launch into HPE.

Another strategy is to start small, with a pilot project, and to move beyond training in one critically important business area. Advocates of change can then follow through on the learners' jobs to improve human performance holistically, gain allies among key decision makers in this process to give the pilot project high visibility, and use the results as a launching pad for an expanded role.

A third strategy is to hitchhike on other continuous improvement efforts. Change advocates can volunteer the training department to help in these initiatives if possible (and if the training department is not otherwise invited to be involved). If the department makes a solid contribution to the effort, it can then use that experience to persuade decision makers that it can assume a broader range of duties, including internal consulting.

Above all, change advocates must take steps to overcome the barriers identified during the process of assessing support.

Creating a Flexible Road Map for Change

Once change agents and training and development professionals have made a convincing case for change, established awareness of a new role for the training department, and assessed and established support, they should then create a flexible road map to guide the transition from traditional training to HPE. To do so, they should consider these questions:

- **Why should the change occur?** How can the results be justified in measurable, bottom-line terms? Use results of previous benchmarking efforts—or small-scale pilot efforts in the organization, if possible—to demonstrate that the benefits of transforming the training department outweigh the cost and time involved. Be prepared to share anecdotal evidence in the absence of convincing financial benefits. However, recall that, according to Thomas Gilbert, the Performance Improvement Potential (PIP) for improvement efforts can be calculated by computing the difference in the value of outputs between exemplars and all other performers.[10] In other words, identify the highest performing worker in an area, decide how much his or her output is worth, calculate the difference between what he or she produces and what others produce, and then forecast the benefits of enhancing the performance of all other workers in the area so that the value of their performance equals that of the best performer. Use that figure as a persuasive point to help make the case for transforming the training department into an HPE department. Involve key operating managers and top managers in this process, if possible, so that they will share ownership in the results.
- **Who should be involved?** Should the process begin with one change agent, or should it begin with a group of change agents and gradually spread out to include a centralized training department, decentralized training departments positioned within operating units, and training and development services provided to customers, suppliers, or distributors? Who should be involved in crafting the flexible action plan to ensure ownership and support?
- **What should be the mission, goals, and objectives of the human performance enhancement department?** Reconsider the mission, goals, and objectives of the training department. Why should an HPE department exist? Whose needs should it serve primarily? Secondarily? What general results should the function seek to achieve, and how can those results be measured?

- **When should the changes occur?** Making transformational change on an organizational scale is extraordinarily difficult to do in a short time. As a result, it makes sense to establish milestones—that is, specific times by which demonstrable results will have been achieved. These milestones should be expressed in measurable terms—for example, "By December 1, the training department will have changed its name to the human performance enhancement department." Link milestones to measurable objectives to be achieved by the HPE function, if possible.
- **Where should the changes occur?** This question overlaps conceptually with the question of who should be involved in the change effort. In fact, decisions about who should be involved, what results should be achieved, and when they should be achieved will influence the answer to this question. Should efforts to transform the training department into an HPE department begin in Greenfield operations (new location startups) where the corporate culture is not so deeply ingrained? Should they begin in the United States or in other locales, depending on the organization's scope of operations? Where will it be possible to achieve the greatest success most quickly? The answer to the last question may provide valuable clues about where to start.
- **How much will the changes cost?** Transforming the training department to an HPE function will not be free. It can be expensive. Examples of expenses include the financial value of the following:
  - the change agent's time in facilitating the change (such as salary, benefits, and costs incurred while gathering evidence, lining up a change champion, making the case for change to training staff, making the case for change to other stakeholders, and participating in planning the change)
  - the change champion's time
  - staff salaries, benefit expenses, and other costs incurred while staff members are being convinced of the need for the change, are collecting evidence of the need for change, assessing and building support, are involved in preparing a flexible action plan, and are being trained or developed for an expanded role as HPE practitioners

Approaches to Flexible Planning

How can the preceding questions be answered? One approach, of course, is to form an action learning team that includes training and development professionals, key customers, suppliers, distributors, and other stakeholders of the training department.

Another approach is to hold a management retreat or a series of employee meetings focused around transforming the training department into an HPE function. The change agent and the change champion may serve as facilitators, or an external consultant who is knowledgeable about HPE may be hired. Participants should include members of the training department, representatives of key groups that depend on training department products and services, and others who support the development of a flexible action plan leading to the transformation of the training department into an HPE department. Participants should carefully develop a flexible action plan to present to top management (see Exhibit 3-5).

Exhibit 3-5. A Worksheet to Guide Flexible Planning

Directions: For each question appearing in the left column, provide an answer in the column at the right. Use this worksheet in the planning process, giving training staff members, key customers of the training function, and others an opportunity to complete it. Then use their responses in finalizing a plan or in developing a well-crafted proposal for consideration by top management.

QUESTIONS	ANSWERS
Why should the training department take a new, more holistic approach to enhancing human performance? (*What business issues may warrant such an expanded role?*)	
Who should be involved? (*In changing the training department into a human performance enhancement function, who should participate in the process?*)	
What should be the mission, goals, and objectives of the human performance enhancement function?	
When should the changes occur? (*What results should be achieved over time?*)	
Where should the changes occur? (*Are some locales or business units more likely than others to achieve quick, highly visible success?*)	
How much will the change cost? (*What expenses will be incurred in the process? What benefits may result from the transformation?*)	

Building Competencies Key to the Change Effort

A critical element of transforming a training department into an HPE department is building the competencies of training and development professionals so that they can assume more challenging roles. One good way to begin this process is to develop an organization-specific competency model for HPE.

Building a Competency Model

There are different ways to build an organization-specific competency model for HPE. One approach is to use an existing team of training and development professionals or form a new one to review existing HPE competency models and adapt them to the organization's unique requirements and expectations. Examples of such models were described at the end of Chapter 2. While the results of this approach are not likely to be rigorous, they will be fast.

Another approach is to use Rapid Results Assessment (RRA). To begin RRA, inform training and development professionals and other stakeholders about HPE (generally) and about HPE competencies. Do that by circulating articles or by providing information about HPE through other means. Then select a group of between eight and thirteen exemplary training and development professionals from the organization and a few of their exemplary supervisors and invite them to attend a focus group meeting lasting between one and two days.

Begin the meeting by explaining to the participants why they were chosen to participate and what they are to do in the meeting. Appoint a facilitator to guide the process, name two or three additional participants to help the facilitator, and arrange the participants in U-shaped seating. Then ask them to reflect on what they read about HPE before the meeting and have them call out activities that they believe would be part of the role of an HPE specialist. Record each activity on a separate 8½" x 11" sheet of paper, and post all the sheets on the wall in front of the participants. Allow them to continue listing activities until they run out of ideas. Then take a break.

During the break, the facilitator and his or her confederates should develop between four and twelve descriptive categories of activities on the left side of the wall and then rearrange all the activity sheets across the wall opposite the categories to which they are best suited. Participants should then be called back from break and asked to verify the categories. (They can change the names of the categories, add to them, subtract from them, or make other modifications.) Once the categories are verified, the facilitator should ask participants to reexamine each activity listed in the first round. They can add, subtract, modify, or combine information. This process, while time-consuming, encourages the participants to reach consensus on the role activities for HPE practitioners in their organization. It is a future-oriented and thought-provoking activity that crystallizes a detailed vision of what the future should be like.

A final product of the meeting will be a matrix of work activities for HPE practitioners unique to the organization. The matrix can be removed from the wall and typed on one sheet. This matrix, which provides a more concrete description of work activities than most job descriptions offer, can become the basis for a detailed, organization-specific competency model of what HPE professionals should do. Additional steps, perhaps conducted by survey, can lead to the identification of underlying HPE competencies, work outputs, job performance standards, selection criteria, and performance appraisal criteria. Of course, electronic means may be substituted for face-to-face approaches.

Conducting an Overall Staff Assessment

Once the organization has established a competency model for HPE, it becomes necessary to assess how well the training and development staff is collectively prepared to meet the new role expectations. In a small organization or in a small training department, it should be possible to construct a total staff assessment on one sheet of paper or on a single computer screen, with competencies/work activities/steps in HPE arranged along the left column, names of staff members arranged along the top, and ratings supplied by the training director and by training and development professionals in each cell of the staff assessment chart (see Exhibit 3-6 for a simple example). The staff assessment can be used to identify common training needs shared by the training staff, and this information can in turn become the basis for a large-scale developmental effort to build HPE competencies in line with new work expectations.

Conducting Individualized Assessments

In large organizations, it is rarely possible to conduct an overall staff assessment on a single sheet of paper; individualized assessments should be conducted by developing an individualized assessment instrument to be completed by both the training and development professional and his or her immediate supervisor. Colleagues—such as organizational subordinates, peers in other areas of the organization, and external customers or family members—can also be asked to complete the same assessment. The scores are then averaged and used to identify individual training needs linked to HPE work requirements. This individualized information may be fed upward so that it can be used to construct a comprehensive total staff assessment and development plan.

Developing Staff Development and Individualized Development Plans

The results of the assessment process can be used to identify areas in which training and development on HPE are needed. The HPE model should inform efforts to build the competencies of training and development professionals.

Eventually, the same approach may be extended to include all executives, managers, supervisors, or employees in the organization. After all, performance enhancement competencies can be important for everyone—not just for trainers-turned-HPE practitioners.

Exhibit 3-6. A Simple Example of a Format for an Overall Staff Assessment

Directions: List HPE competencies for the organization in the left column. Then, in each cell opposite each competency, list the name of training and development professionals. Under each name, rate the training and development professional's level of expertise as follows: 3 = Exemplary; 2 = Adequate; 1 = Needs training and development in this area;
0 = Not applicable.

Competencies for HPE in the Organization	Names and Competency Ratings of Training and Development Professionals in the Organization

Communicating the Need for Change

Key to launching an HPE intervention is to build a compelling business case for change. That is often best done by the senior-most official of the organizational unit that seeks to change. A communication strategy must be established during every step of the change effort to remind people why the intervention has been undertaken, what results are being garnered from it, and why continued participation and effort is essential.

Hence, it is important to pose such questions as these:

- Who needs to be communicated with during the effort? (List all the stakeholders and indicate what they care about.)
- What should be communicated?
- When should communication be undertaken?
- What methods should be used to communicate?
- How can the success of the communication efforts be measured?

Use the worksheet appearing in Exhibit 3-7 to plan a communication strategy for an HPE effort.

Training People to Think Like HPE Professionals

Do not assume that people just naturally know how to think like HPE professionals. Some training may be needed. And, indeed, a particularly helpful strategy is to train such key stakeholders as executives, managers, supervisors, union leaders, and participants in the performance improvement intervention in a model of HPE. It is thus useful to train them in all steps of the HPE model, including the following:

- Distinguish symptoms from root causes.
- Describe conditions systematically.
- Select and clarify criteria.
- Identify metrics by which to assess gaps.
- Determine importance.
- Determine root causes.
- Assess the feasibility (costs and benefits) of possible performance interventions.
- Select the most feasible HPE intervention.
- Plan for communicating about the change effort, building a compelling business case.
- Establish an implementation plan for the HPE intervention.
- Consider possible negative side effects of implementation so as to avert them.
- Evaluate intervention results before, during, and after the intervention.

Such training may be provided by onsite, online, or blended instruction.

Exhibit 3-7. A Worksheet for Developing a Communication Strategy

Directions: For each step in the implementation of a Human Performance Enhancement intervention of any kind, as shown in the left-hand column below, answer each question in the columns to the right to establish a robust communication strategy.

HPE STRATEGY	QUESTIONS TO ADDRESS IN DEVELOPING A COMMUNICATION STRATEGY				
Steps in the HPE Implementation Strategy	Who needs to be communicated with during the HPE implementation?	What should be communicated?	When should communication be undertaken?	What methods should be used to communicate?	How can the success of the communication efforts be measured?

Is It Just the Training and Development Department That Can Become an HPE Function?

Is it just the training and development department or function that can be transformed to focus on HPE? The answer is a resounding "no." While training is often the first area that is considered for conversion to an HPE function, the reality is that any department or function could become an HPE department or function. For instance, the HR department could become the HPE department; the quality department could become the HPE department; the internal audit group could become the HPE department. Where there is a will, there is a way. That applies to HPE as much as to anything else.

Part Two: Troubleshooting Human Performance Problems and Analyzing Human Performance Improvement Opportunities

CHAPTER 1: Why Training Is Not Enough

CHAPTER 2: What Is Human Performance Enhancement (HPE)?

CHAPTER 3: Transforming a Training Department into a Human Performance Enhancement (HPE) Department

CHAPTER 4: Analyzing *What Is* Happening

CHAPTER 5: Envisioning *What Should Be* Happening

CHAPTER 6: Clarifying Present and Future Performance Gaps

CHAPTER 7: Determining the Importance of Performance Gaps

CHAPTER 8: Identifying the Underlying Causes of Performance Gaps

CHAPTER 9: Selecting Human Performance Enhancement (HPE) Strategies

CHAPTER 10: Implementing Human Performance Enhancement (HPE) Strategies to Address Organizational Environment Problems or Opportunities

CHAPTER 11: Implementing Human Performance Enhancement (HPE) Strategies to Address Work Problems or Opportunities

CHAPTER 12: Implementing Human Performance Enhancement (HPE) Strategies to Address Work Environment Problems or Opportunities

CHAPTER 13: Implementing Human Performance Enhancement (HPE) Strategies to Address Worker Problems or Opportunities

CHAPTER 14: Evaluating Human Performance Enhancement (HPE) Strategies

Chapter 4
Analyzing *What Is* Happening

Analyzing present conditions is an essential starting point for any HPE strategy, just as it is for strategic planning. In both cases, an understanding of present conditions provides valuable clues to guide future improvement efforts.[1] Indeed, few improvement efforts can be launched if HPE practitioners or other stakeholders in the change processes lack current, accurate, and reliable information about the organizational environment, the work environment, the work, and the workers. Simply put, you have to know where you are before you can strike out for a different destination.

This chapter focuses on the first step in the new model to guide HPE. The chapter reviews how much and what kind of information is needed to analyze present conditions, what philosophical approaches may underlie the process, how to collect information about what is happening, and what competencies are required by HPE practitioners to carry out the role of auditor.

What Does It Mean to Analyze *What Is* Happening?

Analyzing what is happening means *collecting information about the present level of performance.* The goal of the HPE practitioner and/or other stakeholders is simply to describe existing conditions. This often seems easier to do than it turns out to be in fact.

Facts or Perceptions?

The first question to consider is: *What are we looking for?* Do we want to know what is actually happening or what people perceive to be happening, or both?

Facts can be independently verified. They are not open to debate. Examples of facts include the date the organization was founded, the names of company executives, the organization structure as depicted on an organization chart, last year's profit margin, scrap rates, service levels, inventory, and accounts receivable. If two different people are asked questions about any of these subjects, they will provide identical answers, provided they take time to check existing records and records are not riddled with errors.

Perceptions, on the other hand, cannot be independently verified. They represent opinions, beliefs, and values. Examples of perceptions include opinions about employee morale, work process bottlenecks (and who is to "blame" for them), customer satisfaction levels (in the absence of data), and opportunities for future ventures.

Perceptions may be widely shared, but that does not mean that they are necessarily true or false. People may vary in what they perceive, and the same event may be open to multiple interpretations. If, for example, a CEO announces a widespread downsizing, people may draw different conclusions and thus have different perceptions about what that means. A cynic may remark that "the company is just trying to increase profits so that executives can grant themselves fat bonuses." Another person may say that "the downsizing was prompted to cut the fat to make the company more competitive in a fierce, and often hostile, global marketplace." A third may assert that "the aim of the downsizing is to shake managers and workers out of their complacency and force them to pay more attention to what the customers want." A fourth may view a downsizing as a laudable effort to streamline the organization's (purportedly inefficient) operations—which is often the charitable view taken by financial analysts and stockholders when they hear that a downsizing is in the works. Any—or none—of these perceptions may be "true."

Although perceptions may vary—and may also be deceiving—they are worthy of consideration. Yet many managers say otherwise, asserting that "we never base decisions on what we perceive but only on what we can prove." Nonetheless, most decisions about entering new markets, downsizing organizational units, or promoting individual workers are based on intuition and perception; facts are marshaled only to support those perceptions. As Mark Twain once quoted Benjamin Disraeli, "There are three kinds of lies: lies, damned lies, and statistics."

When managers and employees lack complete facts on which to base decisions, they rely on perceptions. Moreover, perceptions affect reality. Skeptics who do not believe that might consider that the stock market fluctuates on a minute-by-minute basis as a result of investor perceptions about companies' profitability and future prospects. Self-fulfilling prophecies come true because what people perceive influences how they behave.

In examining what is happening, then, it is important to capture information both about *what is actually happening* and about *what people perceive to be happening*. That is particularly true if employee involvement is desired, because employees, like managers, often base their own decisions on perceptions.

The difference between facts and perceptions is similar to the difference in the results obtained by researchers in the physical and the social sciences. Physical scientists seek facts. To determine the number of computers in a building, for example, they tour the building and count them. Their numbers can be independently verified by someone else who takes the same tour and follows the same procedure. Social scientists, on the other hand, rely heavily on people's perceptions. To determine the number of computers in the same building, they might select a random sample of people positioned at different locations in the building, call them, and ask for their independent opinions about the number of computers in the building or in their vicinity. They would then average these opinions to arrive at an approximate number of computers. A second researcher following the same procedure might reach a different conclusion. Social scientists thus tend to measure perceptions, not facts. Yet both the physical scientist's and the social scientist's approaches are worth knowing and can affect or even drive decision making.

Who Is Asking?

When examining what is happening, HPE practitioners are limited by their knowledge at the outset of an investigation. HPE practitioners who are brought in as external consultants to an organization (or a work unit) will need more background information than those who work in the setting.

Clients are often unwilling to spend valuable time orienting HPE practitioners to unfamiliar settings. There are several reasons for this reluctance. First, an orientation can be costly if external HPE practitioners are charging a high daily rate. Second, conducting an orientation takes valuable time, and the client may have neither time nor staff to spare to orient the practitioners. Third, the client may be unsure of the payoffs that will result from the investment; if HPE practitioners prove to be less than helpful, the time and money spent on orienting them will have been wasted.

In most cases, then, HPE practitioners must take proactive steps to orient themselves quickly to their client's environment in ways that are sensitive to the client's needs and are appropriate to the consulting the client has requested.

One way to do that is to gather information quickly about the four environments affecting human performance—the organizational environment, the work environment, the work, and the worker. To perform such a simple analysis, the practitioner can pose the following questions by phone, electronic mail, fax, or videoconference to several knowledgeable people in the work setting and then compare their responses to detect underlying themes:

The Organizational Environment

- What does the organization do better than its competitors?
- How well has the organization been competing against others in the industry? outside the industry? domestically? internationally?
- What issues have been posing the greatest challenges to the organization, and how have they been managed?
- How do customers perceive the organization? How are their perceptions collected?

The Work Environment

- What major changes have been occurring inside the organization?
- What prompted those changes?

The Work

- How does the organization currently achieve results through work methods and processes? How is the customer served?
- What changes in technology, suppliers, distributors, or other factors are most affecting work methods? How?

The Workers

- What is noteworthy about the people who do the work? Why is it noteworthy?
- What is the reputation of the organization among its workers? What is its employment brand?
- Why do people quit the organization, and what is the organization's level of engagement?
- What is the most important issue confronting workers now? Why is it important?
- HPE practitioners may wish to orient themselves to the setting in a more comprehensive way. They can create an interview guide from the list of questions for organizational assessment that appears in Exhibit 4-1 and then interview a cross-section of organizational members.

Exhibit 4-1. Orienting the HPE Specialist to the Performance Setting

Directions: Use the following checklist to orient yourself to a new performance setting. For each question posed in the left column, respond in the appropriate column to the right. Adapt the checklist as necessary by adding notes in the right column.

QUESTIONS *Have you clarified...*	Yes ☒	No ☒	N/A ☒	NOTES
1. The name of the organization?	☐	☐	☐	
2. The location(s) in which the organization operates?	☐	☐	☐	
3. The industry or industries in which the organization operates?	☐	☐	☐	
4. The sector of the economy of which the organization is part (profit, not-for-profit, or public)?	☐	☐	☐	
5. The organization's affiliations to other organizations? (Is it a holding company, a wholly owned subsidiary, an autonomous firm?)	☐	☐	☐	
6. The organization's size?	☐	☐	☐	
7. The organization's financial condition?	☐	☐	☐	
8. The number of stockholders and employees?	☐	☐	☐	
9. Why an initial contact has been made with the prospective client?	☐	☐	☐	

Exhibit 4-1 (continued)

QUESTIONS *Have you clarified...*	Yes ☒	No ☒	N/A ☒	NOTES
10. Your overall first impressions of the situation?	☐	☐	☐	
11. The complaint or symptom that prompted this contact?	☐	☐	☐	
12. The organization's long-range prospects/strategic goals?	☐	☐	☐	
13. The organization's short-range performance?	☐	☐	☐	
14. The organization's history?	☐	☐	☐	
15. Major disasters or problems that have recently affected organizational performance?	☐	☐	☐	
16. The organization's current products and services?	☐	☐	☐	
17. Developments/changes in products/services?	☐	☐	☐	
18. Relative successes and failures in dealings with external stakeholders such as stockholders, customers/clients, suppliers, and distributors?	☐	☐	☐	
19. Special core competencies/strengths of the organization?	☐	☐	☐	
20. Special weaknesses of the organization?	☐	☐	☐	
21. Record of performance/customer service?	☐	☐	☐	
22. Reporting relationships (organization chart)?	☐	☐	☐	
23. Job descriptions/work responsibilities?	☐	☐	☐	
24. Locations/territories/markets covered?	☐	☐	☐	
25. Equipment size, function, age, and ergonomic design?	☐	☐	☐	
26. Age of physical facilities?	☐	☐	☐	

Exhibit 4-1 (continued)

QUESTIONS *Have you clarified...*	Yes ☒	No ☒	N/A ☒	NOTES
27. Financial functioning of the organization?	☐	☐	☐	
28. Match between stated plans and actual results?	☐	☐	☐	
29. Personnel numbers?	☐	☐	☐	
30. Personnel ages?	☐	☐	☐	
31. Personnel distribution by function, occupation, location, and job/work category?	☐	☐	☐	
32. Personnel diversity?	☐	☐	☐	
33. Personnel educational and training achievements?	☐	☐	☐	
34. Personnel tenure with the organization?	☐	☐	☐	
35. Personnel absenteeism and turnover rates and suspected causes of absenteeism and turnover?	☐	☐	☐	
36. Personnel accident rates and likely causes?	☐	☐	☐	
37. Personnel recruitment practices?	☐	☐	☐	
38. Personnel orientation practices?	☐	☐	☐	
39. Personnel training practices?	☐	☐	☐	
40. Personnel appraisal and feedback practices?	☐	☐	☐	
41. Personnel educational reimbursements?	☐	☐	☐	
42. Personnel promotion and transfer policies?	☐	☐	☐	
43. Personnel disciplinary policies?	☐	☐	☐	
44. Compensation and benefit policies?	☐	☐	☐	
45. Supervision of employees (types of supervisors, management styles)?	☐	☐	☐	

Exhibit 4-1 (concluded)

QUESTIONS *Have you clarified...*	Yes ☒	No ☒	N/A ☒	NOTES
46. Personnel safety policies?	☐	☐	☐	
47. Collective bargaining agreements?	☐	☐	☐	
48. Organizational policies, procedures, and plans?	☐	☐	☐	
49. Work cycles by type, work season, plan, and customer impact?	☐	☐	☐	
50. Communication and information practices in the organization?	☐	☐	☐	
51. Approaches to communicating new information in the organization and their relative effectiveness?	☐	☐	☐	
52. Previous studies of the organization's condition?	☐	☐	☐	
53. Management/employee perceptions of problems/opportunities?	☐	☐	☐	
54. Previous efforts to improve the organization and their results?	☐	☐	☐	
55. Relations with stockholders?	☐	☐	☐	
56. Relations with customers/clients?	☐	☐	☐	
57. Relations with suppliers?	☐	☐	☐	
58. Relations with distributors?	☐	☐	☐	
59. Relations with regulatory bodies?	☐	☐	☐	
60. Relations with the local community?	☐	☐	☐	
61. Relations with the industry and with competitors?	☐	☐	☐	
62. Other issues warranting examination:	☐	☐	☐	

What Are the Roles of the HPE Consultant and Their Clients in Analyzing *What Is* Happening?

There are two ways that HPE consultants may approach their work.

One approach is to assume the role of a *management consultant*, one whose value-added to their clients is expert knowledge. A good analogy to the role of the management consultant is a medical doctor, who assumes the role of diagnostician. When a patient visits a physician for the first time, the physician asks many questions with a goal in mind of looking beyond symptoms to identify root causes. If the physician is able to prescribe the medicine or appropriate therapy to address root causes, then he or she will do so. If not, then the physician will refer the patient to a specialist, whose knowledge of diagnosis and therapies in particular specialty areas is greater than that of a general practitioner.

A second approach is to assume the role of an *organization development consultant*, a facilitator whose value added to their clients is process knowledge of group dynamics. A good analogy to the role of a process consultant is a clinical psychologist from the Rogerian school of psychology, who does not assume the role of diagnostician. He or she instead provides an empathetic listener whose role is to "serve as a mirror to the client." The process consultant works with the client to uncover differing perceptions, building group ownership of a problem and approaches to solving it.

The difference in approach is profound and affects how HPE consultants will enact their role. Management consultants will assume responsibility for collecting information. They will then analyze what they find and recommend appropriate interventions to solve the problem by addressing its root causes. But process or OD consultants will keep responsibility on the client, providing guidance about the process in collecting information and feeding it back to the group for review. Differing perceptions can create an impetus for change by confronting people with differences in opinions. HPE consultants enacting the role of management consultant will thus carry out their work much like physicians, focusing attention on collecting information, interpreting what they find, and recommending appropriate solutions. But HPE consultants enacting the role of process consultant will thus carry out their work much like clinical psychologists, collecting information but feeding it back to clients for their interpretation.

What Prompted the Investigation?

HPE investigations typically begin in one of three ways: (1) a client may ask for it *(solicited help)*; (2) HPE practitioners may propose it *(unsolicited help)*; (3) a counterproposal may be made in response to a request for or an offer of help *(negotiated help)*. Both external and internal consultants who serve as HPE practitioners frequently meet with solicited interventions; proactive HPE practitioners, however, strive to increase the ratio of unsolicited and negotiated assignments.

Typical Solicited Help Scenarios

In typical solicited help scenarios, managers face a problem that they have been unable to solve. For instance, they may turn to a training department for help if they feel that the problem can be solved by training and that the training department is a credible source.

Solicited help scenarios may occur when

- managers confront a change in laws or regulations, work methods, or technology that requires the need to train many people;
- managers believe that training (or some other management action, such as firing) is the solution to a problem they have been experiencing with one employee;
- managers are implementing a change to a team-based, quality-based, or reengineered function.

In a solicited help scenario, HPE practitioners must quickly gather as many facts and perceptions as possible. They should therefore ask many questions about what is happening.

On occasion, managers will approach others for help, but they will jump to conclusions about what the solution should be. Then when they ask someone for help, they don't say "my department has this problem, and I think we should do something to solve that problem." Instead, they phrase their request as one for action: "I need [*insert solution*]." That solution could take the form of a request for training—or anything else, such as a request to fire one or many people, raise pay rates, or something else. This situation is akin to a patient visiting a doctor and immediately saying "I need penicillin," or "I need chemotherapy." We can all imagine how a medical doctor would greet such a request, but HPE clients do that because they believe they know what their problems are, what causes their problems, and how best to solve those problems. In reality, that is no more true than the wrongheaded opinion of a medical patient who has jumped to conclusions about what medicine he or she needs. In this situation, the HPE practitioner must back the client off of his or her request for action and systematically examine what prompted that request in the first place. HPE practitioners must perform "due diligence" to make sure that any data and conclusions already collected by managers make sense. The same logic can be seen at work when medical doctors check the medical chart when they take over patient treatment from other physicians.

Typical Unsolicited Help Scenarios

In typical unsolicited help scenarios, HPE practitioners independently encounter a human performance problem or human performance improvement opportunity. They may (for instance) uncover evidence about the situation by talking to employees or managers, scanning exit interviews, reviewing employee performance appraisal forms, conducting training needs assessments, looking at accident reports, or examining the results of customer satisfaction surveys. They look for managers or employees who are, because of their positions, likely to be interested in solving the problem. They arrange with those stakeholders to present what they have found and recommend HPE strategies that can help solve the problem or seize the opportunity.

Unsolicited help scenarios may occur when HPE practitioners

- are aware of a pending change in law or regulations or technology that will necessitate the need to train many people or introduce other changes in the organization;
- detect an isolated performance problem with an individual and wish to offer advice to others on how to handle it;
- believe they can offer help to another change effort underway in the organization.

In these situations, the credibility of the HPE practitioners is on the line. HPE practitioners must make a convincing case—and have the facts at hand to back up what they say. Offering help to those unwilling to acknowledge a problem can be risky, since there is no buy-in for the change and thus not necessarily any backers for it.

Typical Negotiated Help Scenarios

In a negotiated help scenario, a manager asks for help or an HPE practitioner offers assistance. However, rather than immediately accept a solution strategy proposed or the advice offered, the receiver of the request offers more information and suggests an alternative solution.

Examples of negotiated help scenarios are easy to find. They include the following:

- A manager approaches an HPE practitioner requesting a solution (such as training) rather than describing the problem to be solved or the human performance enhancement opportunity to be seized. The HPE practitioner troubleshoots the problem or explores the opportunity. The recommended solution attempts to address the underlying cause(s) of the problem.
- HPE practitioners approach a manager to offer assistance on a problem they have detected. The manager supplies more information that sheds new light on the matter. The manager may then recommend an alternative action, or HPE practitioners must take the new information and offer revised improvement suggestions.

Gathering and Documenting Facts and Perceptions

Whether help is solicited, unsolicited, or negotiated, fact finding and perception hunting are the keys to understanding *what is happening*. But what approaches should be used to gather and document facts and perceptions?

There are essentially two: (1) *the inductive approach* and (2) *the deductive approach*. Both are useful. They are not mutually exclusive.

Inductive Fact Finding and Perception Hunting

Induction means arriving at general principles from specific facts or circumstances. If HPE practitioners have no clues to show what is happening, an inductive approach to fact finding and perception hunting works best. To apply it, HPE practitioners begin by identifying those who are most likely to be concerned about a problem or who are probably most eager to pursue an exciting opportunity. If the focus is on solving an existing performance problem, HPE practitioners should pose the following questions to the individual or group most interested in solving it:

- Who is involved with the problem?
- What is happening now?
- What events led up to the current situation? Can you think of anything that may have contributed to its development?
- What consequences have stemmed from the problem?
- When did the problem first appear? How did you first notice it?
- Where did the problem first appear? Can you track it to one source or locale?
- Why do you think it is happening?
- How did you notice it? What specific situations can you pinpoint in which the problem was evident? Could you describe them?
- How much is the situation costing the organization in tangible (hard) and intangible (soft) measures of performance? Can you place a price tag on what the problem is costing the organization?[2]

These questions may be used whether the problem is large or small or whether the HPE practitioner's help is solicited or unsolicited. It is helpful, however, to discuss what is happening with many people. Such a process, called *triangulation,*[3] helps to get a fix on a problem in much the same way that ancient navigators found their location by consulting several stars. It is also helpful, for the sake of maintaining consistency, to use a structured interview guide to collect information from multiple respondents. A sample structured interview guide appears in Exhibit 4-2.

Exhibit 4-2. A Sample Structured Interview Guide for Problem Solving

Directions: When analyzing performance problems, use this interview guide to maintain consistency in questioning respondents. First, describe the conditions under which this investigation began. Then pose each question appearing in the left column below to several individuals or groups who should be knowledgeable about it. Write their answers in the column to the right.

How was the problem brought to your attention?

Who are you interviewing?

QUESTIONS	ANSWERS
Who is involved with the problem?	
What is happening now?	
What events led up to the current situation? Can you think of anything that may have contributed to its development?	
What consequences have stemmed from the problem?	
When did the problem first appear? How did you first notice it?	
Where did the problem first appear? Can you track it to one source or locale?	
Why do you think it is happening?	
How did you notice it?	
What specific situations can you pinpoint in which the problem was evident? Could you describe them?	
How much is the situation costing the organization in tangible (hard) and intangible (soft) measures of performance? Can you place a price tag on what the problem is costing the organization?	

A similar approach should be used to examine possible performance improvement opportunities. HPE practitioners should begin by identifying those who are likely to be most interested in the opportunity. They should then pose the following questions:

- What is the opportunity, and why do you think it exists?
- Who will be affected by it?
- What events led to discovering the opportunity? Can you think of anything that may affect its realization?
- What consequences are likely to stem from efforts to pursue the opportunity?
- What are the organization's key competitive strengths? How could they be leveraged to greater competitive advantage?
- When and how did evidence of the opportunity first appear? How was that evidence recognized?
- From what trends, business issues, customer needs or expectations, or other issues outside the organization did the opportunity arise?
- Why do you think the opportunity exists, and what would be important about it if it were realized?
- How much is the opportunity worth? What is its possible economic value in tangible (hard) and intangible (soft) measures? How can a price tag be placed on the opportunity to demonstrate its potential future value to the organization?

These questions may be used whether the opportunity is large or small and whether the HPE practitioner's help is solicited or unsolicited. It is helpful, however, to discuss the opportunity with many people. As in problem solving, it is helpful, for the sake of consistency, to use the same structured interview guide to collect information, posing the same questions to everyone. A sample structured interview guide appears in Exhibit 4-3.

Exhibit 4-3. A Sample Structured Interview Guide for Opportunity Finding

Directions: When examining possible human performance improvement opportunities, use this interview guide to maintain consistency in questioning respondents. First, describe the conditions under which this investigation began. Then pose each question appearing in the left column below to several individuals or groups who should be knowledgeable about it. Write their answers in the column to the right.

How was the opportunity brought to your attention?

Who are you interviewing?

QUESTIONS	ANSWERS
What is the opportunity and why do you think it exists?	
What are the organization's key strengths, and how can they be leveraged?	
Who will be affected by it?	
What events led up to discovering the opportunity? Can you think of anything that might affect its realization?	
What consequences are likely to stem from efforts to pursue the opportunity?	
When and how did evidence of the opportunity first appear? How was that evidence recognized?	
From what trends, business issues, customer needs or expectations, or other issues outside the organization did the opportunity arise?	
Why do you think the opportunity exists, and what would be important about it if it were realized?	
How much is the opportunity worth? What is its possible economic value in tangible (hard) and intangible (soft) measures?	
How can a price tag be placed on the opportunity to demonstrate its potential future value to the organization if it is pursued?	

Deductive Fact Finding and Perception Hunting

Deduction is the technique used by the fictional detective Sherlock Holmes. The investigator begins with a theory—sometimes never articulated but evident from the pattern of investigation—about what caused the problem or led to the opportunity. Unlike the less-focused inductive approach, which is open-ended and spontaneous, a deductive investigation is more focused. It is guided by a sense of what should be happening. The HPE practitioner then begins by hypothesizing about what caused the problem or presented the opportunity. Fact finding and perception hunting focus on that presumed cause.

A simple example can illustrate how the deductive approach works in practice. Suppose that turnover has skyrocketed in an organization. That is clearly a performance problem. (It is a presenting problem because turnover is a symptom of some other issue(s).) Using a deductive approach, HPE practitioners would develop a working theory about what is happening and seek to verify the theory or prove it false by collecting and analyzing information. This approach differs from an inductive approach in which no theory of causation is proposed at the outset; instead, general information is collected and analyzed, leading to specific conclusions.

Deductive reasoning can be immensely useful. Increasingly it has been proposed that organizations follow certain *norms* (recommended guidelines). Examples of such guidelines—which may or may not express specific recommendations about *what to do, how to do it,* or *what to measure*—include (among others) ISO Standards, Six Sigma, Lean Manufacturing, the Malcolm Baldrige National Quality Award, the Deming Prize, and the U.S. Department of Labor's criteria for High-Performance Workplaces.[4]

Analyzing Present Conditions

Training and development professionals who use needs assessment results as the basis for training have long been familiar with various data collection methods. (Fewer than 20 percent of organizations conduct any form of training needs assessment, so training and development professionals are not systematically collecting information about training needs.) However, most methods of training needs assessment can be adapted for use as more holistic human performance enhancement needs assessment (HPENA) methods.

HPENA focuses attention on what is happening at all four performance levels: the organizational environment, the work environment, the work, and the workers. A more rigorous and comprehensive analysis than the faster but less valid approach described earlier in this chapter, an HPENA can be carried out using any of the methods summarized in Exhibit 4-4. What follows is a brief description of approaches to HPENA at each performance level.

Exhibit 4-4. Methods for Collecting Data about What Is Happening

Method	Description
Interviews	Discuss one-on-one with people in the organization what is happening. Interviews may be *structured* (planned in advance, with questions written down) or *unstructured* (spontaneous and free flowing). Use structured interviews to ensure consistency in questioning across respondents; use unstructured interviews to permit maximum freedom in probing for information.
Focus Groups	Call together a group of people in an area affected by a performance problem or opportunity, and ask for their opinions about what is happening. Devote no more than two to three hours to the meeting. Pose two or three questions. Try to ensure that no one person dominates the discussion. Make an effort to involve all participants, posing specific questions to those who otherwise remain silent.
Written Surveys	Use written surveys sent by mail or electronic mail to gather information from those who are most likely to have information about what is happening. Structured surveys are planned and use a scale (such as 1–5) so that respondents can answer quickly. Structured surveys are easy to analyze because responses lend themselves to statistical analysis. Unstructured surveys, on the other hand, require respondents to write essay questions. They are usually open ended and allow more freedom for respondents, though they must be analyzed by a technique called content analysis that summarizes the frequency of occurrence of the same word, phrase, or theme across individual essays.
Phone Surveys	Phone surveys are conducted over the telephone. They combine the personalized touch characteristic of interviews with the greater speed of written surveys. Like interviews and surveys, they may be *structured* (planned and scaled) or *unstructured* (unplanned and calling for essay responses). To use them for gathering information about what is happening, ask respondents to describe current conditions.
Observation	Observation is the process of watching what is happening. Observation can be useful when groups disagree about facts, substituting their own perceptions. Decide what is to be observed. Then develop either a structured observation form (to collect information about the frequency of events, such as number of phone calls received) or an unstructured observation form to collect observer perceptions of events.
Document Reviews	Examine forms processed, such as accident reports, files, or other documentary evidence about performance. Develop categories to describe information on the basis of what is found in the documents.
Production Examinations	A production examination is akin to observation. The HPE specialist visits the work site and observes what is happening, such as how the work is transformed from raw material to finished goods or how customers are treated by the organization's employees.

The Organizational Environmental Level

At the organizational level, HPE practitioners should direct their attention to assessing how well the organization is interacting with its external environment. To do this, they should first identify what stakeholders outside the organization consider to be critical to the organization's continued survival and success. Then they can collect information from organizational members and from members of key external groups about how the organization is interacting with those stakeholders. Appropriate data collection methods include interviews, focus groups, written surveys, and phone surveys.[5]

HPE practitioners commonly wonder about what to analyze. They should initially use open-ended approaches to gathering data, posing questions like the following to a cross-section of knowledgeable members of the organization:

- How would you describe the organization's interactions with its customers? suppliers? distributors? stockholders? regulators?
- How does the organization compare to competitors?
- What other groups are critically important to the organization's survival or success? Why are they important? How would you characterize the organization's interactions with those groups? What is happening?
- How well is the organization's strategic plan helping it function in the global business environment?

Then pose similar questions to randomly selected representatives of key stakeholder groups. If asked who should be questioned, organizational members may—or may not—name individuals whose views are representative. It is therefore desirable to use randomly selected respondents.

HPE practitioners should remember that the aim of this questioning is not necessarily to discover problems or opportunities; rather, it is simply to assess what is happening. To say it another way, the goal is sometimes merely to "get the lay of the land"—that is, get the big picture.

Still, it is often the case that problems at one level (such as an individual worker or team) is actually caused by issues at other levels (such as department, division, or organization). As a simple example, high turnover in one department may result from companywide pay practices. It may thus be necessary to start with the big picture, and an overall organizational diagnosis, and work to specific situations, individuals, departments, or teams. *Organizational diagnosis* is a term of art, one used to refer to a systematic process of gathering information about an entire organization in all its complexity. Many books and articles have been published about it.[6] Many models have been published that can provide guidance in "what to look at." (Do a search of the web for that term.)

The Work Environment Level

At the work environment level, HPE practitioners should seek information about how the organization is interacting with its external environment. HPE practitioners should first identify key but broad-scale issues worthy of examination, such as how well the organization matches up to the criteria for high-performance work organizations, what are the key competitive strengths of the organization (that is, how it compares to other organizations in its industry), how well strategic objectives are being achieved, or how well quality programs are working. HPE practitioners should then identify whom to ask about these issues. They should seek an overview of the big picture, trying to get a snap shot of perceptions about the organization from representative groups—including top managers, middle managers, supervisors, professional employees, technical workers, salespersons, clerical employees, and skilled and unskilled hourly workers. They should next collect information from groups likely to have unique perspectives, such as temporary workers, recently retired workers, or others who have intimate and recent first-hand knowledge of the organization. Interviews and focus groups may be the best methods for collecting data quickly about issues affecting performance in the work environment. While response rates can also be used, they can be problematic because response rates for surveys are declining everywhere.

Examples of questions that may be appropriate include the following:

- What is happening in the organization that affects how well people can do their work efficiently and effectively?
- What is happening inside the organization that affects how well people can meet or exceed customer needs? supplier requirements? distributor requirements?
- What conditions presently existing in the organization seem to be the most helpful in sustaining performance, in your opinion? What conditions are least helpful, and why?

The Work Level

At the work level, HPE practitioners should focus their efforts around workflow across departments, teams, or jobs. HPE practitioners should identify what issues are most important in achieving successful work results and then collect information about them, asking for the views of people who represent a cross-section of the organization. Interviews, focus groups, written surveys, and phone surveys may be the most appropriate methods of collecting this information. Observation, document reviews, and production examinations may also be conducted so that HPE practitioners can observe conditions firsthand and double check what they have been told by others.

When examining performance issues at the work level, HPE practitioners should seek answers to questions such as these:

- How well has the organization clarified, and kept updated, job descriptions and other statements (such as performance management documents) of what workers are supposed to do in their jobs?
- Have job performance standards been formulated and expressed to workers so that they know exactly what results are expected of them?

- How well do performers understand, and agree with, the job performance standards?
- How attainable and realistic are the job performance standards, in the opinions of the workers?
- How well are the workers able to recognize when they should take action?
- How free are workers to perform without interference from other tasks, distractions from the work environment, or safety hazards?
- How efficient and effective are existing work policies and procedures?
- How adequate are the resources supplied to do the work? Have workers been given appropriate time, tools, staff, information, and equipment?
- How clear are the consequences of performance? Do performers receive timely, specific feedback on how useful their labors are to customers, suppliers, distributors, and other stakeholders?
- How meaningful are work consequences from the workers' standpoint?
- What value do workers associate with the results of their efforts? How and when are they rewarded for achieving exemplary results? Do they perceive the rewards to be fair and achievable?
- How timely and specific are the consequences of their performance to performers?

The Worker Level

When HPE practitioners examine what is happening with the workers, they are investigating issues affecting the individuals who perform and how well their competencies match up to work requirements. Worthwhile questions to ask during this examination include:

- What kinds of people are doing the work?
- How were people chosen for the work they do?
- How are people hired, terminated, transferred, or promoted?
- What competencies do the people possess?
- How well has the organization achieved an effective match between individual competencies and work requirements?
- How long have the performers been doing their work?
- How often have performers had occasion to practice all aspects of their work?
- How do the performers feel about the work they do? their work environment? the organizational environment?
- How motivated are the performers, and how are they rewarded for what they do?

The Competencies of the Auditor's Role

You may recall from Chapter 2 that trainers-turned-HPE practitioners should be capable of demonstrating the competencies of the auditor role. The competencies linked to that role are described in this section and listed in Appendix I. HPE practitioners should be able to do the following:

- **Examine needs and expectations of customers, suppliers, distributors, and stakeholders.** As explained in this chapter, HPE practitioners should be capable of examining the present needs and expectations of customers, suppliers, distributors, and stakeholders.
- **Formulate, assess, and convert organizational plans to HPE efforts.** Since organizational success is dependent on how well the organization meets the needs of customers and other external stakeholders and converts those needs into organizational plans, HPE practitioners should be capable of formulating, assessing, and converting organizational strategic plans into HPE efforts.
- **Key improvement efforts to organizational mission and strategy.** HPE practitioners can assess HPE needs against the organization's purpose and direction. What HPE efforts are most important strategically to help the organization achieve its stated goals and objectives?
- **Identify organizational strengths and weaknesses.** Analyzing organizational strengths and weaknesses is essential to assessing what is happening. After all, assessing what is happening is the same as *internal appraisal,* which examines existing organizational strengths and weaknesses against the backdrop of other organizations in the industry or "best-in-class" organizations.
- **Examine workflow within and between departments.** HPE practitioners must be capable of helping workers and others examine workflow inside and across departments or other work units. They must possess the knowledge to carry out such examinations on their own as well.
- **Detect bottlenecks in work process.** A *bottleneck* is an area where the workflow is stopped or slowed. Detecting bottlenecks is essential, since they make performance less efficient and effective. HPE practitioners can flowchart and verify work processes and facilitate discussions with supervisors or team members to identify creative ways to streamline workflow by eliminating bottlenecks.
- **Assess present competency levels.** HPE practitioners should be able to examine the competency levels of the workers.
- **Assess workforce supply.** HPE practitioners can assess—or coordinate assessments of—the existing workforce supply in light of workforce needs, taking inventory of the organization's existing human storehouse of talent.

Chapter 5
Envisioning *What Should Be* Happening

Envisioning what should be happening is in some ways similar to analyzing what is happening. Sometimes *what is* and *what should be* are examined simultaneously; sometimes they are examined separately. But information about what is happening and what should be happening are both needed to improve performance because that information will reveal gaps. The same principle applies to human performance enhancement strategies and to HPE practitioners.

Envisioning what should be happening is also similar to *environmental scanning,* the step in strategic planning that examines future trends outside the organization and determines how those trends may pose future threats or opportunities to the organization. Research indicates that organizations that conduct environmental scanning are more profitable and successful than organizations that do not conduct it. Environmental scanning is the counterpart of *internal appraisal,* the step in strategic planning that examines existing conditions inside the organization and discovers the organization's *core competencies* (strengths)[1] and *areas for improvement* (weaknesses). By comparing the results of internal appraisal and environmental scanning, strategists can detect clues to desirable directions for the organization so that it may seize future opportunities, avoid future threats, build on present strengths, or surmount present weaknesses.

Both environmental scanning and envisioning what should be happening address ideals or norms rather than actualities or realities. Envisioning what should be happening can be future oriented, as is environmental scanning. Change rarely occurs unless people are dissatisfied with present conditions, can conceptualize ideal alternatives, and are motivated to change.

This chapter focuses on the second step in the new model to guide HPE: *envisioning what should be happening.* The chapter reviews information sources that provide clues about what should be happening, methods that may be used to collect information about what should be happening, and competencies that are required of HPE practitioners enacting the visionary role.

What Does It Mean to Envision *What Should Be* Happening?

Envisioning what should be happening means *establishing a vision of desired results.* The vision established becomes a norm—a prescribed standard or an *ideal,* a desired end-state. When envisioning what should be happening, HPE professionals and/or other stakeholders delineate the conditions and the results they most want; they describe what performance will look like when the organization is optimally serving its customers and other stakeholders, is meeting legal requirements established by government at all levels, is optimally organized internally to promote a high-performance work organization, is matching (or even exceeding) best practice, and is optimally positioned to encourage efficient and effective work and workers. As with analyzing what is happening, however, this step frequently appears to be easier to do than it turns out to be.

What Are the Roles of the HPE Consultant and Their Clients in Envisioning *What Should Be* Happening?

HPE consultants enacting the role of management consultants will undertake their own investigation to identify the appropriate criteria against which to judge an existing situation or existing symptom of another problem. But HPE consultants preferring to enact the role of process or OD consultants will guide a client group through the discovery of their own relevant criteria. The difference, like in assessing what is happening, is profound. The efficiency (and speed) of acting as management consultants will be greater. After all, HPE consultants—as individuals—can probably move faster in identifying criteria than can a group of client group members, who may require guidance in discovering criteria and researching them. However, the effectiveness of acting as process or OD consultants will probably be greater, since client group members are more likely to "own" what they discover.

What Sources Provide Clues about *What Should Be* Happening?

To envision what should be happening, HPE practitioners and other stakeholders should begin by collecting visions, job performance standards, work expectations, criteria, goals or objectives, and best practices. They may also choose to examine the legal environment affecting the organization.

What Is a Vision?

A *vision* is a clear, coherent view of how the future should appear. It is essential to providing a point of departure for what is happening.

Visions are meant to motivate people and provide a compelling direction for the future. They build *esprit de corps* (teamwork), show the way toward improvement, excite people to act, and create a sense of shared ownership in a collective future.

Visioning can be a creative and imaginative process that can involve many (or all) members of an organization, division, department, work unit, or team in picturing the organization as it should be operating. Or it may be carried out solely by a transformational leader who electrifies others with an image of an ideal future that others do not see. However the vision is created—and there are many ways, from the empowering to the dictatorial—a good vision should answer such questions as these:

- What is the purpose?
- What are the key values?
- What is the organization aspiring to do best—and why?

HPE practitioners may occasionally have to help members of their organizations assess the clarity of vision in their organizations, divisions, departments, work units, or teams. The instrument in Exhibit 5-1 can be used for that purpose; the activity in Exhibit 5-2 can be used to create a vision.

Exhibit 5-1. Assessing the Clarity of a Vision

Directions: Use this activity to assess the clarity of a vision and to pinpoint areas for improvement. For each item in the left column, circle a code in the center. Administer the instrument separately to a group, such as a top management team, an employee standing team, or another group. Ask each person to rate the team's collective vision. When the participants finish, ask them to turn in the instrument. Compile the results, and feed them back to them. Then ask the team to pinpoint areas for improvement and agree on what should be done to achieve a clearer vision of what should be happening in the organization or team.

Rate the Clarity of the Vision	*Very Unclear*				*Very Clear*	**Comments:**
This team...	**1**	**2**	**3**	**4**	**5**	
1. Agrees why the team exists	1	2	3	4	5	
2. Shares a vision of where the team should go	1	2	3	4	5	
3. Shares a vision of how the team should get where it is going	1	2	3	4	5	
4. Agrees on how to measure progress	1	2	3	4	5	
5. Shares the same values about what is and is not important	1	2	3	4	5	
6. Shares beliefs about what the team should be doing best	1	2	3	4	5	

Exhibit 5-2. Formulating a Vision

Directions: Ask the members of a team or group to assemble and work on answering each question appearing in the left column. They may write their responses in the column to the right. Allow between 30 and 60 minutes for this process. Then discuss the results with the team.

QUESTIONS	TEAM'S ANSWERS
What is the purpose of the team? The organization?	
What forces exert the most influence on the team? The organization? Why?	
What are our core values? What should they be?	
What do we want to do best? Why?	
What do we want to accomplish? Why?	
What do we want to change? Why?	
What could we do to work together more effectively?	

What Is a Job Performance Standard?

A *job performance standard* is usually defined as a minimum level of desired performance. In common parlance, a job performance standard is the output level of an average but experienced worker producing at an average pace. That definition stems from the view, as noted in a classic source on job analysis, that "establishing the standard or allowed time for a given unit of work is based on the amount of time required by a qualified worker, using a standard method and working at a standard work pace, to perform a specified task."[2] A *job performance standard* thus represents a floor of (minimum for) acceptable performance. It differs from a vision or a goal or an objective, which represent desired performance targets.

Standards are useful because they are benchmarks of output. Departures from reasonable standards signal that something has gone awry and that corrective action is needed. Achievements beyond standard may signal that workers deserve rewards, since they have performed better than expected.

Performance problems often stem from problems with job performance standards. Perhaps standards have never been established, and as a result, workers do not know how to measure the acceptability of their output levels. Perhaps standards have never been communicated, so workers do not know that measures exist against which to compare their performance. Perhaps standards are set at levels that workers consider to be unfair, and workers view achievement of them as onerous.

Standards are established in many ways. Standards established *scientifically* are based on rigorous approaches such as time and motion studies or work analysis. Standards established *experientially* are based on past practice. Standards established *authoritatively* are based on management, union, or collective bargaining mandates. Standards established *participatively* are established cooperatively between workers or team members and management representatives.

Any or all of these approaches may be used to establish job performance standards, but the basic approach is the same whether standards are centered on the organizational environment, the work environment, the work, or workers. To establish standards, HPE practitioners should work with other stakeholders to

- identify the mission of the organizational unit, job category, or individual that will be the focus of the standard-setting effort;
- identify the outputs (final results or accomplishments);
- identify sub-accomplishments or tasks (what has to be done to achieve the final results);
- define performance requirements;
- determine measurements for each performance requirement;
- determine standards for each requirement.[3]

HPE practitioners can use the assessment form in Exhibit 5-3 to determine how well standards have been established and communicated in their organizations. They may also use the worksheet in Exhibit 5-4 to establish standards when they are lacking.

Exhibit 5-3. Assessing the Clarity of Job Performance Standards

Directions: This activity is geared to HPE practitioners. Pick a job, job category, or team. Then rate the clarity of job performance standards established for the job, job category, or team on the basis of the statements in the left column. Conduct the rating by circling an item in the center opposite each statement. Finally, write comments or notes for improvement in the space at the right.

Would you say that job performance standards have been...	**RATING** *Disagree* 1	2	3	4	*Agree* 5	**Comments/Notes**
1. Clearly stated	1	2	3	4	5	
2. Clearly communicated	1	2	3	4	5	
3. Stated in measurable terms	1	2	3	4	5	
4. Tied to work requirements for individuals and the organization	1	2	3	4	5	
5. Updated in light of changing work methods	1	2	3	4	5	

Exhibit 5-4. A Worksheet for Establishing Job Performance Standards

Directions: Use this worksheet as one approach to establishing job performance standards. Meet with job incumbents and their immediate organizational superiors. In the left-hand column, list the key job tasks, duties, or responsibilities. Take that list from a current job description, if one is available. Then ask the incumbents and their organizational superiors—working separately—to answer the questions in the right-hand column for each task, duty, or responsibility. Note responses in the space below each question. Feed the results of the activity back to the job incumbents and their organizational superiors. Ask them to reach consensus on the job performance standard for each task, duty, or responsibility. Then ask how those standards should be communicated to all job incumbents.

Job Tasks, Duties, or Responsibilities	Questions for Job Performance Standards
	How can this task/duty/responsibility be measured?
	What is the minimum measurable job performance standard for an *experienced* performer working at an average pace?
	How can this task/duty/responsibility be measured?
	What is the minimum measurable job performance standard for an *experienced* performer working at an average pace?
	How can this task/duty/responsibility be measured?
	What is the minimum measurable job performance standard for an *experienced* performer working at an average pace?

What Is a Work Expectation?

A *work expectation* closely resembles a job performance standard, but there is an important difference. Whereas a job performance standard often represents a minimally acceptable output, a work expectation represents an average output. Some managers do not feel that companies should establish minimum output levels, even when they represent the output of average but experienced workers producing at an average pace. They prefer to avoid the word *standard* with its manufacturing overtones in favor of a term with a more neutral connotation.

There is another benefit to discussing work expectations rather than standards. The term *standard* implies that all work requirements can be met if specific output levels are achieved. But that is not necessarily true. Managers and workers can achieve average output levels by means that do not contribute to long-term organizational survival or success of the organization. Workers who are held to a certain quality standard may conceal or steal work that does not match up to the standard, thereby boosting the ratio of acceptable to unacceptable outputs. Managers and workers may achieve desired outputs while sacrificing customer service, quality, and other important measures of success. Since standards imply work results only, they may not encompass all measures of effective performance.

As a consequence, decision makers and HPE practitioners in some organizations prefer to focus on work expectations in all four areas of performance: the organizational environment, the work environment, the work, and worker. They may also examine five areas that can be measured: quality, quantity, time, cost, and customer satisfaction. By doing so, they can establish work expectations that are more comprehensive measures of acceptability than mere job performance standards (see Exhibit 5-5).

Exhibit 5-5. A Worksheet for Establishing Work Expectations

Directions: Use this worksheet as one approach to establishing work expectations. Meet with job incumbents and their immediate organizational superiors. In the left-hand column, list the key job tasks, duties, or responsibilities. Take that list from a current job description, if one is available. Then ask the incumbents and their organizational superiors—working separately—to answer the questions in the right-hand column for each task, duty, or responsibility. Note responses in the space below each question. Feed the results of the activity back to the job incumbents and their organizational superiors. Ask them to reach consensus on the work expectation for each task, duty, or responsibility. Then ask how those expectations should be communicated to all job incumbents.

Job Tasks, Duties, or Responsibilities	Questions for Work Expectations
	How can this task/duty/responsibility be measured?
	What is the average measurable expectation of output for an *experienced* performer working at an average pace?
	How can this task/duty/responsibility be measured?
	What is the average measurable expectation of output for an *experienced* performer working at an average pace?
	How can this task/duty/responsibility be measured?
	What is the average measurable expectation of output for an *experienced* performer working at an average pace?

What Is a Criterion?

A *criterion* represents *what should be.* Examples of criteria include laws, rules, regulations, municipal ordinances, executive mandates, generally accepted accounting procedures, common business practices, best practices, standard operating procedures (SOPs), and organizational policy or procedure statements.

To use criteria to figure out what should be happening, the HPE practitioner and stakeholders should begin by posing this question: *What criteria may have a bearing on what we are doing or on what results we are seeking to achieve?* A key consideration in examining criteria is determining precisely what they mean. How, for instance, should a law be interpreted? What does a general criterion mean in a specific case? What does a procedure mean? How should it be carried out?

Human performance problems may often be solved or human performance improvement opportunities may be realized simply by establishing and communicating criteria. Take a moment to identify some important criteria that affect human performance, broadly defined, in your own organization. Use the worksheet in Exhibit 5-6 for that purpose.

Exhibit 5-6. A Worksheet for Identifying Human Performance Criteria

Directions: Take a moment to clarify what should be happening in your organization. In the left-hand column, you will find words or phrases about important elements in any organization. In the center space, write statements to describe what should be happening in your organization in each area. In the right-hand column, indicate how you can measure each criterion.

Criteria Areas	Questions for Human Performance Criteria
Leadership	What should be happening in your organization? How can you measure this criterion?
Organizational Structure (reporting relationships)	What should be happening in your organization? How can you measure this criterion?
Incentives and Rewards	What should be happening in your organization? How can you measure this criterion?

Exhibit 5-6 (concluded)

Criteria Areas	Questions for Human Performance Criteria
Feedback to workers on how well they are performing on a daily basis	What should be happening in your organization? How can you measure this criterion?
Training	What should be happening in your organization? How can you measure this criterion?
Information/ Communication	What should be happening in your organization? How can you measure this criterion?

What Is a Goal or Objective?

A *goal* is a target for achievement. Often goals are difficult to measure or to achieve in an identifiable time span.[4] An *objective,* on the other hand, does lend itself to measurement. It is also timebound.[5] Goals are typically developed directly from an organization's mission or purpose statement, and objectives are derived from those goals.[6] Goals and objectives may also be used to clarify desired interactions with the organizational environment or to express desired performance targets for the work environment, the work, or workers.

Human beings, it seems, are by nature goal-oriented creatures. They strive to achieve an idealized vision of the future. Often they do that by establishing goals to guide them. As *path-goal theory* suggests,[7] human performance can be improved when people know what goals they should achieve and are confident that they know how to achieve them. HPE practitioners and stakeholders can contribute to enhancing human performance by clarifying and communicating goals and objectives. The worksheet in Exhibit 5-7 can be used to formulate goals and objectives when they have not been clearly established and communicated.

Exhibit 5-7. A Worksheet for Establishing Goals and Objectives

Directions: Use this worksheet to help you and others in your organization establish clear, measurable objectives linked to the organization's purpose (mission). In the left-hand column, describe the purpose of the organization. In the middle column, describe how that purpose can be achieved in terms that are not necessarily measurable or timebound. Then, in the right-hand column, provide specific and measurable results to be achieved during one year. There are no right or wrong answers. However, some answers may be preferable to others.

What is the purpose of the organization?	What goals stem from this purpose?	How can each goal be measured during one year?

What Is a "Best Practice"?

Many organizations have set off in search of best practices through internal and external benchmarking. Their aim is to find what the Japanese call *dantotsu,* the best of the best. By definition, "benchmarking is the search for industry best practices that lead to superior performance."[8] A *best practice* is an exemplar, a practice worthy of emulation because it represents the best approach. Best practices also represent, of course, possible ways of viewing what should be happening in an organization's interactions with its environment, inside the organization, in the work, or with the workers.

To identify and examine best practices, HPE practitioners may have to work with managers of quality, process improvement teams, external consultants, and others assigned to organizational improvement. Begin the benchmarking effort by clarifying what is to be the focus of investigation. Then identify what is happening by clearly describing (even flowcharting) existing practices in the organization. Next choose the scope of benchmarking: Will the scope be *comprehensive* (looking at many things) or *focused* (restricted to a few things)? What are the most important issues to benchmark; how were they identified, and by whom? Of course, many issues lend themselves to benchmarking, among them:

- *Organizational mission*—How should an organization state and communicate its purpose?
- *Organizational strategy*—How should an organization formulate, implement, and evaluate the way it will compete?
- *Organizational structure*—How should an organization establish reporting relationships contributing to strategy?
- *Customer requirements*—How should an organization pinpoint what its customers need or value most?
- *Distributor or supplier requirements*—How should an organization establish efficient and effective relationships with those supplying materials or services and those selling or distributing products/services?
- *Production processes or service delivery methods*—How should an organization transform raw materials to finished goods? Most effectively serve customers?
- *Measures of success*—How should success be measured?
- *Products or services purchased*—How should products or services be purchased by an organization?

Benchmarking may also focus around key elements contributing to human performance. These elements may include the following:

- feedback systems
- incentive and reward systems
- selection methods

- training
- job or work design
- organizational design
- supervision
- job performance standards
- work measurement methods
- tools and equipment[9]

Best practices may be found inside an organization, in the industry, or outside the industry. Identify best-practices organizations by conducting organized searches of databases, by consulting experts, by talking to vendors, or by networking with colleagues in other organizations who may have conducted their own previous best practices studies.

HPE practitioners can envision what should be happening by comparing practices in their organizations to best practices inside or outside the industry. Use the worksheet in Exhibit 5-8 to decide whether benchmarking is warranted; use the worksheet in Exhibit 5-9 as a starting point for envisioning what should be happening that could affect human performance.

Exhibit 5-8. Assessing the Need for Human Performance Benchmarking

Directions: Use this worksheet to decide whether benchmarking is warranted. For each question appearing in the left column, check yes, no, or N/A (not applicable) in the right column. Conduct benchmarking only if you can answer "yes" to every question.

Questions about Benchmarking	Yes ☒	No ☒	N/A ☒
1. Have you clearly examined current practices in your own organization?	☐	☐	☐
2. Have you conducted enough background research on the practice that you are familiar with major issues?	☐	☐	☐
3. Has your organization clarified what results are desired from the practice?	☐	☐	☐
4. Have you lined up decision makers who are willing to visit a best-practices organization to see firsthand "how it is done"—and why it is done that way?	☐	☐	☐

Exhibit 5-9. A Worksheet for Benchmarking Human Performance

Directions: Use this worksheet as the starting point to develop an interview guide for a best-practices organization. Pose each question provided in the left-hand column. Then write the response of the best-practices organization in the space at the right. When you finish, form a team and discuss how best practices in another organization may be adapted to the unique corporate culture of your organization.

QUESTIONS ***How does the organization attempt to enhance human performance by improving...***	**ANSWERS**
• Feedback systems?	
• Incentive and reward system?	
• Selection methods?	
• Training?	
• Job or work design?	
• Organizational design?	
• Supervision?	
• Job performance standards?	
• Work measurement methods?	
• Tools and equipment?	
• Other areas (list them):	

What Is a *Key Performance Indicator* (KPI)?

In recent years, many organizations have tried to align organizational strategic goals, as identified by the Balanced Scorecard, with targets for performance established for divisions, departments, teams or work groups, and individuals. The Balanced Scorecard has four traditional strategic components—financial, marketing, operations, and learning/growth. Authors Norton and Kaplan identified these components to emphasize that there is more to organizational success than mere financial measures that are determined on a daily basis (based on stock prices) or quarterly (based solely on earnings reports).[10] Although this approach looks new, it is clear that each of the four categories of the scorecard align to the traditional functions of management—finance (financial), marketing (customer), operations (operations and production), and learning/growth (human resources).

Key performance indicators take organizational targets and cascade them down to lower levels on the organization chart. In one sense, thinking about the scorecard and KPIs may be regarded as the latest generation of management by objectives (MBO) in which each part of the organization is shown to be related to, and dependent on, the others.[11]

KPIs are typically determined during a planning period (when strategy is established or updated) and then negotiated at each subsequent level. KPIs become part of the individual's performance management system. While many books and articles have been written about how to determine KPIs,[12] the goal here is not to discuss those. Instead, it is important to realize that KPIs provide valuable information about "what should be"—that is, desired performance targets. Comparisons between those targets and actual performance will yield possible differences between *what is* and *what should be.* Some organizations have detailed information about the targets and how well they were achieved and reasons for any differences.

It is possible to relate the organization's strategic goals, as identified in the Balanced Scorecard, with each division, department, team, or job in the organization. They may also be related to competencies tied to jobs. That may be done from top down (that is, organizational Balanced Scorecard strategic goals to job descriptions) or from bottom up (that is, job description activities to organizational Balanced Scorecard strategic goals.) Use the worksheets appearing in Exhibits 5-10 and 5-11 to help to do that.

Exhibit 5-10: A Worksheet to Integrate the Balanced Scorecard Strategic Goals of the Organization, Job Descriptions, Job Competencies, and Key Performance Indicators

Directions: In the box below the directions, list the four components of the organization's Balanced Scorecard to clarify the organization's strategic goals. Then, under Column 2, list all activities/duties from the job description for a targeted position. Under Column 3, identify the competencies tied to the work activities. Finally, under Column 4, identify the job description activities or competencies that are most closely associated with the Balanced Scorecard organizational strategic goals. Make sure that there are no more than 5 to 7 Key Performance Indicators listed under Column 4. Add more lines or pages if necessary.

Job Title:

COLUMN 1	COLUMN 2	COLUMN 3	COLUMN 4
Which of the four parts of the Balanced Scorecard may this activity relate to? (The four parts of the Balanced Scorecard are: Financial, Customer, Business Operations, and Learning/Growth.)	What are the work activities, duties, or responsibilities of the job? (Describe the work.)	What are the characteristics of the person who can perform the work adequately or outstanding? (Describe the person who does the work.)	Which 5 activities/competencies for the job are most important? (Identify the Key Performance Indicators, making sure they indicate a measurable target to be achieved over a period of time.)

Exhibit 5-11: A Worksheet to Integrate Job Descriptions, Job Competencies, Balanced Scorecard Strategic Goals, and Key Performance Indicators

Directions: In the box below the directions, identify the job title that you wish to describe (for example, secretary). Then, under Column 1 in the section below the job box, place the work activities, duties, or responsibilities of the job in the left column. If you do not know them, refer to the job in the *Dictionary of Occupational Titles* (find that online at http://www.occupationalinfo.org/). Under Column 2, describe the characteristics—knowledge, skills, attitudes, or others—of the person who does the job adequately or outstandingly. Under Column 3, list one of the four components of the organization's Balanced Scorecard to which that activity and competency may be related. Under Column 4, pick no more than 5 activities/competencies for the job and indicate that they are key performance indicators (KPIs). Add more lines or pages if necessary.

Job Title:

COLUMN 1	COLUMN 2	COLUMN 3	COLUMN 4
What are the work activities, duties, or responsibilities of the job? (Describe the work.)	What are the characteristics of the person who can perform the work adequately or outstanding? (Describe the person who does the work.)	Which of the four parts of the Balanced Scorecard may this activity relate to? (The four parts are Financial, Customer, Business Operations, and Learning/ Growth.)	Which 5 activities/competencies for the job are most important? (Identify the Key Performance Indicators, making sure they indicate a measurable target to be achieved over a time period.)

What about the Legal Environment?

Clearly, every organization must adhere to governmental requirements as expressed in laws, rules, and regulations. While HPE practitioners should not be expected to be trained lawyers, they should remember to ask questions about the laws that affect an organization and how well the organization is meeting those requirements. That may be easier than it sounds because international organizations may have to worry about laws across national borders. Even firms doing business in the United States may have to be concerned about differences spanning 50 states and many different local governments.

Consider posing questions such as these:

- What laws, rules, and regulations affect your organization, and how well is your organization complying with them?
- What evidence exists of departures from legal requirements as demonstrated by fines or other actions?
- What evidence exists of exceeding government expectations by being noted as an exceptional employer or by winning competitive government funding efforts?

What Methods May Be Used to Collect Information About *What Should Be Happening?*

As we noted in Chapter 4, training and development professionals have long had to be familiar with data collection methods to conduct training needs assessment. Just as most methods of training needs assessment can be adapted to more holistic human performance enhancement needs assessment (HPENA), they may also lend themselves to formulating visions, job performance standards, work expectations, criteria, goals, or objectives. Various futuring methods, also used in strategic planning, can be adapted to establish descriptions of what should be happening.

To provide a basis for comparing what is with what should be, focus attention on each level of the performance environment: the organizational environment, the work environment, the work, and the workers. Exhibit 5-12 summarizes key data collection methods that may be used in formulating what should be; Exhibit 5-13 summarizes key futuring methods that may be used in formulating descriptions of what should be. What follows is a brief overview of key issues to consider when deciding what should be happening at each performance level.

Exhibit 5-12. Methods for Collecting Data about What Should Be Happening

Method	Description
Interviews	Discuss one-on-one with people in the organization what should be happening.
Focus Groups	Call together a group of people and pose questions about what should be happening. Conduct focus groups about what should be happening either as standalone efforts (geared to visioning) or as comparative efforts designed to uncover specific differences between what is happening and what should be happening.
Written Surveys	Use written surveys sent by mail or by electronic mail to gather information from those who are most likely to have information about what should be happening. Use surveys to gather information about facts and perceptions of desirable conditions.
Phone Surveys	Conduct phone surveys on what should be happening by randomly calling customers, suppliers, distributors, and/or employees. Ask them open-ended questions, such as: What should the organization be doing more of? less of? why? Then analyze results using content analysis.
Observation	Use observation creatively to get ideas about more effective ways to do the work. Involve several people in the process so that they may compare their observations, and develop flowcharts of what people should be doing to function most efficiently and effectively. Then show the findings to the workers and ask for their opinions and suggestions.
Document Reviews	Examine forms to discover ways to streamline them—or eliminate them. Collect forms from other organizations to determine whether they suggest new ways documents should be processed. Also, use documents to examine work processes to discover hidden opportunities for major improvements in productivity. Identify key documents in your organization, and use them to construct new, more efficient, and more effective ways to achieve the same results.

Exhibit 5-13. Futuring Methods Useful in Assessing What Should Be

Method	Description
The Delphi Procedure	Form an expert panel. Draft a questionnaire that lists all of the important trends or issues that could affect the organization in the future. Then send the questionnaire to participants. Compile the results and mail them back to the respondents with a second questionnaire. Continue the process until the group agrees what will probably happen in the future. The same method may be used to identify desirable approaches to handling those trends.
Nominal Group Technique	Form an expert panel. Ask participants to meet. Give each participant a 3" x 5" card. Ask for one major trend that is likely to affect the organization in the future. Then compile the cards. Feed the results back to participants and ask them to vote on which trend will be most important. Repeat the procedure to identify the likely consequences of the trend on the organization and best strategies for addressing the trend.
Force Field Analysis	Form a small group. On a flipchart, create three vertical columns. Above the first column, write "trends or issues"; above the second column, write "driving forces"; and above the third column, write "restraining forces." Explain to participants that "driving forces" force change to happen and that "restraining forces" keep change from happening. Ask the participants to list all the trends or conditions that they can think of that will require the organization, division, department, work unit, or team to change. Write those trends or conditions in the first column. Then, for each trend or condition listed, ask participants to list everything that is likely to impel change below the column labeled "driving forces." For each trend or condition listed, ask participants also to list everything that is likely to impede change (retain the status quo). Finally, ask participants what must be done to strengthen the force of driving forces or weaken the force of restraining forces.

The Organizational Environment Level

At the organizational level, HPE practitioners should collect information to detect what should be happening in the organization's interactions with its external environment. HPE practitioners should identify what groups outside the organization should be considered most important to the organization's survival and success. They should then collect information to determine what should be happening in the organization's interactions with those stakeholders. They should ask both organizational members and members of external groups either as part of, or separate from, strategic planning efforts. To that end, they may use methods such as interviews or focus groups.

HPE practitioners may pose questions such as the following to a cross-section of stakeholders from inside and outside the organization:

- How should the organization be interacting most effectively with its customers? suppliers? distributors? stockholders? regulators?
- What other groups are critically important to the success of the organization?
- How should the organization be interacting with those groups?
- What should be happening to capitalize on external interactions?

The aim of this questioning is to discover the most desirable interactions with each external stakeholder group with which the organization must interact to be successful. The information obtained from this data collection effort should prove valuable in formulating a vision or establishing job performance standards, work expectations, criteria, goals, or objectives.

The Work Environment Level

At the work level, HPE practitioners should examine what should be happening on a broad scale inside the organization. HPE practitioners should first identify key issues to examine in the way the organization is managing its operation. For each issue area, they should then describe what should be happening.

Then, as when determining what is happening, the practitioners should identify whom to ask about these issues. The aim should be to take a snap shot of perceptions about what should be happening from representative groups within the organization, including top managers, middle managers, supervisors, professional employees, technical workers, salespersons, clerical employees, and skilled and unskilled hourly workers. Information gathering should be restricted to members of the organization only. Interviews, focus groups, written surveys, and phone surveys may be the best methods for collecting data about the work environment.

HPE practitioners should pose questions such as the following to the representatives of the organization:

- What should be happening in the organization that will improve how well people perform?

- What should be happening in the organization that will improve how well people meet or exceed customer needs? Supplier requirements? Distributor requirements?
- What conditions should exist in the organization that do not presently exist? Why should these conditions exist?

The Work Level

At the work level, HPE practitioners should lead efforts to develop models to govern effective work and workflow. They should first identify what issues are likely to become more important in doing the work over time. For example, what trends in work methods may be identified from outside the organization? What breakthrough productivity improvements can be identified by examining these trends or by examining best practices in other organizations?

In examining the work level, HPE practitioners should answer questions such as these:

- What job descriptions and/or competency models should exist, and how effective are they expected to be in guiding performance?
- What job performance standards should exist, and how should they be communicated?
- How well should performers understand the performance standards?
- How well should performers recognize occasions when they should take action—or refrain from taking action?
- What policies and procedures should exist that do not presently exist?
- What resources should be supplied by the organization so that workers may perform more efficiently and effectively? What time, tools, staff, information, and equipment should workers be given to function competently?
- What feedback should performers receive on their performance to meet or exceed the needs of customers, suppliers, distributors, and other stakeholders?
- How meaningful should be the consequences of performance from the workers' standpoint?
- What value should workers associate with the results of their efforts?

The Worker Level

When HPE practitioners examine what should be happening with the workers, they are investigating the desirable future competencies of those who perform. Worthwhile questions to ask during this examination include the following:

- What kind of people should be doing the work in the future? Why?
- How should performers be selected?
- What competencies should performers possess to perform most competently? What evidence exists to support the need for these competencies?
- How should performers feel about the work they do? the work environment? the organizational environment?
- What specific rewards and incentives should be tied directly to the results the workers are expected to achieve?

The Competencies of the Visionary Role

You may recall from Chapter 2 that applying the new model for HPE calls for trainers-turned-HPE practitioners to display specific competencies to enact the role of visionary. The competencies related to envisioning what should be happening are briefly described in this section and are summarized in Appendix I. They include the following:

- **Ability to identify customer needs and expectations.** How should the organization serve customer needs and meet or exceed expectations? What evidence exists to show that the organization has been meeting those needs and expectations? The ability to answer these questions is key to success in HPE, since power often follows those who serve the customer. HPE practitioners must be capable, as their training and development counterparts frequently have not been, of basing what they do on what customers need and expect of the organization.
- **Ability to detect threats and opportunities in the organizational environment.** HPE practitioners should exert the leadership to help their organizations detect future threats and opportunities stemming from external environmental change. How should the work environment, the work, and the workers be most efficiently and effectively organized to avert future threats and seize future opportunities stemming from external environmental change? How should preparation for averting threats and seizing opportunities be translated into HPE strategy integrated with organizational plans?
- **Ability to locate world-class benchmarks of organizational performance.** To perform competently, HPE practitioners can lead—or participate in—benchmarking efforts designed to formulate descriptions of the ways their organizations should be interacting with their external environments, organizing internally, and managing the work and the workers.
- **Ability to modify the criteria of high-performance work organizations to one corporate culture.** The criteria of high-performance work organizations are not universally applicable; differences do exist among corporate cultures. Hence, HPE practitioners should possess change agent competencies. They

must be able to lead or facilitate efforts to transform the general criteria of high-performance work organizations into terms that make sense in the culture of their organizations. Doing that requires essentially the same competencies as are required of organization development professionals,[13] those who focus on improving group interactions and facilitating change in organizational settings.

- **Ability to identify employee needs and expectations.** What do employees need and expect so that they can perform efficiently and effectively? What conditions are ideal for high performance? Answering these questions requires HPE practitioners to surface employee needs and expectations in the same way that they surface customer needs and expectations.[14]
- **Ability to clarify ways to improve workflow to achieve breakthrough productivity increases.** HPE practitioners must be capable of leading—or coordinating—efforts to reengineer workflow to achieve major improvements in productivity. They should possess the ability to imagine how work should flow through work units and how work should be organized most effectively and to convey their ideas to others. That may require the ability to influence others, reduce resistance to change, elicit employee creativity, and stimulate management efforts to improve productivity.[15]
- **Ability to forecast future competency needs.** What competencies should employees and managers possess to achieve breakthrough productivity? How can strategic plans, organizational structure, and work processes be effectively integrated with the competencies required of workers in the future? To answer these questions, HPE practitioners should lead or coordinate innovative efforts to assess the competencies that will be needed by the workforce in the future. Once known, those competencies can become the focal points for HPE strategies.
- **Ability to assess future workforce needs.** How many and what kind of people will the organization need to achieve its work, work environment, and organizational goals? To answer that question, HPE practitioners should work with other stakeholders to assess when, where, and how to obtain the performers needed to meet performance needs. That may require a combination of skillful and innovative staffing methods, such as the judicious use of external consultants, temporary workers, and transferred workers. It may also require innovative approaches to planning and managing human resources.[16]

Part Three: Finding Opportunities for Improving Human Performance

CHAPTER 1: Why Training Is Not Enough

CHAPTER 2: What Is Human Performance Enhancement (HPE)?

CHAPTER 3: Transforming a Training Department into a Human Performance Enhancement (HPE) Department

CHAPTER 4: Analyzing *What Is* Happening

CHAPTER 5: Envisioning *What Should Be* Happening

CHAPTER 6: Clarifying Present and Future Performance Gaps

CHAPTER 7: Determining the Importance of Performance Gaps

CHAPTER 8: Identifying the Underlying Causes of Performance Gaps

CHAPTER 9: Selecting Human Performance Enhancement (HPE) Strategies

CHAPTER 10: Implementing Human Performance Enhancement (HPE) Strategies to Address Organizational Environment Problems or Opportunities

CHAPTER 11: Implementing Human Performance Enhancement (HPE) Strategies to Address Work Problems or Opportunities

CHAPTER 12: Implementing Human Performance Enhancement (HPE) Strategies to Address Work Environment Problems or Opportunities

CHAPTER 13: Implementing Human Performance Enhancement (HPE) Strategies to Address Worker Problems or Opportunities

CHAPTER 14: Evaluating Human Performance Enhancement (HPE) Strategies

Chapter 6
Clarifying Present and Future Performance Gaps

Clarifying present and future performance gaps is the process of comparing *what is* and *what should be.* Without this step, HPE practitioners and other stakeholders will be unable to rectify existing human performance problems or seize future performance improvement opportunities. By carrying out this step, HPE practitioners dramatize the need for HPE strategies designed to solve problems or capitalize on improvement opportunities. In this way, they create an impetus for change and for closing performance gaps.

This chapter reviews what it means to clarify present and future performance gaps. What is a performance gap? What approaches can clarify present and future performance gaps? What competencies are required for HPE practitioners to enact the role of gap assessor?

Defining a *Performance Gap*

A *performance gap* is a *difference between what is happening and what should be happening.* A performance gap can also be regarded as a *difference between the way things are and the way they are desired to be.* Six gaps are possible:

1. A present positive gap
2. A present negative gap
3. A present neutral gap
4. A future positive gap
5. A future negative gap
6. A future neutral gap (see Exhibit 6-1)

Exhibit 6-1. Ways to Conceptualize Performance Gaps

Time	Positive Gap	Neutral Gap	Negative Gap
Present	The organization presently excels in any or all performance quadrants.	The organization presently equals comparative reference points in any or all performance quadrants.	The organization is presently deficient in any or all performance quadrants when *what is* and *what should be* are compared.
Future	If trends continue as expected, the organization will excel in any or all performance quadrants.	If present trends continue as expected, the organization will equal comparative reference points in any or all performance quadrants.	If present trends continue, the organization will eventually become deficient in one or all performance quadrants.

Present Positive Gap

A present positive performance gap is the most desirable. It may also appear to be unusual. Representing a strategic or tactical strength (an organizational *core competency*), "a positive gap is indicative of internal operations showing a clear superiority"[1] over points of comparison. That means that the organization currently enjoys advantages over competitors, "best-practice organizations," or other reference points in the organizational environment, work environment, work, or workers. A present positive gap indicates that the organization has exceeded its reference points and is outperforming them. Verifying a present positive gap is important to avoid wishful thinking. The burden of proof is greatest when uncovering present positive performance gaps, because decision makers may greet the news with hearty skepticism. When a positive gap is confirmed, the danger also exists that decision makers will become complacent.

In recent years, much attention has focused around strengths-based or positive-based change thinking.[2] That is quite relevant to present and future positive gaps. The idea is that building on strengths is often easier, and more likely to lead to success, than focusing on "what's wrong" (that is, on negative gaps). One major reason is that a focus on "what's wrong" usually leads to *blamestorming*, a process of looking for the culprit (or scapegoat) to blame for problems. Focusing on strengths requires a process in which the organization's members are tasked to think about what they are doing right and then envisioning how they could leverage those strengths to greater competitive advantage.

Present Negative Gap

A present negative performance gap represents a strategic or tactical weakness. It is properly classified as a performance problem. Such a gap means that the organization suffers from disadvantages when compared to its competitors, "best-practice organizations," or other reference points. A present negative gap suggests that the organization is not performing as well as others. Further analysis and corrective action are warranted.

When first identified, present negative gaps may tempt decision makers to take hasty (and sometimes ill-advised) action. That is to be avoided. Further analysis may be needed to clarify the exact cause(s) of the problems, to distinguish symptoms from cause(s), and to target corrective action at cause(s) rather than at symptoms.

Present Neutral Gap

A present neutral gap is neither a strategic or tactical strength nor a weakness. It is neither a performance problem nor a performance improvement opportunity. It means that the organization currently matches—but neither surpasses nor falls behind—competitors, "best-practices organizations," or other reference points. It may, for instance, comply with legal requirements but not go beyond or fall even slightly below governmental requirements codified in law, rule, or regulation. A present neutral gap suggests that the organization is matching expectations or else is performing about the same as others.

Present neutral gaps are usually neglected because decision makers are inclined to believe that such gaps are neither candidates for corrective action nor avenues for dramatic improvements. However, that view can be mistaken. Organizations that experience breakthrough improvements in productivity are sometimes able to distinguish themselves by applying innovation to a neutral gap.

Suppose that the average response time to fill a customer order in a fast food restaurant is three minutes. All fast food restaurants may fall near that time. It is thus a neutral gap. But if it were possible to find ways to respond in one minute or less, an organization could distinguish itself in the industry—and take full marketing advantage of that.

Future Positive Gap

Any future gap incorporates information about expected changes over time. A future positive gap represents a strategic or tactical opportunity for achieving competitive superiority in any performance quadrant. A future positive gap suggests that the organization has potential over time to exceed its reference points and achieve breakthrough results in human performance.

Achieving future positive gaps is one goal of most planning efforts. What is important, however, is to find ways to convert desired organizational results into future realities. That requires leadership from the top, employee commitment from the bottom, and innovative HPE strategies.

Future Negative Gap

A future negative gap represents a strategic or tactical threat. The organization is in peril, falling behind competitors or other reference points in any performance quadrant. A future negative gap should stimulate strategies for corrective action over time. Averting future negative gaps is a secondary goal of most planning efforts.

Future Neutral Gap

A future neutral gap represents neither a strategic nor a tactical threat or opportunity. It means that, if trends unfold as expected, the organization will merely keep pace with competitors, best-practice organizations, or other reference points in the four performance quadrants. A future neutral gap suggests that the organization will probably end up performing about the same as others.

Like present neutral gaps, future neutral gaps may be overlooked because decision makers are likely to believe that they are not worth much attention. However, that view may be in error. Indeed, future neutral gaps may be the most promising of all areas to examine for breakthrough improvement opportunities because competitors may tend to overlook them.

Identifying Performance Gaps

Identifying performance gaps resembles training needs assessment. Key differences do exist, of course. One difference is that the focus of identifying performance gaps is not restricted to uncovering only knowledge, skill, or attitude deficiencies; human performance enhancement needs assessment (HPENA) identifies *any* deficiency or proficiency affecting human performance. Another difference is that the focus of the gap need not be restricted to the past or present, as is often the case with training needs assessment. A third difference is that identifying performance gaps may be a solitary pursuit by HPE practitioners or a process that involves, empowers, and energizes stakeholders in a way that is not typical of traditional training needs assessment.

The Solitary Analyst Approach

In the solitary analyst approach, HPE practitioners undertake comparisons of *what is* and *what should be* on their own, either after they have been requested to do so or after they have noticed possible gaps. Such an approach is worthwhile when a quick response is needed, such as when a new law is passed, an urgent new policy is introduced, or a competitor takes surprise action that demands a swift response. In today's fast-paced, downsized (and sometimes highly stressful) work environments, too, key decision makers are not always available to participate personally in analytical projects designed to compare *what is* and *what should be.* In these cases it falls to HPE practitioners to take the initiative.

When functioning as a solitary analyst, use the worksheet in Exhibit 6-2 as a starting point. Collect information sufficient to fill in the grids shown in the exhibit. Then identify performance gaps. This process, while fast and largely intuitive, is not rigorous. But it will satisfy those who want prompt action based on analysis.

Exhibit 6-2. A Worksheet for Solitary Analysts to Use in Comparing *What Is* to *What Should Be*

Directions: Use this worksheet to compare ***what is*** happening to ***what should be*** happening and to identify the performance gap that appears to exist. Then identify the performance gap that appears to be exerting the most influence on the present and future performance of the organization. Mount corrective efforts to solve identified problems; mount improvement efforts to take advantage of identified performance improvement opportunities.

Performance Quadrants	***What Is*** **Happening?**	***What Should Be*** **Happening?**
Organizational Environment		

What is the difference between *what is* happening and *what should be* happening? (Describe the difference and classify it as Present Positive, Present Negative, Present Neutral, Future Positive, Future Negative, or Future Neutral)

Performance Quadrants	***What Is*** **Happening?**	***What Should Be*** **Happening?**
Work Environment		

What is the difference between *what is* happening and *what should be* happening?

Exhibit 6-2 (concluded)

Performance Quadrants	*What Is* Happening?	*What Should Be* Happening?
Work		

What is the difference between *what is* happening and *what should be* happening?

Performance Quadrants	*What Is* Happening?	*What Should Be* Happening?
Worker		

What is the difference between *what is* happening and *what should be* happening?

The Team, Task Force, or Committee Approach

In team-based corporate cultures, something can be said for conducting comparisons of *what is* and *what should be* by using one or more teams, task forces, or committees. Members of a team, task force, or committee form a core of change champions who can build an impetus for an HPE strategy based on their findings. Members have broad ownership resulting from their participation. The team, task force, or committee effort is also a development opportunity in its own right.

Different categories of teams may be used in making comparisons between *what is* and *what should be. Standing teams* consist of work group members who work together to achieve common goals. *Cross-functional teams* represent several standing teams, groups, or departments sharing common concerns. When selecting teams to make comparisons between *what is* and *what should be,* target the teams that are well suited to examine the issues. For instance, the board of directors or the top management team may be especially well suited to examine the organizational environment. Top and middle managers may be especially competent to examine the work environment. Other teams may be well suited to examine the work and the worker environments.

Task forces are *ad hoc* groups assembled to focus on an issue of common concern. Their charters are restricted to a few issues only. Most task forces have limited life spans and disband once they have completed their assigned tasks. A *vertical-slice task force* uses members from many hierarchical levels and thus differs from a *horizontal-slice task force* composed of people from the same level. A vertical-slice task force, chaired by an HPE practitioner, may be particularly useful in making broad comparisons between *what is* happening and *what should be* happening among the four performance quadrants. Members should be chosen for their abilities (what they can contribute) as well as their organizational placement (where they come from), their interest level (how willing they are to participate), and their development needs (what competencies they can build through task force participation).

A *committee,* unlike a task force, endures beyond one project. In other respects, committees and task forces have common features. A *steering committee* guides efforts; an *advisory committee* offers only recommendations and suggestions for action. A human performance enhancement committee may be a committee that sets policy and priorities on HPE or one that merely advises others.

To use a team, task force, or committee to best effect in comparing *what is* and *what should be,* HPE practitioners should do the following:

1. Take steps to identify the team or members of a task force or committee.
2. Clarify the group's mandate, having obtained approvals from senior management as necessary (it is desirable if a member of top management participates in the group as well).
3. Organize the group, taking steps to clarify the role of the group and individual responsibilities within the group.

4. Brief members as necessary on issues affecting human performance and on the need to distinguish training from other HPE strategies.
5. Help group members become acquainted with each other (if necessary) and develop a project plan to guide the group's efforts to
   - gather information about what is happening in each performance quadrant;
   - gather information about what should be happening in each performance quadrant;
   - compare and analyze the results of Steps 1 and 2;
   - conduct subsequent steps so as to identify worthwhile HPE strategies, set priorities, or make recommendations to others about desirable priorities for HPE.

To use a group most effectively, HPE practitioners should give group members opportunities to participate in collecting information about *what is* happening and *what should be* happening. That may mean, for instance, that group members must participate in framing what issues to examine, conducting benchmarking studies by phone or by site view, or surveying employees to clarify their perceptions. When group members are involved in this way, they will have strong ownership in their findings and possess a clear understanding of them. When such personal involvement is not possible, HPE practitioners will usually have to supply more information to overcome objections and build acceptance for possible HPE strategies.

The Management Retreat

Some corporate cultures remain top-down oriented even as management theorists on all sides preach the gospel of employee involvement and empowerment. In such cases, HPE practitioners are well advised to begin their HPE strategies at the top and to work down. An excellent way to do that is to make HPE the focus of a management retreat.

A management retreat is, as the name implies, a getaway for executives, middle managers, and supervisors. The goal of many retreats is to set aside time to examine important issues. Most retreats last several days and are conducted off-site so that participants will not be interrupted to handle momentary crises or routine requests. (However, shorter retreats and on-site retreats can be conducted.)

Management retreats are carried out for many purposes. Some focus on strategic planning, succession planning, total quality, business process reengineering, employee involvement or empowerment, or organizational learning. They may also be helpful in formulating vision statements, establishing action plans to realize them, or evaluating the results of organizational efforts.

The flexibility of the management retreat makes it an almost ideal venue for examining differences between *what is* and *what should be* happening in human performance. Given the widespread use of management retreats, they are also nearly ideal for directing attention to HPE strategies. By engaging many or all members of management, retreats can be powerful ways to introduce and consolidate widespread change, at least in the management ranks.

How should a management retreat be planned to direct attention to differences between *what is* and *what should be?* While there are many possible approaches, one way is for HPE practitioners to assume leadership for planning the retreat. They should then enlist the personal involvement of top managers, if that is possible. Working by themselves or in a team with stakeholders, HPE practitioners should then identify *what is* happening and *what should be* happening in all four performance quadrants. That information may be gathered from management employees themselves before the meeting. HPE practitioners should then organize a highly participative group meeting that will make the business case for enhancing human performance, describe many ways to do that, identify *what is* happening and *what should be* happening, verify that information with retreat participants, and ask them to clarify differences between *what is* and *what should be.* Exhibit 6-3 provides a possible agenda for a management retreat on HPE.

Exhibit 6-3. A Possible Agenda for a Management Retreat Focused on Clarifying Present and Future Performance Gaps

---

I. Introduction

Describe the purpose of the retreat and the results to be achieved (objectives).

II. Identifying Present Challenges

A. Form small groups and ask participants to create a list of the top five challenges confronting the organization. Allow 20 to 30 minutes for the activity. Ask each group to appoint a spokesperson and to list the challenges it identified. The facilitator should write the challenges on a flipchart or overhead transparency.

B. Describe key issues affecting human performance with the participants.

C. Present the new model to guide HPE to the participants (see Exhibit 2-5 in this book).

D. Ask participants to form new small groups and identify the current "status" of human performance that stems directly from the challenges confronting the organization. Allow 20 to 30 minutes for the activity. Ask each group to appoint a spokesperson and list the "status" they identified. The facilitator should write the problems on a flipchart or overhead transparency.

E. Ask participants to remain in the same small groups and, for each description of *"what is happening"* identified in the previous activity, write *"what should be happening."* Allow 20 to 30 minutes for the activity. Ask each group to appoint a spokesperson and to list its visions of *what should be* happening. The facilitator should write the visions on a flipchart.

F. Ask participants to categorize the gaps as present positive, present negative, or present neutral. Carry out this activity with the large group.

G. Summarize present challenges.

III. Identifying Future Challenges

Repeat the same procedure as summarized in Step II, focusing attention on future challenges.

The Large-Scale Change Effort Approach

Of growing popularity is the large-scale group change effort,[3] sometimes called whole systems transformational change, an event that involves as many key stakeholders from inside and outside an organization as possible. One large-scale change effort is the *search conference* in which participants work together collaboratively to build a preferred future for the organization.[4]

Such gargantuan meetings are advantageous because they build a critical mass for change among many key decision makers at one time. These meetings do have disadvantages, of course: They are difficult to organize effectively; they pose a succession-planning risk to the organization when so many decision makers are gathered in a central location; and they can make it a challenge for the organization to conduct business when so many key decision makers are out for an extended time. (Some organizations meet the last challenge by simply shutting down the business for one or more days, which implies immense top management support and commitment. Such an approach is sometimes called *immersion assessment.*)

A large-group change effort approach requires careful planning. Meeting facilitators

- contract with the organization's leadership team to secure commitment for the change effort;
- build alignment, ownership, and commitment to the process in the leadership team;
- develop an organizational strategy to guide the change effort;
- design the real-time strategic-change event;
- plan for the meeting that is the centerpiece of the event;
- plan for follow-up initiatives after the event;
- rehearse the event;
- hold the event;
- implement the follow-up on change initiatives.

Additional steps may include evaluating the results and providing information about the results to prompt real-time improvements in the change effort.

The same approach can be modified to compare *what is* and *what should be* as a starting point for identifying human performance problems, identifying human performance enhancement opportunities, building an impetus for human performance enhancement strategies linked to organizational strategy, and setting priorities for the strategy (or strategies).

When the large-scale change effort approach is used in this way, HPE practitioners function as meeting planners and group facilitators. They secure top management support for moving beyond training to focus on long-term strategies for enhancing human performance. They establish a team to help them plan and execute the large-scale change effort event. Team members, drawn from a cross-section of the organization, conduct background research to identify *what is* happening and *what should be* happening in each performance quadrant. They then prepare a presentation and briefing materials to summarize the results of their research.

When the background research has been completed, a large-scale meeting is planned to include representatives from all stakeholders, such as stockholders, customers, management employees, union representatives, government regulators, suppliers, and distributors. Representatives from these groups are handpicked for their superior performance and then assembled for a briefing on *what is* and *what should be* happening in all four of the organization's performance quadrants.

Assembled in small groups of between eight and ten that form a microcosm of the organization's external and internal environments, these representatives work together to verify or modify information about what is happening and what should be happening. They also compare the two and thereby identify performance gaps. Their goal in this process is to achieve broad consensus on the gaps and on HPE strategies designed to narrow or close the gaps.

Clarifying Present and Future Performance Gaps

It is worth emphasizing that there is a big difference between present and future performance gaps. What could be a small gap at present could turn into a large one in the future as conditions change outside and inside an organization. It is thus worth asking these questions, among others:

- What will happen if no action is taken on closing a gap at present? Will it increase in the future, decrease in the future, or remain the same? Why?
- What will be the drivers that lead a performance gap to change over time?
- What is the present and future value of the money required to close a gap? What is the present value of closing a gap at present, and what is the discounted value of the money required to close the gap for the future?

To assess the value of gaps, it may be necessary to conduct some scenario planning. What will happen in the future that will affect existing gaps today?

Once the gaps have been identified, it may be helpful to place them on one or more visual aid of some kind. The visual aids could take the form of one or more pictures to show present and future negative, neutral, and positive performance gaps. Some HPE practitioners may choose to summarize the gaps on a SWOT (strengths, weaknesses, opportunities, and threats) grid or something that looks like that. Of course, neutral gaps should not be forgotten, and that will usually mean that a SWOT grid may have to be modified to one or more 3 x 3 grids.

The Competencies of the Gap Assessor Role

In Chapter 2, we said that applying the new model for HPE requires trainers-turned-HPE practitioners to display specific competencies. The competencies related to clarifying present and future performance gaps are linked to the gap assessor role. For the section of the competency model pertaining to that role, see Appendix I. Brief descriptions of each competency follow:

- **Ability to compare *what is* and *what should be* in the organization's interactions with the external environment.** HPE practitioners can compare *what is* and *what should be* happening in the organization's interactions with the external environment. They must detect shortcomings in the company's ability to meet or exceed the needs of customers, suppliers, distributors, and other key stakeholder groups. That means more than merely facilitating the efforts of others to do so—such as facilitating strategic planning retreats—though that competency is also included.
- **Ability to compare *what is* and *what should be* in the organization's internal operations.** HPE practitioners can spearhead efforts to compare *what is* and *what should be* in the organization's internal operations, what is called the work environment. They can analyze how well the organization and its parts are structured and are internally interacting. In short, HPE practitioners can independently examine policy, structure, leadership, and other key factors affecting organizational performance. They must also be able to help others who carry out such examinations, such as cross-functional process improvement teams.
- **Ability to compare *what is* and *what should be* in work processing.** HPE practitioners can analyze the way work is processed. They must possess sufficient skills to analyze the way work is transformed from inputs to outputs. They should also be capable of facilitating teams assigned to reengineer work processing operations.
- **Ability to compare the difference between *what is* and *what should be* at the individual level.** HPE practitioners can recognize—and lead—efforts to compare the difference between actual and ideal individual performance. They should thus be capable of troubleshooting gaps in individual performance.
- **Ability to detect mismatches between individuals and the jobs in which they are placed.** Despite the egalitarianism that has been fashionable in recent years, individuals are not created equal. They differ dramatically in abilities and experiences. As a result, not every person is ideally suited for every job. HPE practitioners can compare individual talents, abilities, and motivations to work requirements. That may also require them to identify *essential job functions,* as the term is used in the Americans with Disabilities Act, and to assess how well an individual can perform those functions. Identifying possible ways to make *reasonable accommodation* for individuals who are physically, psychologically, or learning disabled is also included in this competency area.

Chapter 7
Determining the Importance of Performance Gaps

Once performance gaps have been identified, HPE practitioners should spearhead efforts to determine their importance. Determining the importance of performance gaps is a starting point for setting priorities for human performance enhancement strategies. With resources scarce, it may not be worth the time, people, money, or opportunity costs of addressing gaps of little importance.

Determining importance is, in part, a matter of *measuring* importance. The value of gaps must be determined, and it is best to do that before taking action because human performance enhancement efforts are essentially investment decisions. Nobody invests money if they expect to lose it, and nobody invests time, money, or effort if they believe the payoff will not be worthwhile. It is critical to forecast the benefits of an HPE effort before implementing a solution.

Defining *Importance*

To determine importance means to assign value to a performance gap. The word *value* is derived from the Latin word *val re,* meaning "to be of worth." Value can refer to the relative worth or usefulness. Both denotations apply when determining the importance of performance gaps.

Quantitative Measures of Importance

Most training and development professionals and HPE practitioners probably think that *valuing* means assessing the financial desirability of investing in an HPE strategy. That *is* one meaning, and, in fact, much attention has been devoted to calculating the financial return on training investments. Forecasting the financial return on training before making an investment and estimating the financial return after making the training investment are examples of determining importance. Some call this the process of assessing *hard* (monetary) returns. Examples of hard measures are listed in Exhibit 7-1. However, any effort to measure results can be equated with assessing importance.[1]

Exhibit 7-1. Hard Measures of Importance

OUTPUT	TIME
• Units produced	• Equipment downtime
• Tons manufactured	• Overtime
• Items assembled	• On-time shipments
• Money collected	• Time to project completion
• Items sold	• Processing time
• Forms processed	• Supervisory time
• Loans approved	• Break-in time for new employees
• Inventory turnover	• Training time
• Patients visited	• Meeting schedules
• Applications processed	• Repair time
• Students graduated	• Efficiency
• Tasks completed	• Work stoppages
• Output per hour	• Order response
• Productivity	• Late reporting
• Work backlog	• Lost time days
• Incentive bonus	
• Shipments	
• New accounts generated	

COSTS	QUALITY
• Budget variances	• Scrap
• Unit costs	• Waste
• Cost by account	• Rejects
• Variable costs	• Error rates
• Fixed costs	• Rework
• Overhead costs	• Shortages
• Operating costs	• Product defects
• Number of cost reductions	• Deviation from standard
• Project cost of savings	• Product failures
• Accident costs	• Inventory adjustments
• Program costs	• Time card corrections
• Sales expenses	• Percent of tasks completed properly
	• Number of accidents

Source: Jack J. Phillips. *Handbook of Training Evaluation and Measurement Methods,* 2nd ed. (Houston: Gulf Publishing, 1991), p. 154. Copyright © 1991, Gulf Publishing Company, Houston, Texas. Used with permission. All rights reserved.

Qualitative Measures of Importance

There can, however, be more to determining importance than simply calculating financial value. Nonfinancial measures of worth reflect values. Values are important because they drive decision making and perceptions of worth. In one study of executive development programs, for instance, chief executive officers (CEOs) indicated that their chief means of assessing the value of these programs was whether people were available when needed.[2] Availability of executive talent became, for them, the chief measure of importance, rather than some short-term or arbitrary measure of the financial value of investments in executive development. Examples of soft, nonfinancial measures are listed in Exhibit 7-2 on the following page.

Assessing Consequences

Assessing consequences is important in determining the value of performance gaps.

What Is a Consequence?

A *consequence* is a *predicted or actual result of a performance gap.* It is the answer to the question "What happens if the gap is left alone and no action is taken?" Consequences may, of course, stem from action or inaction.

A simple example can illustrate the importance of consequences. Suppose that decision makers of an organization are forced to fill all executive vacancies from outside because no internal candidates are available. That is *what is* happening. However, that is not what decision makers believe *should be* happening. Having benchmarked with other organizations, they discover that approximately 80 percent of all executive vacancies should be filled from within. The gap is thus between the desired state (filling 80 percent from within) and the actual state (no vacancies filled from within).

What are the consequences of this difference? The financial costs of recruiting externally can be assessed by examining fees paid to executive recruiters, relocation fees, and related expenses. Less easily determined for comparative purposes are the costs of recruiting internally, since no executives are currently recruited in that way. However, those costs can be *estimated.* Possible costs include the expenses of finding replacements for the vacancies created by promotions.

Consequences Stemming from Taking Action and Not Taking Action

Consequences stem both from taking action and from not taking action. In the example, consequences can stem either from taking action to recruit more executives internally or from choosing not to take action and leave matters as they are. Taking action to recruit more executives may require an investment in a planned executive development program. That is a cost. Benefits should also flow from taking action—not the least of which would be a gradual reduction in expenditures for executive search fees. Less tangible costs will result from, for example, investing time in developing executives internally; an intangible benefit may be reduced turnover among high-potential middle managers who see that internal advancement is possible.

Exhibit 7-2. Soft Measures of Importance

WORK HABITS	NEW SKILLS
• Absenteeism • Tardiness • Visits to the dispensary • First aid treatments • Violations of safety rules • Number of communication breakdowns • Excessive breaks	• Decisions made • Problems solved • Conflicts avoided • Grievances avoided • Counseling problems solved • Listening skills • Interviewing skills • Reading speed • Discrimination charges resolved • Intention to use new skills • Frequency of use of new skills
WORK CLIMATE	**DEVELOPMENT/ADVANCEMENT**
• Number of grievances • Number of discrimination charges • Employee complaints • Job satisfaction • Unionization avoidance • Employee turnover • Reduced litigation	• Number of promotions • Number of pay increases • Number of training programs attended • Requests for transfer • Performance appraisal ratings • Increase in job effectiveness
FEELINGS/ATTITUDES	**INITIATIVE**
• Favorable reactions • Attitude changes • Perceptions of job responsibilities • Perceived changes in performance • Employee loyalty • Increased confidence	• Implementation of new ideas • Successful completion of projects • Number of suggestions submitted • Number of suggestions implemented • Work accomplishment • Setting goals and objectives

Source: Jack J. Phillips. *Handbook of Training Evaluation and Measurement Methods,* 2nd ed. (Houston: Gulf Publishing, 1991), p. 156. Copyright © 1991, Gulf Publishing Company, Houston, Texas. Used with permission. All rights reserved.

Consequences Stemming from Different Types of Gaps

Consequences may vary depending upon the type of performance gap. *Neutral gaps* are easiest to work with, since their consequences are not significant. A *present negative gap* means that a problem exists, so the negative consequences of inaction may be most severe, and corrective action, while costly, may be warranted. A *future negative gap* means that a problem may exist if the future unfolds as expected; negative consequences may stem from inaction, but those consequences are less certain. A *present positive gap* means that an opportunity for improvement exists. This should be treated as a possible investment, so taking action warrants the careful scrutiny accorded any other investment. A *future positive gap* means that an opportunity for improvement may exist in the future if the future unfolds as expected. Like its present-oriented counterpart, a future positive gap is subject to scrutiny. It may also be time-sensitive, meaning that taking action at one time may be more desirable or more cost-beneficial than doing so at other times.

Who Determines Importance?

Value depends on perspective. Who considers taking action worthwhile? Who prefers inaction? What accounts for these differences in opinion? These questions are critically important in determining importance.

In speaking to training directors, I have frequently made the point that the fundamental flaw in calculating returns on training investments is treating the matter as a simple accounting problem. If only a single, magic formula could be found, too many training directors reason, then skeptical managers would always be convinced that training is worth the investment. As a result, many efforts to examine return on training investments take an accounting-oriented approach. Numbers are given more importance than the people who give them meaning; the quest is on for bottom-line, bullet-proof financial measures divorced from the people who interpret them.

But meanings are in people, not in numbers. (That is a paraphrase of a quotation from the great communication theorist Count Alfred Korzybski, who said that "meanings are in people, not in words."[3]) Instead of viewing return on training investments as an accounting problem, training and development professionals and HPE practitioners should view the issue as akin to a legal problem. After all, trial lawyers know too well that they can supply a jury with as much evidence as they wish. The evidence may be compelling, or it may be weak. Whatever its persuasive strength, evidence does not become proof until the jury accepts it.

The same principle applies to showing the return on training investments and other HPE strategies. Among the key questions to ask are these:

- Who has the biggest stake in the performance gap? Why?
- What results do stakeholders most want to achieve now and in the future?

- When are the stakeholders most interested in finding out about the performance gaps: now or in the future? Why?
- What evidence will be most persuasive to those who must decide whether to take action?
- What approaches to presenting evidence will the chief stakeholders find most persuasive as they decide whether to act?
- How willing are the stakeholders to participate in troubleshooting a performance problem or seizing a performance enhancement opportunity? Why?

By asking these questions, HPE practitioners can direct attention to finding the human meanings that form the foundation for perceptions of importance. The worksheet appearing in Exhibit 7-3 can help HPE practitioners identify the key stakeholders of a performance problem or an improvement opportunity and consider ways of answering these questions.

Exhibit 7-3. A Worksheet for Addressing Issues of Concern to Stakeholders

Directions: Use this worksheet to help structure your thinking about who has the most self-interest in addressing a performance gap and issues of concern to address with them.

QUESTIONS	ANSWERS
Who has the biggest stake in the performance gap? Why?	
What results do stakeholders most want to achieve now and in the future?	
When are the stakeholders most interested in finding out about the performance gaps? Now or in the future? Why?	
What evidence will be most persuasive to those who must decide whether to take action?	
What approaches to presenting evidence will the chief stakeholders find most persuasive as they decide whether to take action?	
How willing are the stakeholders to participate in troubleshooting a performance problem or seizing a performance enhancement opportunity? Why?	

Forecasting Importance

To forecast the future importance of a performance gap, HPE practitioners should assume leadership. They may use any one of several approaches: the solitary analyst approach; the team, task force, or committee approach; the management retreat approach; or the large-scale change effort approach. No matter how the forecasting process is carried out, however, six important questions should be addressed.

Question 1: What Consequences Stem from the Performance Gap? What *is* the difference between *what is happening* and *what should be happening*? What does that difference mean? Refer to the hard measures listed in Exhibit 7-1 as one way to think about measurable values to use in pinpointing the consequences. Which ones are most applicable? Least applicable? Not at all applicable?

Question 2: What Costs and Benefits Can Be Estimated for the Gap? Examine the consequences of the gap and the measurable values associated with it. What is the gap's present annual cost to the organization? What is the gap's projected cost to the organization over the next one to five years? What is the present value of that money?

What benefits, if any, are flowing from the gap? Are there any? (Problems often have a positive side.) Subtract the benefits derived from the gap from the costs associated with it. The remainder should equal the *benefits of inaction.*

Question 3: What Costs and Benefits Can Be Pinpointed for Taking Action to Close the Performance Gap? Focus attention on possible corrective actions or performance enhancement opportunities. Since nothing is free, costs and benefits will result from taking action. Review the estimated costs and benefits of HPE strategies intended to solve performance problems or improve performance, such as providing training, improving feedback, or providing job aids. Estimate the costs of mounting each effort and the benefits accruing from it. Then subtract the benefits derived from the gap from the costs associated with it. The remainder should equal the *benefits of action.*

Question 4: How Do the Costs and Benefits Compare? Compare the costs and benefits estimated for taking action to those for taking no action. How do they compare? Which ratio yields the higher present advantage? The higher ratio over time? Why?

Question 5: What Nonfinancial Measures May Be Important? Avoid making decisions based solely on financial, or hard, measures. Consider also the soft measures. What intangible issues are at stake? Will taking action to close a performance gap produce intangible costs or benefits? If so, what are they? Will inaction yield intangible costs or benefits? If so, what are they?

Question 6: What Is the Importance of the Performance Gap? How advantageous is it to take action? not to take action? The gap is important only if the benefits of taking action exceed those of inaction or if nonfinancial measures of taking action are likely to outweigh the costs. In those cases, the gap should be regarded as a human performance enhancement priority. On the other hand, consider the gap unimportant if the benefits of taking action are less than those of not taking action or if the nonfinancial benefits of inaction are apparent.

The Competencies of the HPE Facilitator Role

Applying the new HPE model described in Chapter 2 calls for trainers-turned-HPE practitioners to display competencies linked to determining the importance of performance gaps. These competencies, listed in Appendix I and described briefly here, are associated with the role of HPE facilitator:

- **Ability to determine the importance of gaps between *what is* and *what should be* in the organization's interactions with the external environment.** HPE practitioners must possess the ability to detect, or to lead others to detect, mismatches between *what is* and *what should be* happening in the organization's interactions with the external environment. This means exercising strategic thinking skills and having a keen ability to compare an idealized vision of the future to present events.
    - HPE practitioners can examine the sectors in, and the stakeholders of, the external environment and find important differences between what is happening and what should be happening. Key questions to consider in this process may include the following:
        - How will the most important present challenges facing the organization eventually play out in its dealings with customers, stockholders, suppliers, distributors, and other important external groups?
        - How will the most important future challenges facing the organization eventually unfold in its dealings with customers, stockholders, suppliers, distributors, and other important external groups?

While answering these questions, it may be helpful to use a grid like that shown in Exhibit 7-4.

Exhibit 7-4. A Grid for Uncovering Human Performance Enhancement Opportunities

Directions: For each sector or issue area listed in column 1, describe, in column 2, important trends that you feel are likely to change the external environment in which the organization is functioning. Then, in column 3, describe what changes are most likely to result from the trends over the next one to three years. In column 4, identify human performance enhancement opportunities that might present themselves because of the trends. Be creative. There are no right or wrong answers. In the spirit of employee empowerment and involvement, you may wish to involve organizational stakeholders, decision makers, and employees in this creative activity.

COLUMN 1: ***Sector or Issue Area***	**COLUMN 2:** ***What important trends are emerging in the sector or issue area?*** **(List them below)**	**COLUMN 3:** ***What changes are most likely to result from the trends over the next one to three years?*** **(Describe them below)**	**COLUMN 4:** ***What possible human performance enhancement opportunities may present themselves because of the trends?*** **(List them below)**
National/International Economic Conditions			
The Industry			
Competition			

Exhibit 7-4 (continued)

COLUMN 1: *Sector or Issue Area*	COLUMN 2: *What important trends are emerging in the sector or issue area?* (List them below)	COLUMN 3: *What changes are most likely to result from the trends over the next one to three years?* (Describe them below)	COLUMN 4: *What possible human performance enhancement opportunities may present themselves because of the trends?* (List them below)
Law and Regulations			
Geography			
Product/Service Cycle Time			
Work Methods			

Exhibit 7-4 (continued)

COLUMN 1: *Sector or Issue Area*	COLUMN 2: *What important trends are emerging in the sector or issue area?* (List them below)	COLUMN 3: *What changes are most likely to result from the trends over the next one to three years?* (Describe them below)	COLUMN 4: *What possible human performance enhancement opportunities may present themselves because of the trends?* (List them below)
Customer Needs/ Preferences			
Social Trends			
Workforce Trends			
Supplier Trends			

Exhibit 7-4 (concluded)

COLUMN 1: *Sector or Issue Area*	COLUMN 2: *What important trends are emerging in the sector or issue area?* (List them below)	COLUMN 3: *What changes are most likely to result from the trends over the next one to three years?* (Describe them below)	COLUMN 4: *What possible human performance enhancement opportunities may present themselves because of the trends?* (List them below)
Distributor Trends			
Other (please specify):			

- **Ability to determine the importance of gaps between *what is* and *what should be* happening within the organization.** HPE practitioners can lead, coordinate, or participate in organization-wide performance enhancement efforts to detect important gaps between *what is* and *what should be* happening. In this case, *important* means *having major consequences.* As part of this process, HPE practitioners should examine organizational structure and policy; this step is essential to discovering real or perceived consequences to the organization.
- **Ability to determine the importance of gaps between *what is* and *what should be* in work processing.** HPE practitioners can lead, coordinate, or participate in efforts at the work level to examine workflow, work processing, and the inputs, outputs, and transformation processes involved in producing the work or delivering the organization's services. As part of this competency, they should possess the fundamental ability to examine the following:
  - how work flows into a division, department, or work unit/team and the raw (untransformed) states in which materials, people, and information flow into a division, department, work unit, or team
  - how materials, people, and information should flow into the division, department, work unit, or team
  - the gaps that exist between what is happening and what should be happening
  - the consequences that stem from existing gaps between *what is* and *what should be* happening in workflow
  - the importance of those consequences
- **Ability to determine the importance of gaps between what workers can do and what they should be able to do.** HPE practitioners can lead, coordinate, or participate in matching work requirements to worker competencies. They can discover answers to questions such as these:
  - What competencies are available among workers to function effectively in the organization's internal and external environment and to deal with the work processing requirements?
  - What competencies should be available among workers to function effectively in the organization's internal and external environment and to deal with the work processing requirements?
  - What gaps exist between worker competencies required now and those available now?
  - What gaps exist between worker competencies required in the future and those available now?

- How important are the gaps in worker competencies?
- What consequences stem from—or are expected to stem from—these competency gaps?

Determining the Importance of Performance Gaps

The HPE consultant's role is key to the process of determining the importance of performance gaps. HPE consultants enacting the role of management consultants will tend to draw their own conclusions about what is important. They will then seek to persuade clients of that importance by discovering appropriate financial and nonfinancial measures. But HPE consultants enacting the role of process consultants will tend to involve their clients in discovering how much a performance gap is important. Indeed, process consultants are keenly aware that perceptions of importance can vary, depending on who draws the conclusion. What is important to top managers may not be important to frontline employees, and what is important to customers may not be perceived as important to some members of the organization. Hence, a challenge of HPE consultants who enact the process consultant role is to encourage people to feel importance from the perspective of others.

Chapter 8
Identifying the Underlying Causes of Performance Gaps

The most important step in HPE is identifying the underlying causes of performance gaps. Appropriate performance enhancement strategies can be selected only after the underlying causes have been identified. Yet no other step is more difficult. One reason is that human performance problems and opportunities may stem from multiple causes. In addition, causes are easily confused with symptoms. Pinpointing underlying causes is thus extraordinarily difficult—and admittedly sometimes impossible.

This chapter defines *cause,* explains how to distinguish a cause from a symptom, identifies many different causes for human performance problems, explains who determines causes, suggests when causes should be assessed, summarizes my research on the causes of human performance problems, offers some advice about how and why causes may change over time, reviews approaches to determining the causes of human performance gaps, and summarizes the core competencies linked to the strategic troubleshooter role.

Defining *Cause*

A *cause* is the *ultimate reason (or reasons) for the existence of a human performance gap.* It is the root determinant for a mismatch between *what is* and *what should be.*

Traditional Views of Cause

Historically, theorists have focused on three possible causes of all human performance problems. Robert F. Mager and Peter Pipe, for example, distinguish among *skill deficiencies, management deficiencies,* and a combination of them.[1] Thomas F. Gilbert distinguishes among *deficiencies of knowledge, deficiencies of execution,* and a combination.[2] In a classic and still-relevant work, Geary A. Rummler and Alan P. Brache trace the causes of all human performance problems to three needs: *training needs, management needs,* and a combination of training and management needs.[3]

The terms share common meanings. *Skills deficiencies, deficiencies of knowledge,* and *training needs* are essentially synonymous. They refer to problems traceable to individual performers that prevent them from functioning properly and that stem directly from lack of the appropriate knowledge, skill, or attitude. They are thus addressed by performance enhancement strategies geared to individuals and intended to correct the deficiencies or meet the needs. *Management deficiencies, deficiencies of execution,* and *management needs* are also essentially synonymous. They refer to problems with the performance environment and with management, which is ultimately responsible for setting the tone for interactions with the organizational environment and for controlling the work environment, the work, and the workers.

Gilbert, Mager and Pipe, and Rummler and Brache reduce all performance problems to three causes to maintain analytical simplicity and economy. Their approaches make it easier to explain to decision makers that training is not the panacea for all ills. Only problems traceable to skills deficiencies, deficiencies of knowledge, and training needs lend themselves to training as a human performance enhancement strategy. Problems traceable to management deficiencies, deficiencies of execution, and management needs must be corrected by management action, such as reengineering job design, organizational design, rewards and incentives, feedback, or job and performance aids. Many other management actions are, of course, possible.

A Dissenting View

Although much can be said for simplicity, reducing all causes to just three may emphasize simplicity at the expense of reality. Many human performance problems simply cannot be traced to a single cause. Such problems may, in fact, stem from strategic mismatches (such as not doing what customers want), work environment mismatches (such as not structuring functions properly), or a host of other causes.

Traditional views of performance problems emphasize negative performance gaps and focus on troubleshooting only. In this view, a problem must exist before corrective action is initiated by HPE practitioners, managers, or employees. While that may be the easiest view—people are usually motivated to solve a problem once it has been recognized—it may not be the most productive approach. A more desirable approach is to avoid performance problems before they occur. That means that HPE practitioners should be alert to seizing performance enhancement opportunities even when no problems are immediately apparent. Alternatively, HPE practitioners may discover the organization's (or individual's) unique strengths and then leverage them to competitive advantage.

A trend of the future is to focus on creativity and innovation rather than problem-solving alone. *Creativity*, the ability to think in new ways, is the raw material; *innovation* means the application of creativity to business success. Numerous methods have been described to describe or spur creativity and encourage innovation. Classic books on the topic include (1) Michalko, M. (2006). *Thinkertoys: A handbook of creative-thinking techniques*, 2nd ed. Berkeley: Ten Speed Press; (2) Rogers, E. (2003). *Diffusion of innovations*, 5th ed. New York: The Free Press; and (3) Van Gundy, A. (1988). *Techniques of structured problem-solving*, 2nd ed. New York: Van Nostrand Reinhold. While Van Gundy's and Michalko's books describe techniques to foster creative thinking and thereby move to creative solutions to problems, Rogers's classic book explains how new ideas are gradually accepted.

Rogers's ideas are all about the acceptance, or willingness to experiment, with new ideas. He believed that new ideas are accepted along a bell curve. Some people look for innovative solutions (about 2.5 percent of any group are innovators). Early adopters are those prone to accept new ideas more readily than others (about 13.5 percent of any group). Innovation is then gradually accepted by the early majority (about 34 percent of any group), late majority (about 34 percent of any group) and laggards (about 16 percent). The acceptance of new ideas depends on many factors. Among them: adopters' awareness, interest, evaluation, trial, and adoption.

HPE practitioners should care about creativity and innovation for several reasons. First, some observers of the contemporary business scene believe that the world's economy is moving toward one in which innovation becomes key to competitive advantage. It is not the business with the most resources that will win but rather the one with the best ideas that reaches the market first. Second, some critics claim that HPE is past-oriented and reactive. These critics claim that HPE practitioners wait until a problem comes up before they take action to solve it. But creative, innovative solutions will outpace a reactive mode. If HPE practitioners are willing to accept creative approaches, they will become more proactive. By doing so, they will move beyond the reactive and become proactive.

A New View of Causes

A *present cause* is the difference between what is and what should be happening now; a *future cause* is the difference between what is happening now and what should happen in the future if present trends unfold as expected. A *positive cause* suggests that conditions are better than desired; a *negative cause* indicates that conditions are worse than desired.

Distinguishing a Cause from a Symptom

A *symptom* is evidence of a performance gap. It is often identical to the consequences of a problem. Symptoms are usually evident to everyone and prompt interest in corrective action. Consultants call them *presenting problems*.

Examples of symptoms include unacceptable levels of absenteeism or scrap rates or lower than desired customer satisfaction ratings. Loss of market share is a symptom of a problem in organizational-environmental interactions. Management conflicts about overlapping responsibilities are symptoms of problems in the work environment. Bottlenecks in processing are symptoms of problems at the work level. Complaints about individuals who are performing poorly are symptoms of problems at the worker level.

Distinguishing Causes from Symptoms

Although novices find it difficult to distinguish causes from symptoms, more experienced HPE practitioners rely on one simple method. Whenever they are presented with evidence of a human performance problem, they list what they believe to be the causes of the problem. They then review the list, posing the following questions about each cause:

- Is that the *ultimate* reason (root cause) for the problem, or is that only the *consequence* of another problem?
- Would an effort to deal with the "cause" really improve the situation, or might it only change the situation without improving it?

Obviously, this approach is subjective. However, it can help assess root causes. Possible causes of human performance problems are summarized in the left-hand column of Exhibit 8-1. For each cause, HPE practitioners should describe its implications for performance in the remaining columns.

Exhibit 8-1. Possible Causes of Human Performance Problems

Directions: For each general cause of human performance problems listed in the left-hand column below, address what the cause can mean in each of the remaining columns. When you finish, review your list. Identify causes that lend themselves to training solutions.

GENERAL CAUSE	WHAT THE CAUSE MEANS...			
	In Organizational Environmental Interactions	In the Work Environment	In the Work	With Workers
People don't know why they should do it.				
People don't know how to do it.				
People don't know what they are supposed to do.				
People think your way will not work.				
People think their way is better.				
People think something else is more important.				
There is no positive consequence for people to do it.				
People think they are doing it.				
People are rewarded for not doing it.				

Exhibit 8-1 (concluded)

GENERAL CAUSE	WHAT THE CAUSE MEANS...			
	In Organizational Environmental Interactions	In the Work Environment	In the Work	With Workers
People are punished for doing what they are supposed to do.				
People anticipate a negative consequence for doing it.				
People experience no negative consequence resulting from poor performance.				
People face obstacles beyond their control.				
The personal limits of people prevent them from performing.				
Individuals are experiencing personal problems.				
No one could perform the work as it has been structured.				

Source: The characteristics listed in the left-hand column are adapted from Ferdinand F. Fournies, *Why Employees Don't Do What They're Supposed to Do and What to Do About It.* (Blue Ridge Summit, PA: Tab Books, 1988). Used by permission of F. F. Fournies & Associates, Inc., Tab Books, Inc., Blue Ridge Summit, PA. 17294–0214.

An Example of Distinguishing a Cause from a Symptom

Suppose you are an HPE practitioner who has been approached by an operating manager whose department is experiencing a 10 percent annual turnover rate. The level of turnover answers the question "What is happening?" According to the manager, company turnover averages 5 percent and other companies in the industry are averaging 4 percent annual turnover. That information answers the question "What should be happening?" To clarify the gap, consider that the difference amounts to 5 to 6 percent. The cost of training a new employee is $2,300 annually. Twenty people were hired into the department last year. The gap is thus important, since above-average turnover is apparently costing the company about $23,000 annually.

What is the cause of the turnover? List all the possible causes you can think of. Consult sources of information that may help isolate possible causes. Suppose, in this case, that company exit questionnaires reveal that terminating employees listed the following reasons for leaving: (1) the necessity of following a spouse to another geographical location for employment, and (2) salary and wage rates that are too low.

On their face, the reasons for leaving *appear* to be the causes of turnover. But are they? Or could it be that turnover is only a symptom of another, still hidden, problem?

The answer is that excessive turnover is thus only a *presenting problem.* It is a consequence or symptom of another problem. It compels management attention and action, but it is not the real problem. The real problem remains elusive, because the reasons listed on exit questionnaires may or may not be merely *socially acceptable causes.* Employees are inclined to provide socially acceptable responses because they may wish to return to the company for employment. They may not wish to reveal their real reasons for leaving. These real reasons may include the following:

- problems dealing with coworkers or supervisors
- fear of layoff
- excessive job stress and workload
- lack of promotional opportunities

To identify the real causes, you as an HPE practitioner should work with the department manager. Begin by listing all the causes you can think of that may account for dissatisfaction among employees. Then collect more evidence, perhaps by talking to employees or others (such as management employees or union representatives), to isolate the cause(s). The chances are good that turnover stems from several causes, not one.

Who Determines the Causes of Human Performance Gaps?

HPE practitioners should be able to troubleshoot the causes of human performance problems or anticipate human performance improvement opportunities. However, the stakeholders of the problems or opportunities must be involved in isolating the cause(s) if they are to accept the causes identified and the corrective actions subsequently taken.

When Should Causes Be Identified?

Causes should be identified when problems are recognized and when the organization's stakeholders, decision makers, and employees embark on improvement efforts. Identify causes when

- problems (or symptoms of problems) present themselves in any of the four performance quadrants;
- planning for future improvements in any of the four performance quadrants;
- conducting strategic planning for the organization;
- conducting planning for departments, divisions, units, or teams;
- benchmarking differences between organizational practices and "best-in-class" or common business practices.

What Is Known about the Causes of Human Performance Problems?

There are many possible causes of human performance problems. Consider: How many ways can human performance go wrong in organizational settings? That question can be considered from the perspective of how many different issues affect productivity in organizational settings. That number would be very large.

It is very much akin to the problem that medical doctors face. How many ways can the human body go wrong? That number is also staggeringly large. HPE practitioners should approach diagnosis of organizational problems in much the same way as medical doctors approach diagnosis of problems with the human body.

Consider some of the possible root causes of human performance problems described in the following paragraphs:

- *Lack of feedback on consequences* means that performers are not being given feedback on the results of their work activities. They are performing in a vacuum. They take action but hear little about how well the fruits of their labors are contributing to meeting customer needs, helping the organization achieve its goals, or helping the team meet production or service delivery standards.
- *No timely feedback* means that the time lag is excessive between worker performance and feedback received about that performance. People cannot improve quickly if they have to wait a long time to hear how well they are doing.
- *Lack of assigned responsibility* is clearly a failure of management. People do not know what they are responsible for doing or what results they should be achieving. Hence, they are not accountable for what they do. Since management's role is to assign responsibility, this cause can be traced to management deficiencies. Lack of assigned responsibility often follows in the wake of downsizing and work restructuring because management does not explicitly reallocate the work.
- *Lack of timely information* means that performers are not being briefed on a timely basis. They may, for instance, lack information about new organizational policies or plans at the time they need it to act. Similarly, they may not have been told about new work procedures, customer needs, supplier problems, or other key issues affecting their performance.
- *Lack of knowledge* is frequently traceable to an employee training need. If people cannot perform because they lack knowledge, they should be trained so that they will have the knowledge they need.
- *Lack of rewards for performing* suggests a mismatch between performer activities/results and rewards. Although the organization may espouse "pay for performance," for instance, it remains to be seen whether exceptional performance leads to exceptional pay increases. (Frequently it does not.)

- *Lack of information* is not identical to "lack of timely information." Instead, it means that performers receive no information and remain in the dark about changes affecting the organization.
- *No practice* means that performers are not given the opportunity to practice important but infrequently performed work tasks. Hence, they have difficulty remembering what to do when the time comes. Some infrequently performed work duties may be critically important to organizational success or to personal safety. The average worker, for instance, has little need to perform cardiopulmonary resuscitation on a daily basis. But if a worker has a heart attack, it is essential that someone remembers what to do, even though there may have been few opportunities to practice.
- *Fear for job security* indicates that performers are paralyzed with fear for their jobs. As a result, they are unwilling to take risks and may devote more time to finding other jobs or protecting their existing jobs than to improving performance, meeting or exceeding customer needs, or engineering leaps in productivity improvement. In the wake of forced layoffs, this issue can be a key cause of human performance problems.
- *Lack of motivation* means that performers know what to do and how to do it but are simply unwilling to do it. They just refuse to perform. Often, this suggests some personal or organizational problem. Some organizations address problems of insubordination, sabotage, or deliberate incompetence through employee discipline.
- *Lack of clear organizational policy* indicates a failure of management. Performers are not performing properly because no guidelines have been established to indicate what performance is acceptable. If managers do not know what they want, they may get anything.
- *Lack of organizational plans* means that decision makers have not clarified how the organization should compete in the industry or what goals it should achieve. Crisis management is the norm, and "shooting from the hip" is the usual management approach to problem solving.
- *Lack of tools* means that workers are asked to perform without being given the tools they need to do so. On occasion, tools may be lacking because the organization's decision makers are unwilling to make the necessary investment.
- *Rewards for not performing* means that workers are deriving some benefit or reward—financial or nonfinancial—from not performing as desired. Much like a prizefighter who throws a fight for a bribe, a worker who is rewarded for not performing is receiving some benefit from not meeting job performance standards. These benefits may come from coworkers (who urge the worker not to make them look bad by overachieving) or from management (which establishes a

work environment in which good performance leads only to more work and no other reward).

- *Lack of clear reporting relationships* suggests that employees do not know to whom they report. Authority relationships are unclear. Consequently, when important decisions must be made and employees feel uncomfortable about taking risks, they may choose to avoid making decisions. The reason: they have nobody authoritative to turn to for help.
- *Inadequate equipment* means that employees are furnished with outdated or obsolete equipment other than tools for doing their work. They may, for instance, be asked to perform their work on outdated personal computers or use a phone system that does not function properly. When poor performance stems from inadequate equipment, worker performance is impeded by management's unwillingness to provide adequate equipment.
- *Inadequate tools* make performance difficult. This means employees are not given the right tools to do the work. An auto mechanic asked to turn a screw with a hammer (because screwdrivers are not available) is being asked to perform with inadequate tools.
- *Lack of equipment* is similar to lack of tools. Workers do not possess the right equipment to do the work. In one state agency, three employees were expected to share a telephone, which each employee needed to perform daily work. In that case, poor performance was easily traced to lack of equipment—and to poor management.
- *Lack of ability* means that a mistake was made during employee selection. An individual was hired, transferred, or promoted into a job that he or she lacked the ability to perform—or to learn. In one organization, an employee was promoted to executive secretary. She was unable to type—and was also unable to learn how to type. That is lack of ability.
- *Poor ergonomic design* means that the relationship between the worker and the technology or equipment necessary to do the work is not optimal. If an employee is asked to sit eight hours a day on a hard chair, that may eventually create back problems and hinder performance. Poor ergonomic design of chairs, desks, computer equipment, and other machinery may cause human performance problems.

Identifying the Causes of Human Performance Gaps

How can HPE practitioners detect the causes of human performance gaps? What approaches may be used by HPE practitioners working as solitary analysts or with teams, committees, task forces, or other groups?

Three approaches are particularly promising for identifying causes of human performance gaps—root cause analysis, the Ishikawa fishbone diagram, and portfolio analysis. Other approaches may also be used; they are reviewed briefly.

Root Cause Analysis

Root cause analysis traces the causes and effects of accidents or other problems. It tends to be past oriented and focused only on pinpointing the causes of negative performance gaps.

The basic approach is simple enough. When a problem becomes apparent or an accident has happened, key stakeholders and participants are assembled in a room. They are asked to recount the chronology of events leading up to the problem. As they speak, someone writes the description of each contributing event on a sheet of paper. This confederate sticks the pages to the wall as the relationship of one event to the others becomes clear. This process continues until all possible contributing events have been identified. The result is a wall-sized flowchart that shows all events leading up to the problem. Participants are then questioned carefully to pinpoint the one event or sequence of events that is the apparent *root cause* of the problem or accident. Once the cause is known, corrective action can be taken.

The Ishikawa Fishbone Diagram

The *Ishikawa fishbone diagram technique,* sometimes called the cause-and-effect diagram method, has been widely used in process improvement. Like root cause analysis, it is usually past oriented and focused on closing negative performance gaps.

The approach is as simple as that for root cause analysis. When a problem becomes apparent, an HPE practitioner assembles a team of people who are familiar with it. Several hours are set aside for this meeting. Participants are given a diagram like the one in Exhibit 8-2. The basic idea is that all causes can be traced to people, policies/procedures, equipment, and climate. (It is also possible to add other dimensions or to modify the diagram to reflect other categories.) Considering the typical causes of human performance problems identified by the author's research, HPE practitioners may find it appropriate to create a troubleshooting cause-and-effect diagram like the one shown in Exhibit 8-3.

Exhibit 8-2. A Sample Cause-and-Effect Diagram

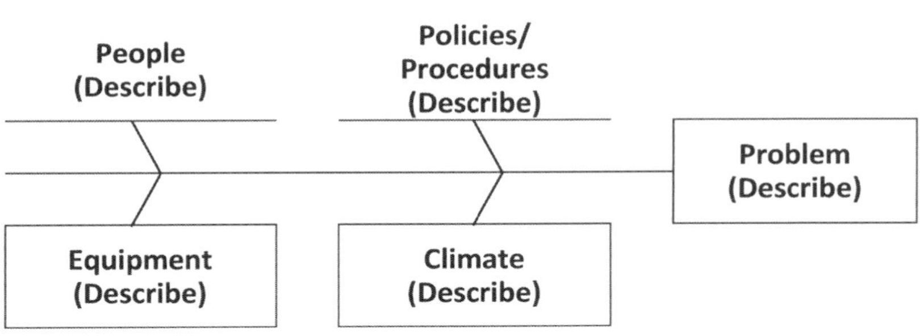

Exhibit 8-3. A Sample Cause-and-Effect Diagram Applied to Human Performance Problems

Directions: When a human performance problem is encountered, conduct troubleshooting. Give this diagram to a group (or team) of individuals who are familiar with the problem. Ask them to describe the problem first in the box at the far right. Then ask them to describe how each possible cause in the other boxes may be contributing to the problem. When the activity is finished, use the results as a starting point for determining appropriate HPE strategies to address the root cause(s) of the human performance problem.

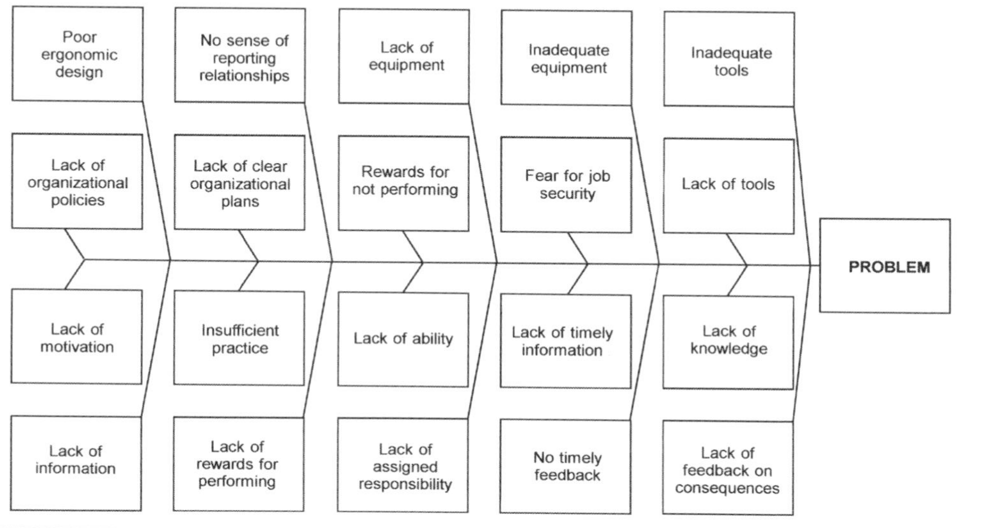

By presenting participants with hints about areas that may be contributing to the cause(s) of a problem, the cause-and-effect-diagram approach provides participants with a valuable troubleshooting tool for discovering the underlying cause(s) of human performance problems.

Portfolio Analysis

Portfolio analysis has been widely used by financial managers to examine the past performance of investments as a basis for making decisions.[4] It may therefore be considered a future-oriented approach. Unlike root cause analysis and cause-and-effect diagrams, portfolio analysis can focus on *positive* performance gaps.

To use this method, prepare a grid like the one shown in Exhibit 8-4. Then follow the instructions provided in the exhibit. The idea is to make decisions based on opportunities for human performance enhancement that will have the greatest likelihood of payoff. The portfolio analysis approach works best when key stakeholders are involved in deciding which HPE strategies are likely to have the greatest payoffs. However, a solitary HPE practitioner may also make these decisions, using the results of portfolio analysis to justify HPE strategies as they are implemented.

Exhibit 8-4. Applying Portfolio Analysis

Directions: Some causes of human performance problems are more important than others. Use this activity to rank the most important causes of human performance problems now and in the future. On the portfolio grid below, one side is labeled "Causes of Present Performance Problems," and the other side is labeled "Causes of Likely Future Performance Problems." On each side you will also find the labels "High Importance" and "Low Importance." Divide the workers on a team into small groups. Give them symbols to represent each cause of human performance problems identified in Exhibits 8-2 and 8-3. (Examples of symbols may include ★, ◆, ●, ■.) Then ask the members of each small group to position the causes of human performance problems on the grid. Advise them that they may use any, all, or none of the "causes." While the groups are at work, the facilitator should prepare a large grid on the flipchart. When the groups finish, their causes should be placed on the grid in front of the large group. Then a spokesperson for each group should be asked to explain why his or her group answered as it did—and what it believes can be done to address the underlying cause(s) of human performance problems now and in the future.

Causes of Present Performance Problems

Causes of Likely Future Performance Problems		HIGH	LOW
	HIGH		
	LOW		

Other Approaches

Root cause analysis, cause-and-effect diagrams, and portfolio analysis are not the only ways that HPE practitioners may troubleshoot the underlying causes of human performance problems or discover improvement opportunities. Many other approaches may also be used. Such common data-gathering methods as interviews, surveys, observation, document reviews, and focus groups may also be applied to detecting underlying cause(s). Other analytical approaches, commonly associated with Total Quality Management or process improvement practices, may also lend themselves to use in identifying the underlying cause(s). Exhibits 8-5 and 8-6 list and describe some of them.

Exhibit 8-5. Techniques for Detecting Underlying Causes of Performance Problems

Technique	Brief Description
"The Five Whys"	Ask someone, *"Why does that problem exist?"* When the response is given, ask *"Why is that?"* Continue this process until the question *"why"* has been posed a total of five times. The idea to get at the root of problems by continually probing to get beyond superficial responses or the mere consequences of a problem.
Magnification	Ask a team to investigate a problem. Start by asking the team members to exaggerate its importance. Then ask the team to exaggerate what is causing the problem. When the team members have had some fun with the problem, ask them to ponder their comments to troubleshoot the problem's cause.
Brainstorming	Ask a team to think of as many possible causes of a problem as possible. Conduct brainstorming face-to-face or by electronic mail. Caution members that they should not evaluate or criticize any ideas during the first round, no matter how unusual they may seem. When the group members run out of ideas, go back over all the ideas generated and present them to the group members. Ask them to review each idea and vote on the likelihood that it is a primary cause of a problem. When finished, tally the scores. Identify the top three to five possible causes of a problem. Then ask group members to generate ideas about possible HPE strategies to address those causes.

Exhibit 8-6. Four Classic Tools for Examining Problems

Tool	Description	Uses	How to Use the Tool	Tips
Flowchart	A picture of the sequence of steps in a process	Flowcharts are used to depict all steps involved in completing a task, examining the relationships between steps or decisions in a task, and identifying bottlenecks or important missing steps in a process.	Construct a flowchart by gathering a team that represents various groups involved in performing a process, deciding on a starting and ending point for the process, listing the key activities and decision points involved in a process. Listing the activities and decisions in the order they are performed, and drawing a diagram to represent the activities and decisions.	• When preparing a flowchart, use a box to represent an activity or process step, a diamond to depict a decision, and an arrow to indicate the flow of events. • Avoid excessive detail. • Look for loops in decision points, since they represent needless redundancy. • Be sure to involve those who do the work. • Use notes with glue on the back to construct a draft flowchart; then draw it.
Histogram (frequency distribution)	A chart that distributes the frequency of data	Uses a histogram to depict frequencies or variations.	Identify the highest and lowest points in a set of data, divide the range by an odd number (3, 5, 9, etc.) and separate the values equally. Count the values in each interval, and construct a bar chart that shows the data. Use the intervals along the x-axis (bottom) and data along the y-axis (side of chart).	• This approach works only with a variable that is measurable. • The value of the chart is to look for shape. • A shape other than a normal distribution (bell curve) suggests multiple causes of a problem. • This approach does not help identify the exact nature of a problem. • A disadvantage of this approach is that it depicts ranges of data but loses the sequence of occurrence.

Exhibit 8-6 (concluded)

Tool	Description	Uses	How to Use the Tool	Tips
Pareto Chart	A bar graph showing the importance of elements of a condition	Use a Pareto chart to focus improvement efforts, depict the progress of problem solving, and display the relative significance of different problem elements.	Select a condition to be studied; agree on a unit of measurement and a time period; collect information about the elements; construct a bar chart using elements on the x-axis (bottom of chart) and occurrences on the y-axis (left vertical line to side of chart); order the bars on the graph from high to low.	• Clear definitions will make it easier to construct a chart. • Focus attention on defects, if nothing else. • Cost or time may be substituted for occurrences on the bar's y-axis.
Run Chart	Displays data over time in which the data occur	Use a run chart to monitor a process of system for its relative stability and to identify trends or shifts in process characteristics.	Determine what characteristic will be measured; plot the time on the x-axis of a chart (bottom of chart) and the unit of measurement on the y-axis (left side of chart); collect data; connect the observations by a line.	• A run chart will not reveal the underlying cause(s) of variance. • A normal process should exhibit random variation. • Patterns may reveal that "something is happening" at a specific time or step in a process. • Identify the highest and lowest points from the center line to get a fix on the amount of variation.

How and Why Do Causes Change Over Time?

Nothing remains static; the world is a dynamic place. The underlying cause or causes of human performance problems may change over time.

Examining problems or opportunities can be compared to shooting at a moving target. Just as the HPE practitioner approaches the cause, the target moves. Major reasons for this *moving target effect* include changes in the four performance quadrants (the organizational environment, the work environment, the work, and the workers).[5] Most important of these is the organizational environment. Changes outside the organization exert pressure that, in turn, affect how the organization structures itself and carries out its work. At the same time, workers—and leaders—come and go.

Years ago, the organizational theorists Michael Cohen, James March, and Johan Olsen coined a classic term that is just as useful today as it was when he coined the phrase. They called organizations *garbage cans,* and they emphasized that the dynamic nature of change led to a *garbage can model of decision making.*[6] Their point was that decisions are complicated because people, solutions, and problems are fluid and changing during daily operations. People come and go; solutions and problems are randomly and chaotically matched up due to work pressures and other reasons. The result is a mess—a garbage can.

To thrive amid such chaos, HPE practitioners should become accustomed to *leading the target.*[7] They must anticipate the consequences of action or inaction. Although many factors play a part in what change occurs, some of which cannot be foreseen, it is important to make an effort to do just that. As present causes are identified, HPE practitioners should attempt to anticipate possible changes in the people, solutions, and causes that affect their efforts.

To that end, try out the activity in Exhibit 8-7. Use it to help you assess whether (or how much) future changes may affect identified causes. Then step back into the present and plan for those changes as much as possible. In other words, make an effort to lead the target.

Exhibit 8-7. Scenario Preparation: A Tool for Assessing Change in Cause(s) Over Time

Directions: Ask participants to plan for changes in people, methods, or problems/solutions as they affect their efforts to solve performance problems or seize performance enhancement opportunities. For a given problem or opportunity, form a team of five to eight people who are knowledgeable about it. Then ask them to meet or to ponder the following questions by electronic mail or by other means.

1. What is the problem you are trying to solve or the opportunity you are trying to take advantage of? (*Describe it.*)

2. Over what period do you plan to take action? (*Provide a specific time. Will it be one day? One month? One year?*)

3. What changes do you expect to be likely over the timeframe indicated in response to question #2? (*Describe as many changes relevant to the problem or opportunity as you can think of. Describe the future as you expect it to exist at the end of the timeframe indicated in response to question #2.*)

4. How do you believe your solution or strategy should be modified now to anticipate the likely changes that you expect to happen? List suggestions and justify them.

The Competencies of the Strategic Troubleshooter Role

To detect the underlying causes of human performance problems, HPE practitioners should be able to carry out the role of strategic troubleshooter. The competencies associated with that role are listed in Appendix I. They are also summarized briefly here.

- **Ability to isolate strategic mismatches in the organization's interactions with the external environment.** A frequent cause of organizational problems is a mismatch between customer, supplier, or distributor needs and organizational responses. Strategic planning focuses on averting such problems or seizing future opportunities. HPE practitioners must be sufficiently aware of organizational strategy to isolate these mismatches when they occur and to mobilize appropriate responses to them.
- **Ability to benchmark other organizations in the industry or "best-in-class" organizations.** A frequent cause of performance problems is the organization's inability to compete effectively with other organizations in the same industry. When that is suspected as a possible cause of performance problems, HPE practitioners should conduct benchmarking to identify "best practices" or even "typical practices" and compare those to the organization's current practice. Such an effort can provide the basis for improvement.
- **Ability to isolate large-scale and small-scale causes of gaps within the organization.** Setting priorities is an essential competency. Not all human performance gaps are of equal magnitude, nor are their consequences identical over time. HPE practitioners should be able to isolate large-scale and small-scale causes of performance gaps whenever possible.
- **Ability to troubleshoot the causes of gaps in the work or workflow.** What causes contribute to slower-than-desired workflow? What approaches can be used to streamline workflow? The ability to spearhead organizational efforts to answer these questions is essential to success in HPE. HPE practitioners should be able to identify the causes of gaps in work or workflow, using such methods as root cause analysis, cause-and-effect analysis, and portfolio analysis.
- **Ability to troubleshoot the causes of performance gaps between worker and other performance environments.** To what causes are mismatches between workers and the work environment attributable? Are the best people in the best positions now? Will the same people be the most appropriate for those positions in the future? The ability to lead others in answering these questions is essential to success in HPE.

What Are the Roles of the HPE Consultant and Their Clients in Identifying the Underlying Causes of Performance Gaps?

As in carrying out other steps in the HPE model, the roles of the HPE consultant and their clients depend on how HPE consultants approach their roles. If HPE consultants enact the role of management consultants, they will tend to shoulder responsibility for troubleshooting root causes. They will then justify their findings by pointing to evidence that they gather. Clients will enact the roles of judges, determining whether the evidence is sufficient—and persuasive.

Alternatively, if HPE consultants enact the role of process consultants, they will tend to work with representatives of the client group to troubleshoot root causes. They may do that by forming project teams to gather evidence, benchmark other organizations, or apply a range of problem-solving tools to a problem. They will not attempt to justify their findings but will, instead, focus on working with members of the client organization to find evidence that will be persuasive to those in the organization. Clients working with HPE consultants who adopt this approach will be their own information gatherers, and they will act with confidence on the evidence that they themselves gather.

Part Four: Selecting and Implementing HPE Strategies: Intervening for Change

CHAPTER 1: Why Training Is Not Enough

CHAPTER 2: What Is Human Performance Enhancement (HPE)?

CHAPTER 3: Transforming a Training Department into a Human Performance Enhancement (HPE) Department

CHAPTER 4: Analyzing *What Is* Happening

CHAPTER 5: Envisioning *What Should Be* Happening

CHAPTER 6: Clarifying Present and Future Performance Gaps

CHAPTER 7: Determining the Importance of Performance Gaps

CHAPTER 8: Identifying the Underlying Causes of Performance Gaps

CHAPTER 9: Selecting Human Performance Enhancement (HPE) Strategies

CHAPTER 10: Implementing Human Performance Enhancement (HPE) Strategies to Address Organizational Environment Problems or Opportunities

CHAPTER 11: Implementing Human Performance Enhancement (HPE) Strategies to Address Work Problems or Opportunities

CHAPTER 12: Implementing Human Performance Enhancement (HPE) Strategies to Address Work Environment Problems or Opportunities

CHAPTER 13: Implementing Human Performance Enhancement (HPE) Strategies to Address Worker Problems or Opportunities

CHAPTER 14: Evaluating Human Performance Enhancement (HPE) Strategies

Chapter 9
Selecting Human Performance Enhancement (HPE) Strategies

What is an HPE strategy? What is the range of possible HPE strategies? What assumptions guide their use? How often are they used, and how often should they be used? How should HPE strategies be selected? What competencies are necessary to function in such roles as HPE methods specialist, forecaster of consequences, and action plan facilitator? This chapter answers these questions. In doing so, it paints HPE on a large canvas and provides the foundation for the remaining chapters in Part Four.

What Is a Human Performance Enhancement Strategy?

An *HPE strategy,* synonymous with a *human performance improvement strategy,* is any effort intended to close a human performance gap by addressing its underlying cause. It is a *strategy* because it implies a long-term direction for change, just as a strategic plan does. Indeed, the term *strategy* is used precisely because it is not a quick fix.

Types of Strategies and Types of Gaps

HPE strategies vary by the types of gaps they are designed to close. Present negative performance gaps have received the most attention in writings on human performance improvement,[1] partly because people are greatly motivated to solve problems that are pressing and urgent, as gaps of this kind often are. Closing a negative performance gap amounts to identifying the cause of a present problem and solving it.

HPE strategies may also be applied to present positive, future negative, and future positive performance gaps. (Neutral performance gaps usually warrant no action.) Closing a present positive gap means taking advantage of an existing strength by intensifying it. Closing a future negative performance gap means averting a problem expected in the future. Closing a future positive performance gap means capitalizing on trends that will allow the organization to strengthen its competitive position.

Regardless of the kind of gap, appropriate HPE strategies may include the redesign of jobs, organizational structure, training, rewards or incentives, job or performance aids, employee selection methods, and employee feedback. The key point is that the appropriate use of HPE strategies differs, depending on the kind of gap.

Types of Strategies and Causes of Gaps

The appropriate HPE strategies depend on the causes. That point cannot be overemphasized. If strategies treat only the symptoms of performance problems, they will not be effective. It is critically important to identify, as closely as possible, the underlying causes of the performance gaps.

Types of Strategies and Moving Targets

Just as human performance problems do not remain static, so must HPE strategies avoid being static. HPE practitioners and the stakeholders they involve in selecting and implementing HPE strategies should consider the conditions that are likely to change as the HPE strategy is implemented. The aim is to lead the target, anticipating (rather than merely reacting to) changing conditions that affect HPE strategies and the performance gaps they are designed to close.

What Assumptions Guide the Selection of HPE Strategies?

Several key assumptions guide the selection of HPE strategies:

1. **Employee training should be viewed as an HPE strategy of last resort.**[2] One reason is that training is expensive. A second reason is that as little as 20 percent of off-the-job training transfers back to work settings. A third reason is that the critical mass of people needed to introduce large-scale change can rarely be mustered when using training as a solitary HPE strategy. A fourth reason is that most human performance problems stem from the work environment, not from individual performers. Since training is an individually oriented change strategy, it is rarely appropriate for addressing problems that are organizational in their scope. (It can serve that purpose if combined with other efforts.)
2. **HPE practitioners should usually begin their HPE strategies in the outer circle of the four performance quadrants and move inward.** As systems theory suggests, most performance problems are attributable to flawed interactions between the organization and its external environment. Most HPE strategies should therefore focus on the needs of customers, suppliers, distributors, stock owners, and other key external stakeholders. This assumption is bolstered by recent research suggesting that seasoned HPE practitioners examine the work environment for causes of performance problems *before* they examine workers.[3]

What Is the Range of Possible HPE Strategies?

Much has been written about possible HPE strategies.[4] For purposes of simplicity, we will examine them as shown in Exhibit 9-1. By using this organizing scheme, HPE practitioners should be able to structure their thinking about strategies for influencing the four performance quadrants affecting organizational performance. Descriptions of these strategies are provided in Exhibit 9-2.

Exhibit 9-1. A Scheme for Organizing Human Performance Enhancement Strategies

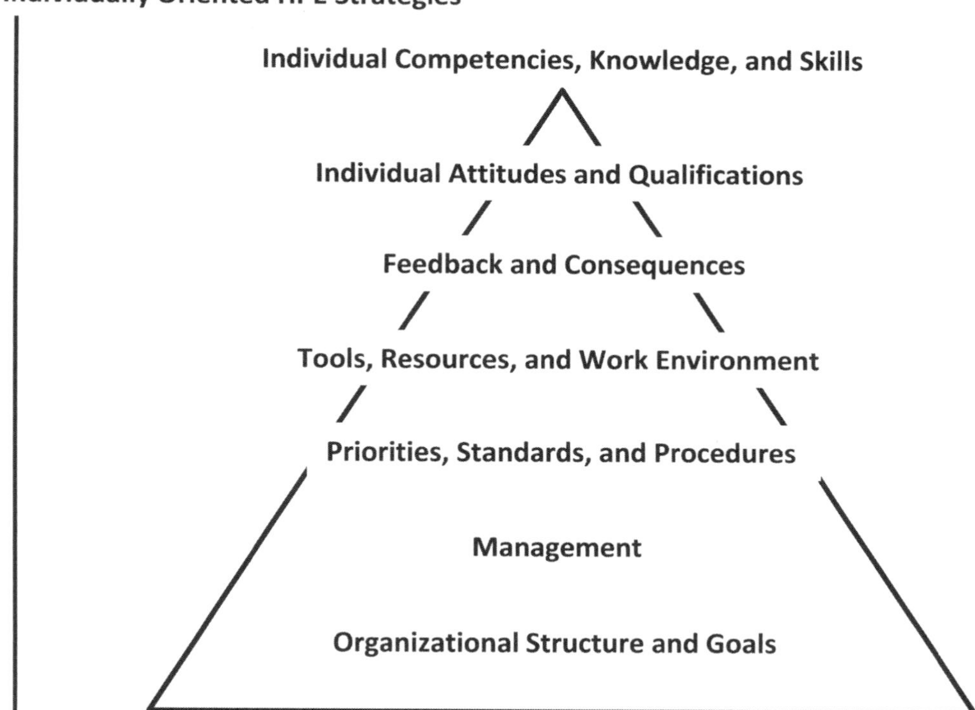

Source: P. Harmon, "A Hierarchy of Performance Variables," *Performance and Instruction, 23,* no. 10 (1984): 27–28. Used by permission of *Performance and Instruction.*

Exhibit 9-2. Possible Human Performance Enhancement Strategies

Strategy	Key Issues to Examine	Brief Descriptions of Specific HPE Strategies
Organizational Structure and Goals	• How well has organizational strategy been translated into effective structuring of work efforts (reporting relationships) within the organization? • How well has organizational strategy been translated into clear and effectively communicated goals within the organization?	• Improve strategic planning efforts. • Review interactions with external stakeholders for improvement opportunities. • Reorganize reporting relationships to improve accountability. • Improve goal setting and goal-related communication.
Management	• How effectively has management established a climate (high-performance workplace) in which individuals are capable of performing competently? • How well do the values of the existing management match up to the competencies required by the organization to achieve its strategic goals and function effectively with external stakeholders?	• Change the management when mismatches exist between required and existing competencies. • Change the management when existing strategy, having been tried for a reasonable time, is not working. • Improve management competencies/skills through targeted management development and organization development efforts.
Priorities, Standards, and Procedures	• How clearly has management established and communicated organizational priorities? • How clearly has management established a means to formulate and communicate work standards or work expectations by division, department, work group/team, and job? • How clearly has management established a means to clarify and communicate work procedures? • How well has management involved employees in setting priorities, establishing work standards or expectations, and clarifying procedures?	• Establish methods of formulating and communicating priorities, work standards/expectations, and procedures while involving employees in those methods.

Exhibit 9-2 (continued)

Strategy	Key Issues to Examine	Brief Descriptions of Specific HPE Strategies
Tools, Resources, and Work Environment	• How well are performers equipped with appropriate tools to do the work? • How well is the equipment/machinery supporting the work and the workers? • How well does available time link to important work? • How well are materials matched to work requirements? • How well do tools and equipment lend themselves to effective, ergonomic use by performers?	• Analyze and improve the tools employees have been given to do the work. • Analyze and improve the equipment employees have been given to do the work. • Analyze the time necessary to do the work and, when necessary, reallocate priorities to match realistic time expectations to achieve quality and customer standards. • Analyze how well tools and equipment match up to ergonomic needs of users and, when necessary, redesign tools and equipment to allow for human factors.
Feedback and Consequences	• How often and how well do individuals receive developmental feedback? • How often and how well do individuals receive feedback designed to recognize competent and/or exemplary performance? • How often and how well do individuals receive corrective feedback? • How often and how well are performance expectations made clear? • How often and how well are performance criteria established and communicated? • How often are procedures clarified and communicated? • How supportive is the work group or team culture to performance enhancement?	• Establish improved methods of obtaining feedback from external stakeholders, internal customers, and other groups. • Establish improved methods of developmental feedback and recognition feedback. • Improve methods of communicating performance criteria. • Examine and, when necessary, begin efforts to improve the supportiveness of work climate through organization development interventions. • Examine and, when necessary, begin efforts to improve the match between feedback, rewards, and performance.

Exhibit 9-2 (concluded)

Strategy	Key Issues to Examine	Brief Descriptions of Specific HPE Strategies
Feedback and Consequences (concluded)	• How much are performers rewarded for poor performance? • How much are performers rewarded for good performance? • How much are performers punished for poor performance? • How much are performers punished for good performance?	
Individual Attitudes and Qualifications	• What physical capacity is required for workers to perform? • What emotional capacity is required for workers to perform? • What intellectual capacity is required for workers to perform? • What technical ability is required for workers to perform?	• Establish work qualifications based on detailed work analysis. • Examine policies on selection, transfer, promotion, and use of temporary workers.
Individual Competencies, Knowledge, and Skills	• What competencies lead to exceptional performance? • What knowledge and skills are required for performance? • What experience is required for competent performance?	• Assess individual competencies. • Clarify the work outputs associated with exceptional performance. • Identify the political knowledge

How Often Are HPE Strategies Used?

Very little information is available about how often various HPE strategies are used. It is likely that most root causes are not subjected to any form of systematic match, since managers—even those trained professionally with MBA degrees—are not trained on how to diagnose problems with human performance and how to identify the best, most efficacious or cost-effective strategies to address them.

Some such strategies are described briefly in this chapter and treated in greater detail in the remaining chapters in Part Four.[5]

Providing information to perform means giving performers the information they need to function competently. If performers lack such information, they are unable to function effectively. Significant performance gains can be achieved by improving the flow of information about the work. Methods to do that may include staff meetings, electronic mail messages, procedure manuals, memos, and one-on-one discussions.

Training is a work-related HPE strategy designed to build the competencies that workers need to perform. Generally, training is appropriate only when performers lack the knowledge, skill, or attitude that they need.

Providing clear feedback means establishing a work environment in which performers are given clear, unambiguous feedback about how well they are doing. Feedback may flow from customers, suppliers, distributors, coworkers, or other stakeholders. Methods for providing clear feedback include periodic employee performance appraisals and customer, supplier, and distributor satisfaction surveys. Simply asking if feedback has been understood can also be helpful in improving its *clarity.*

Improving timely feedback to performers means providing individuals with information about how well they are performing on a timely basis. The sooner that people know how well (or how poorly) they are doing, the faster they can improve. Timely feedback refers to HPE strategies designed to close the feedback loop faster and to give individuals as well as teams and organizations prompt feedback. Methods to improve the timeliness of feedback include providing daily or weekly performance reviews and daily or weekly follow-ups with customers, suppliers, distributors, coworkers, and other stakeholders.

Supplying job or performance aids means giving performers real-time aids so that they can improve as they perform. Such aids may range from sophisticated expert systems and electronic performance support systems to checklists, procedure manuals, reference cards, and other "instant help" aids.

Clarifying work responsibility means giving individuals, teams, and work groups clear accountability for who does what. Often work is restructured but responsibilities in the new work environment are left vague. As a result, nobody is sure who is supposed to do what for whom and when, and performance suffers. To address this management problem, decision makers should clearly establish responsibilities. They may engage workers in this process through responsibility charting and procedure writing.

Providing opportunity to practice is appropriate when performers need to know what to do but perform a work task irregularly so that they may have forgotten what to do when the need arises. Appropriate HPE strategies of this kind involve establishing opportunities for structured practice. Such opportunities may be arranged on or off the job. For example, managers may set up a word processing station near the work site so that employees who have forgotten how to type efficiently or effectively can sharpen their skills and build up their speed or accuracy. When planned, such practice opportunities are called *structured practice opportunities.*

Providing adequate tools means giving workers the tools they need to perform. Nobody would expect automobile mechanics to overhaul engines without the appropriate tools. If workers function with outdated or improper tools, they cannot achieve the desired results. An HPE strategy focused on this issue must address the appropriate tools required for performance and the relative availability of those tools to performers when needed.

Providing tools means giving workers the appropriate tools they need to perform. Some organizations make it a policy to require workers to supply their own tools. Some automobile repair shops, for example, expect mechanics to bring their own tools. However, organizations have an important stake in the tools used by the workers. Therefore, some employers make it policy to supply the tools that workers need to perform. Such an HPE strategy focuses on ensuring that performers are given tools to do the work.

Clarifying organizational plans is, of course, a management responsibility. But if managers have not clarified—and communicated—how the organization is expected to compete now and in the future, performers will have difficulty knowing what to do. There is an old saying that "if you don't know where you are going, it is tough to say where you will end up." The same principle holds true with planning. An HPE strategy focused on clarifying organizational plans may include establishing, communicating, and following a unified strategic vision.

Clarifying policy means providing clear direction and coordination across the organization on important issues involving its interactions with customers, suppliers, distributors, and other organizational groups. What is the organization's policy, for example, on accounts receivable? on accounts payable? on handling sexual harassment issues? on hiring? on orienting workers? on training? on disciplining? on rewarding? Without clear policy, achieving improvements is problematic. *Policy analysis* is the process of determining what policies exist, what their impact is and will be, and what guidelines for performance should be established.

Using progressive discipline (sometimes called by the more euphemistic phrase *corrective action*) means holding workers accountable for what they have been assigned to do. Progressive discipline is appropriate only when people know what to do but deliberately refuse to do it. Progressive discipline usually begins with one-on-one discussions between employees and their immediate supervisors. In team settings, discipline may be conducted by coworkers or an entire team. In union settings, the union itself may discipline members. The aim is to bring individual behavior into compliance with accepted group norms and organizational policy.

Providing equipment other than tools means giving workers access to additional technological support beyond what they need to use to perform their immediate work tasks. Common equipment items include telephones, fax machines, personal computers, and calculators. In some occupations, these items may qualify as tools; in others, they are used irregularly but may still be essential to successful performance. An HPE strategy geared to this level will examine whether workers have access to up-to-date equipment that is necessary for performance.

Providing equipment overlaps with *providing equipment other than tools.* It means giving workers the equipment they need to perform.

Addressing job insecurity has to do with what total quality management guru W. Edwards Deming calls "driving fear from the workplace."[6] Workers are unlikely to perform well if they remain in constant fear for their jobs. Numerous human performance problems can stem from job insecurity. Among them increasing violence in the workplace; increasing employee sabotage; growing turnover; the concealment of vital information to give individuals the illusion of job security; and an increasingly selfish perspective among workers. To address this problem, an organization's management must diminish fears by setting a positive tone and showing that risk taking is rewarded rather than punished.

Clarifying reporting relationships means clarifying who reports to whom. That is a management responsibility. It is particularly important following the introduction of teams or in the wake of forced layoffs and reengineering efforts.

Changing reward systems and *changing reward systems to address problems with performance* mean improving the match between individual or team results and rewards. Organizational approaches to changing reward systems may involve the introduction of bonus plans, piece rates, broad banding, pay-for-knowledge, and other innovative compensation and recognition efforts.

Providing ergonomically supportive equipment means assessing the relationship between work demands and the human factors required to work effectively. HPE strategies of this kind include making reasonable accommodations for the disabled and improving the relationship between humans and technological applications.

Transferring workers ill-suited to their jobs means moving employees who lack ability to perform the work to other areas for which they are better suited. This HPE strategy amounts to a form of reselection. It typically results from selection error.

Terminating wrong hires also results from a selection error in which an individual who lacks essential qualifications or abilities is selected and/or trained to perform and then is found to be unable to do so. While terminating workers is often a strategy of last resort, it is sometimes necessary. Many corporate downsizings have included terminations of many people who were ill equipped by knowledge, skill, ability, or attitude to perform as necessary.

Changing reward systems to address providing rewards for nonperformance means altering reward systems so that performers are not rewarded for avoiding desired performance. It is the least frequently encountered HPE strategy, according to those who responded to my survey.

How Should HPE Strategies Be Selected?

The key to selecting an appropriate HPE strategy—or combination of strategies—is identifying the causes of the performance gaps. Is the performance gap a present negative, a present positive, a present neutral, a future negative, a future positive, or a future neutral? How do we know what causes the gaps, and how widely is that view shared? Only after answering these questions can an appropriate HPE strategy (or combination of strategies) be selected for present or future action.

Selecting HPE strategies can be done in many ways. It is more art than science, so there is no precise way to do it. In many respects it is akin to formulating and implementing an organizational strategic plan. HPE too is a form of strategizing. Whatever HPE strategy that is chosen should also be consistent with organizational initiatives as specified in an organization's strategic plans.

Selecting an HPE Strategy Using a Matrix

One approach to selecting an HPE strategy is to construct a matrix (see Exhibit 9-3). Write possible causes of performance gaps in the left column. Then write possible HPE strategies across the top row. Examine each cause carefully. If it is a source of a performance gap, mark it with a number to indicate how important it is perceived to be to improve organizational and/or individual performance, with 1 meaning "most important." Then examine the possible HPE strategies listed in the top row. For each strategy that may contribute to addressing the cause of the performance gap, write in another number, with 1 again indicating "most important." The same approach could be used to rank the possible causes of one performance problem or to choose HPE strategies appropriate to unique conditions in different divisions, groups, work teams, or with individuals.

Exhibit 9-3. A Human Performance Enhancement Strategy Selection Matrix

Directions: Read the possible causes of performance gaps in the left-hand column. Then write possible HPE strategies across the top row. Examine each cause carefully. If it is a source of a performance gap, mark it with a number to indicate how important it is perceived to be to improve organizational and/or individual performance. Use 1 to equal most important. Then examine the possible strategies listed in the top row. For each strategy that may contribute to addressing the cause of the performance gap, mark it with another number. The strategy believed to be most effective in addressing the cause should be prioritized as 1 to indicate greatest importance.

Continued →

Exhibit 9-3 (continued)

Possible Causes of Performance Gaps	Provide Information	Train Employees	Provide Feedback	Improve Timeliness of Feedback	Provide Job Performance Aids	Clarify Work Responsibilities	Provide Adequate Tools
Lack of feedback on work consequences							
Lack of timely feedback							
Lack of assigned work responsibility							
Lack of timely information							
Lack of knowledge							
Lack of rewards for performing							
Lack of information							
Lack of opportunity to practice infrequently performed work activities							
Fear for job security							
Lack of motivation							
Lack of clear organizational policy							
Lack of clear organizational plans							
Lack of tools							
Rewards for not performing							
Rewards for nonperformance							
Lack of clear reporting relationships							
Inadequate equipment							
Inadequate tools							
Lack of equipment							
Lack of ability							
Poor ergonomic design							
Other (list below):							

Possible HPE Strategies

Exhibit 9-3 (continued)

Possible Causes of Performance Gaps (continued)	Possible HPE Strategies (continued): Provide Tools	Clarify Organizational Plans	Clarify Organizational Policy	Use Employee Discipline	Provide Equipment Other than Tools	Address Feelings of Job Insecurity	Clarify Reporting Relationships
Lack of feedback on work consequences							
Lack of timely feedback							
Lack of assigned work responsibility							
Lack of timely information							
Lack of knowledge							
Lack of rewards for performing							
Lack of information							
Lack of opportunity to practice infrequently performed work activities							
Fear for job security							
Lack of motivation							
Lack of clear organizational policy							
Lack of clear organizational plans							
Lack of tools							
Rewards for not performing							
Rewards for nonperformance							
Lack of clear reporting relationships							
Inadequate equipment							
Inadequate tools							
Lack of equipment							
Lack of ability							
Poor ergonomic design							
Other (list below):							

Exhibit 9-3 (concluded)

Possible HPE Strategies (concluded)

Possible Causes of Performance Gaps (concluded)	Change/Improve Reward System	Provide Ergonomically Supportive Equipment	Transfer Workers Who Are Ill Suited to Their Jobs	Terminate Wrong Hires	Change Reward System to Address Problems of Providing Rewards for Non-Performance	Other (please list):
Lack of feedback on work consequences						
Lack of timely feedback						
Lack of assigned work responsibility						
Lack of timely information						
Lack of knowledge						
Lack of rewards for performing						
Lack of information						
Lack of opportunity to practice infrequently performed work activities						
Fear for job security						
Lack of motivation						
Lack of clear organizational policy						
Lack of clear organizational plans						
Lack of tools						
Rewards for not performing						
Rewards for nonperformance						
Lack of clear reporting relationships						
Inadequate equipment						
Inadequate tools						
Lack of equipment						
Lack of ability						
Poor ergonomic design						
Other (list below):						

Another approach to selecting an HPE strategy is to use a worksheet (see Appendix III for such a worksheet).

Who Should Select an HPE Strategy?

Selecting an HPE strategy may be carried out by a solitary HPE practitioner, by top managers, by a committee or task force, by those affected by the gap, or by stakeholders. Decision makers should be chosen on the basis of corporate culture, constraints on action (time, money, and available people), and degree of desired ownership by affected groups. The worksheet appearing in Exhibit 9-4 on the following page can help decide who should select HPE strategy.

The Competencies of the HPE Methods Specialist Role, the Forecaster of Consequences Role, and the Action Plan Facilitator Role

Applying the new model for HPE calls for trainers-turned-HPE practitioners to act as HPE methods specialists, forecasters, and action plan facilitators. The competencies related to these roles are summarized in Appendix I and are also described here.

The HPE methods specialist role is linked to selecting the HPE strategy (or strategies) that narrow or close performance gaps by addressing their underlying cause(s).

- **Ability to identify possible HPE strategies.** What HPE strategies can best address the underlying cause(s) of performance problems? That is the essential question tied to this competency. HPE practitioners can apply many diagnostic, troubleshooting models and select one or more approaches to narrow or close the performance gaps. This is often a creative process that also relies heavily on an ability to deal effectively with political and interpersonal realities in an organizational setting.
- **Ability to benchmark/compare the application of HPE enhancement strategies in other organizations.** How do other organizations make use of HPE strategies? Which organizations represent best practices in a given HPE strategy? How did those organizations select the strategies? HPE practitioners can apply benchmarking to answer these important questions. They should also be able to translate effective practices in other organizations to the unique corporate culture of their own organizations.
- **Ability to excite enthusiasm among others about planning and implementing HPE strategies on an organizational scale.** It is one thing to select an HPE strategy; it is quite another to excite enthusiasm about planning and implementing the HPE strategy in an organization. HPE practitioners should be capable of persuasively communicating about HPE strategies.

Exhibit 9-4. A Worksheet for Determining Who Should Be Involved in Selecting HPE Strategy

Directions: Selecting HPE strategy may be carried out by a solitary HPE specialist, by top managers, by a committee or task force, by those affected by the gap, or by stakeholders. Select decision makers according to corporate culture, constraints on action (time, money, and available people), and degree of desired ownership by affected groups. Answer these questions to decide who should select HPE strategy.

1. Who is the most affected by the existing human performance problem or opportunity?

2. Who stands to gain or lose the most by implementing the HPE strategy?

3. Who controls or affects the HPE strategy or strategies chosen? (*For instance, addressing reward systems may necessitate involving compensation specialists from inside or outside the organization.*)

4. How does corporate culture provide guidance about desirable people to include in selecting HPE strategy?

5. What constraints exist in selecting HPE strategy? (*Describe what constraints may or may not affect the choice of an HPE strategy.*)

- **Ability to involve and empower others in the process of selecting HPE strategies on an organizational scale.** HPE practitioners should be able to empower and involve stakeholders and prospective participants in selecting a chosen HPE strategy. That may mean that HPE practitioners can apply the action research model, which undergirds organization development.[7] *Action research* uses a cyclical process to involve stakeholders in identifying the problems or opportunities facing an organization and in planning to take action. In this role, HPE practitioners facilitate the stakeholders' efforts to pinpoint problems and surface solutions.
- **Ability to excite enthusiasm among others about planning and implementing human performance enhancement strategies specific to work methods or processes.** Just as HPE practitioners should exert positive influence over others and create infectious enthusiasm for HPE strategies on an organizational scale, so too should they possess the ability to excite enthusiasm for improvement efforts among the members of work units or teams. Essential to this competency is *credibility,* the sense among followers that a leader has their best interests at heart. From credibility stems the ability to influence others.[8]
- **Ability to involve and empower others in the process of selecting HPE strategies linked to the work.** HPE practitioners should empower others while selecting HPE strategies at the work process level. That often means that they should collaborate with workers to select what the workers believe to be the most effective methods of narrowing or closing performance gaps.
- **Ability to identify and apply HPE strategies at the individual worker level.** HPE practitioners can identify and apply HPE strategies to individuals, deciding when training—or another individually oriented change effort—is most appropriate to close a performance gap and when alternatives to training should be used. This competency may also require HPE practitioners to counsel one or more individuals about their performance.
- **Ability to involve and empower the worker in the process of selecting human performance enhancement strategies linked to the individual.** Individuals want to know how they will be affected or will benefit from any change, and they usually want to have a say in decisions affecting them. HPE practitioners should be skilled in involving individuals in selecting HPE strategies affecting them.

The forecaster of consequences role assesses the likely outcomes of HPE strategy once it is implemented. The aim is to minimize negative side effects and maximize positive results. HPE practitioners in this role try to think ahead to assess what consequences will stem from the HPE strategy before it is implemented. Once the consequences have been assessed, HPE practitioners can then step back into the present and try to prevent the negative side effects of their efforts.

In the action plan facilitator role, the HPE practitioner establishes a flexible action plan to guide implementation of HPE strategy once it has been selected. To fill this role successfully, HPE practitioners should do more than conduct solitary planning: they should involve and empower others so that they create their own action plans. A possible starting point for action planning is the development of a written proposal delivered to stakeholders that

- describes the background of the plan;
- establishes measurable objectives for a project designed to solve a problem or seize an opportunity;
- describes exactly how the objectives will be achieved, usually step by step;
- provides a schedule tied to the steps;
- projects measurable gains and the bottom-line value of results to be achieved.

The proposal can then be summarized orally to key decision makers as a starting point leading to action (see Appendix IV for a worksheet that can help guide proposal preparation).

What Are the Roles of the HPE Consultant and Their Clients in Selecting and Implementing HPE Strategies?

The roles of the HPE consultant and their clients in selecting and implementing HPE strategies depend on how HPE consultants enact their roles. If they act like management consultants, they will select an appropriate HPE strategy and then attempt to persuade the client that it is a correct—and cost-effective—strategy based on the evidence gathered.

Chapter 10
Implementing Human Performance Enhancement (HPE) Strategies to Address Organizational Environment Problems or Opportunities

The *organizational environment* is the world outside the organization. It includes customers or clients, competitors in the same or related industries, stockholders, suppliers, distributors, regulators, and other key stakeholders. Organizations survive and prosper only when a net gain results from their interactions with the external environment. Businesses and industrial companies traditionally measure their success with the external environment in terms of profits, return on investment, return on equity, and other financial measures. Government agencies rely on indications of constituent, executive, judicial, and legislative satisfaction (in government, the relative willingness of the legislative body to grant the agency's appropriation request is often an important signal of how well the agency is perceived to be doing its job). Nonprofit organizations look to numbers of clients served, favorable returns on investments, and client satisfaction to judge their success.

Few traditional training departments have had significant interaction with groups outside their organizations. That may be one reason that so many training and development professionals lack power, since power seems to stem from the proximity of an organizational function to key external stakeholders. It may also explain why, at least in U.S. corporations, so much power resides with marketing, finance, and the executive team, which enjoy the greatest external visibility. Lower levels of visibility have traditionally been associated with such internally focused functions as human resources, training, production/operations, accounting, and management information systems.

To have the greatest impact on organizational performance and, therefore, on group or individual performance, training departments that are shifting their emphasis to human performance enhancement should move from an internal to an external focus, beginning with efforts to improve interaction between the organization and its external environment. Such a shift implies that trainers-turned-HPE practitioners can gain appropriate top management support (of course, without top management support, any improvement effort is usually doomed).

Who are the most important external stakeholders? How well is the organization interacting with its most important external stakeholders(s)? What HPE strategies can improve an organization's interactions with its external stakeholders? How should such

HPE strategies be implemented? What HPE competencies are necessary to select, plan, and implement organizational environment HPE strategies? This chapter addresses these questions.

Who Are the Most Important External Stakeholders?

The key to selecting the most powerful externally oriented HPE strategies is identifying and gaining a consensus about the most important external stakeholders.

Identifying Key External Stakeholders

Organizations interact with many external stakeholders (see Exhibit 10-1).

Exhibit 10-1. Possible Key External Stakeholder Groups

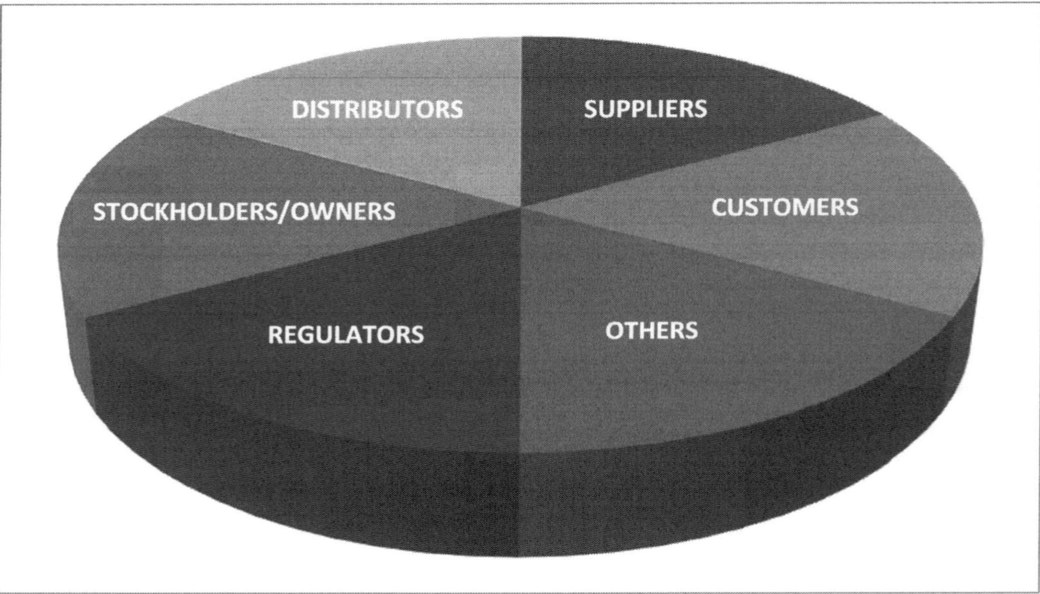

Identify the groups above for your organization:

- Who are the distributors?
- Who are the suppliers?
- Who are the customers?
- Who are the stockholders/owners?
- Who are the regulators?
- Who are the other key external stakeholders?

Without agreement on who those key external stakeholders are and what they need, establishing effective HPE strategies can be difficult, if not impossible. It is therefore essential that HPE practitioners identify the key external stakeholder groups and gain consensus on them.

To identify key external stakeholders, ask organizational members these questions:

- "If you had to choose the most important groups outside this organization that influence its success or failure, who would those groups be?"
- "Why did you choose the groups you listed?"

If necessary, distribute a questionnaire like the one shown in Exhibit 10-2 for this purpose.

Exhibit 10-2. A Worksheet for Identifying Key External Stakeholders

Directions: Answer the two questions appearing below. When you finish, return this worksheet to the individual whose name appears at the bottom. Responses from the worksheets will be compiled and fed back to all participants. Your responses to these questions will be anonymous, so feel free to be frank.

1. If you had to choose the most important groups outside this organization that influence its success or failure, who would those groups be?

   Answer:

2. Why did you choose the groups you listed in response to question 1? (*Explain briefly.*)

   Answer:

Thank you for your cooperation! Please return this worksheet to [name] *at* [address] *by* [due date].

Gaining Consensus on the Key External Stakeholders

To gain consensus on the identities of the most important external stakeholders, summarize the questionnaire results, feed them back to participants, and ask the participants to agree on the most important groups. This process can be conducted by itself or combined with efforts sponsored by a process improvement team.

Sometimes decision makers are unable to reach agreement on *one* key stakeholder group and insist that two or even three groups are the most important external stakeholders. In most cases, key decision makers select one or more customer groups as the most important external stakeholders. That is appropriate, since everything begins with the customer. It is no exaggeration to say that effective human performance, like quality, resides in the eyes of the customer.

How Well Is the Organization Interacting with the Most Important External Stakeholders?

The starting point for any HPE strategy should be the collection of information about how well the organization is interacting with the most important external stakeholders. To that end, consider:

- How is the organization presently collecting information about interactions with key external stakeholder groups?
- How could information collection efforts be improved?
- How could the results of information collection efforts be used to justify HPE strategies? How could they best be summarized and fed back to employees and managers to prompt self-initiated HPE strategies?

Ask participants to brainstorm on these issues, using the worksheet in Exhibit 10-3.

Exhibit 10-3. A Worksheet for Brainstorming about Interactions with Key External Stakeholder(s)

Directions: Use this worksheet to structure your thinking about ways to improve interactions with key external stakeholders. Using the worksheet by yourself or working with others in a meeting, training session, or other venue, answer the questions below.

1. How is the organization presently collecting information about interactions with the key external stakeholder groups?

   Answer:

2. How could information collection efforts be improved?

   Answer:

3. How could the results of these information collection efforts be used to justify HPE strategies? How could they best be summarized and fed back to employees and managers to prompt self-initiated HPE strategies?

   Answer:

What HPE Strategies Can Improve the Organization's Interactions with External Stakeholders?

Any HPE strategy described in Chapter 9 can be applied, individually or collectively, to improve the organization's interactions with external stakeholders in general, as well as with specific individual key external stakeholders. The aim of any of these strategies should be to close present negative, present positive, future negative, or future positive performance gaps. Customer service interventions and strategic planning interventions are perhaps the most obvious HPE strategies to improve organizational-environmental interactions and so warrant examination.

Customer Service Interventions

Customers are usually identified as the key external stakeholder group. Customer service should be regarded as highest priority. Paying attention to customers requires constant effort and is the source of all meaningful human performance enhancement. It gives the organization an appropriately external orientation to improvement efforts.

It is important to track what is happening with customer satisfaction. To begin, consider the following issues:

- Who are the customers?
- How were the customers selected by the organization, and why were they selected?
- What do the customers want?
- How are customer preferences and needs changing over time?
- How do customers feel about the organization's products? services?
- What issues are important to customers, and how well satisfied are they with the organization's handling of those issues?
- How do customers perceive the representatives of the organization with whom they come in contact? How competent do customers perceive them to be? How do they compare to competitors' representatives?
- How is the organization collecting, tracking, and measuring information about customer satisfaction?
- How does the organization handle such issues as customer complaints, customer compliments, and gains or losses of customers? Why are such strategies chosen, and how well are they implemented and evaluated?

The organization's decision makers should then compare what is happening with customers and what should be happening. They should consider these questions:

- Who should be the customers?

- How should customers be selected, and why should they be selected that way?
- What should the customers want, in the opinion of the organization's decision makers, and why should they want what they do?
- How should the organization handle changing customer preferences and needs?
- How should customers feel about the organization's products and services?
- How well should the organization be satisfying customer needs? tracking customer satisfaction? measuring customer satisfaction?
- How should customers perceive the organization's representatives? How competent should they be perceived as being? How should the organization's representatives compare to competitors' representatives?
- How should the organization handle such issues as customer complaints, customer compliments, and gains or losses of customers? Why should such strategies be chosen, and how well should they be implemented and evaluated?

Once these questions have been answered, it is necessary to clarify performance gaps with customers by determining what gaps exist between what is happening and what should be happening with customers or any other key external stakeholder group identified for the organization. Exactly what is the gap? What is its current status, and how is it changing over time?

Once the performance gap has been clarified, HPE practitioners should lead their organizations to determine the importance of present and future performance gaps. They need to determine how important the gaps are in addressing the needs and expectations of customers or another key external stakeholder group and what their implications are for achieving the organization's strategic goals and for divisions, departments, work groups or teams, and individuals.

Once the relative importance of the performance gap has been determined, HPE practitioners should help their organizations pinpoint the causes of the gaps. What are the chief symptoms, underlying causes, and consequences of performance gaps? What has happened that has prompted a problem to occur? What is expected to happen that will prompt an opportunity to arise? As part of this process, HPE practitioners should consider whether problems arise from lack of agreement or lack of clarity about these factors:

- who the customers are or should be
- how customers are or should be selected
- what customers want or should want
- how customer preferences and needs are changing over time
- how customers feel about the organization's products or services and the reasons they feel as they do

- how customers do (or should) perceive the representatives of the organization with whom they come in contact
- how the organization handles or should handle such issues as customer complaints, customer compliments, and gains or losses of customers
- how the organization is and should be collecting, tracking, and measuring information about customer satisfaction

Finally, HPE practitioners should lead their organizations to establish HPE strategies to narrow or close the performance gaps: What HPE strategies can address the causes of human performance gaps stemming from customer service? What problems and opportunities exist? What should be done about them?

Use the worksheet in Exhibit 10-4 to answer these and other questions about improving customer service, recalling that any efforts to improve interactions with the organization's key external group is an excellent starting point for driving HPE strategies into the organization, creating widespread impetus for improvement throughout.

Exhibit 10-4. A Worksheet for Assessing Customer Service as a Starting Point for Human Performance Enhancement Strategy

Directions: Use this worksheet to organize your thinking about how customer service can become the starting point to drive HPE strategy. For each question appearing in the left column, write a response in the space at the right. If necessary, circulate this worksheet among decision makers and employees in the organization as a starting point for using customer service to drive HPE strategy.

QUESTION	ANSWER
1. What is happening with the organization's dealing with customers? How do we know?	
2. What should be happening with the organization's dealing with customers? Why do we think so?	
3. What is the nature of the performance gap (or gaps) between *what is* and *what should be* happening with customers? Exactly what are the gaps now? How may they change in the future?	

Exhibit 10-4 (concluded)

QUESTION	ANSWER
4. How important is the performance gap, or how important are the performance gaps?	
5. What HPE strategies undertaken by the organization could help close the performance gaps? (*Consider strategies geared to improve employee feedback, training, organizational policy, structure, plans, work design, work process, rewards, job or performance aids, and any combination of them.*)	
6. How should HPE strategies intended to improve customer service be formulated? implemented? evaluated?	

Strategic Planning Interventions

How well have the organization's decision makers established and communicated a clear, realistic, and achievable competitive plan? HRD professionals responding to a 2004 survey identified lack of clear organizational plans as one cause of human performance problems. An effective strategic plan can be a powerful tool for addressing (and even anticipating) external environmental trends affecting the organization, integrating and coordinating internal organizational efforts, and providing direction to work activities and employees.

HPE practitioners can compare the organization's strategic planning efforts against best practices obtainable through benchmarking, using a model of strategic planning like that shown in Exhibit 10-5 as a point of departure and asking how well the organization's decision makers and employees have done the following:

- Established a clear mission statement of why it exists and what it should be doing?
- Formulated clear goals and measurable objectives that are logically derived from the organization's mission?

- Identified and addressed future threats and opportunities resulting from external environmental change?
- Identified and addressed the organization's present strengths and weaknesses? (Strengths may represent the organization's *core competencies.*[1])
- Considered possible grand strategies to guide the organization? (Examples of grand strategies include growth, retrenchment, integration, diversification, turnabout, or a combination of any or all of these in different parts of the organization simultaneously.)
- Selected a realistic, optimal grand strategy, given the constraints within which the organization must operate?
- Implemented the grand strategy over time by ensuring that
  - the organization's reporting relationships (structure) match the strategy?
  - appropriate leaders have been identified and empowered based on the competencies required to make the strategy successful?
  - appropriate rewards have been tied to desired results?
  - policies have been formulated (or revised) so that internal coordination exists among divisions, departments, work groups, or teams and individuals?
  - the strategy is effectively communicated to employees and other relevant groups?
- Established a means by which to evaluate the strategy before, during, and after implementation?

Exhibit 10-5. A Model of the Strategic Planning Process

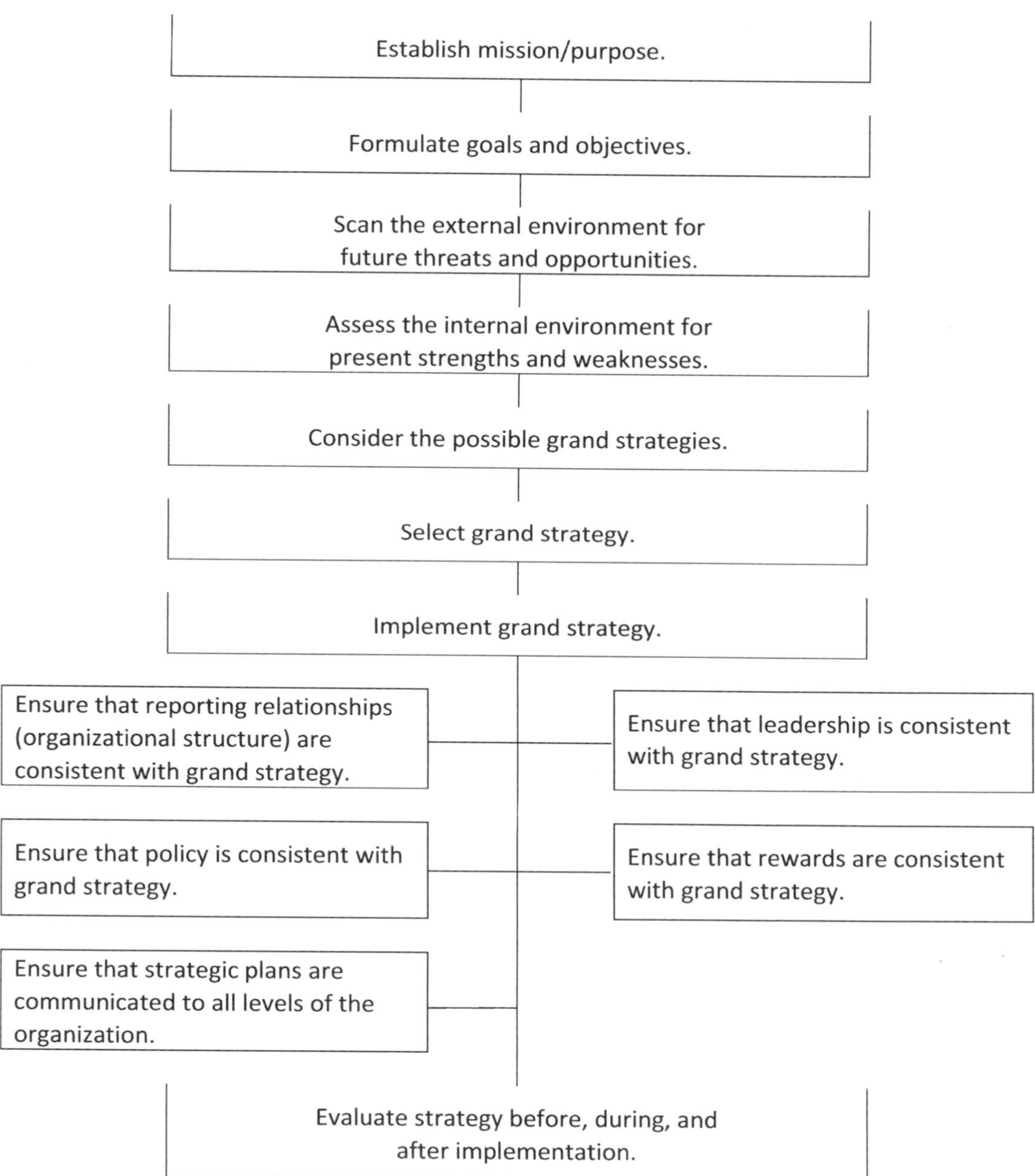

Use the worksheet in Exhibit 10-6 to assess the relative success of strategic planning practices in the organization. If it is not as successful as it should be, then formulate a new approach using the worksheet in Exhibit 10-7 through discussions with key decision makers inside the organization and key external stakeholders (as appropriate). Use the strategic planning process itself as a means to identify and justify HPE strategies that are directly tied to the organization's competitive initiatives or strategic objectives and that can build on the organization's core competencies or cultivate new ones.

Exhibit 10-6. A Worksheet for Assessing the Organization's Strategic Planning Process

Directions: Use this worksheet to assess the strengths and weaknesses of the organization's strategic planning process. For each step in strategic planning listed in the left column, rate the effectiveness of the step as it currently exists. Use the following scale:

6 = very effective
5 = effective
4 = somewhat effective
3 = somewhat ineffective
2 = ineffective
1 = very ineffective

Step in the Strategic Planning Process	Very Ineffective		Somewhat Ineffective		Very Effective	
How well have the organization's decision makers and employees:						
1. Established a clear mission statement of why the organization exists and what it should be doing?	1	2	3	4	5	6
2. Formulated clear, specific goals and measurable objectives that are logically derived from the organization's mission?	1	2	3	4	5	6
3. Identified and addressed future threats and opportunities resulting from external environmental change?	1	2	3	4	5	6
4. Identified and addressed the organization's present strengths and weaknesses?	1	2	3	4	5	6
5. Considered possible grand strategies to guide the organization?	1	2	3	4	5	6
6. Selected a realistic, optimal grand strategy, given the constraints within which the organization must operate?	1	2	3	4	5	6

Exhibit 10-6 (concluded)

Step in the Strategic Planning Process	Very Ineffective		Somewhat Ineffective		Very Effective	
7. Implemented the grand strategy over time by ensuring that						
a. the organization's reporting relationships (structure) match the strategy?	1	2	3	4	5	6
b. appropriate leaders have been identified and empowered based on the competencies necessary to make the strategy successful?	1	2	3	4	5	6
c. appropriate rewards have been tied to desired results?	1	2	3	4	5	6
d. appropriate policies have been formulated (or revised) so that internal coordination exists across divisions, departments, work groups or teams, and individuals?	1	2	3	4	5	6
e. the strategy is effectively communicated to employees and other relevant groups?	1	2	3	4	5	6
8. Established a means by which to evaluate the strategy before, during, and after implementation?	1	2	3	4	5	6

Exhibit 10-7. A Worksheet for Planning Improvements to Organizational Strategic Planning Practices

Directions: Use this worksheet to help plan improvements to organizational strategic planning practices. There is space below each question to provide your answer. There are no right or wrong answers. If you wish, circulate this worksheet among decision makers and employees to gain the benefit of their perspectives on these issues.

1. What areas of the strategic planning process deserve improvement?

   Answer:

2. How should those areas of strategic planning be improved?

   Answer:

3. How can strategic planning become the basis for planning human performance enhancement strategies? What strategies would be particularly useful in encouraging the formulation and implementation of strategic planning itself?

   Answer:

4. How should those HPE strategies be implemented?

   Answer:

How Should HPE Strategies Be Implemented?

As the competency model of HPE indicates, HPE practitioners should anticipate the consequences of their HPE strategies, establish action plans, and implement those plans. Essentially, implementing HPE strategy requires the same steps as implementing organizational strategy.[2] For each HPE strategy, HPE practitioners should work with key decision makers and employees to do the following:[3]

1. Clarify the purpose or mission of the HPE strategy.
2. Establish HPE goals and measurable objectives.
3. Assess future threats and opportunities outside the organization that may affect the relative success of the HPE strategy in the organization.
4. Assess present strengths and weaknesses of the organization in relation to the HPE strategy.
5. Select an HPE strategy or strategies to achieve desired enhancements to human performance.
6. Assess the likely outcomes or side effects of the HPE strategy or strategies and plan to avoid negative side effects.
7. Establish an implementation action plan.

Kathleen Whiteside has also indicated key factors in implementing interventions.[4] These factors include the following:

- plan the intervention
- ensure communication
- analyze the target population
- plan for the politics
- assess for events or issues that may interfere with the intervention rollout
- make sure to sequence the rollout steps appropriately

The Competencies of the HPE Implementor

When enacting the role of *human performance enhancement implementors,* HPE practitioners are required to demonstrate specific competencies (see Appendix I). These competencies include the following:

- **Ability to implement or coordinate implementation of HPE strategies, integrating them with organizational strategic plans.** Organization strategic plans articulate how the organization will interact with its external environment. HPE practitioners should be able to effectively link HPE strategy to organizational strategy.

- **Ability to implement, or coordinate implementation of, HPE strategies, integrating them with organizational culture, structure, and politics.** Implementation of HPE strategy cannot be carried out effectively unless it is consistent with the organization's culture, structure (reporting relationships), and politics. HPE practitioners should be able to link HPE strategy to these key issues inside the organization.
- **Ability to implement, or coordinate implementation of, HPE strategies, integrating them with work processes and work methods.** Work is the point at which individual and organization meet. To be effective, HPE strategy must be implemented in ways that are sensitive to the existing—and desired—work processes and methods of the organization.
- **Ability to implement, or coordinate implementation of, HPE strategies, giving each worker a say in decisions affecting him or her.** HPE practitioners must implement HPE strategies in ways that empower individual workers and allow them to participate in implementing strategies designed to improve the match between individual competencies and work requirements.

Chapter 11
Implementing Human Performance Enhancement (HPE) Strategies to Address Work Problems or Opportunities

This chapter focuses on HPE strategies designed to narrow or close human performance gaps in the work environment. These broad-based strategies may affect an entire organization, division, department, work unit, or work group. They include formulating, clarifying, or communicating organizational policies, procedures, and organizational design. While apparently unrelated, these HPE strategies lend themselves to large-scale, and often long-term, improvement.

Formulating, Clarifying, and Communicating Organizational Policies and Procedures

Formulating, clarifying, and communicating organizational policies and procedures is an apt starting point for enhancing human performance within organizations because policy establishes guidelines, blueprints, expectations, and desired results. Policy also flows from a strategic plan.

What Are Policies and Procedures?

A *policy* coordinates the activities of different organizational functions or work methods to achieve common and desired ends. Policy answers the two questions: "What should be done?" and "Why should it be done?"

A *procedure* is naturally related to a policy and flows from it. A procedure answers the question "How should the policy be implemented?" Most procedures provide step-by-step guidance on exactly how to enact policy.

Both policy and procedure represent statements of what should be happening. They are points of departure against which to assess variation, performance problems, and measurement. Differences between policy or procedure and actual practice often represent performance problems, just as differences between future plans and present practices often represent performance enhancement opportunities.

Policies provide guidance across several organizational functions, although they may also provide coordination within one division, department, work unit or team, or among several jobs. Examples of policy with organizational scope include executive compensation policies, employee selection or promotion policies, and collective bargaining agreements. Examples of policies with more restricted scope include policies on handling returned goods, customer complaints, supplier shipments, product warranties, and computer access. Virtually any area of organizational activity can be guided by a policy and related procedures.

What Are the Differences between Formal and Informal Policies and Procedures?

Interest in documenting policy and procedure has been stimulated by ISO (short for International Standards Organization) 9000 requirements, which affect businesses involved in international trade. ISO requires businesses to document their procedures.

Formal policies and procedures are documented in writing and stem from deliberate management or employee decisions. The need for a policy is identified because of a new law, past problems in handling the work within a unit or team, or past problems stemming from poor coordination across the organization. Such problems lead to efforts to clarify exactly what results are desired and how they should be achieved.

In contrast, *informal policies and procedures* are not documented in writing and represent precedent or group norms. If a customer is given a refund on a returned product with no questions asked and if no written policy governs that action, it is an informal policy. That action may establish a precedent; future customers may expect similar treatment, or employees may rely on that precedent as guidance for solving similar problems in the future.

Group norms, much like policy stemming from precedent, are usually established from the bottom up. Employees may decide among themselves, for instance, that production levels should be very high early in the week and then should fall off later in the week. That will become an informal policy if practice follows that expectation and is guided by it. Much evidence suggests that group norms exert considerable impact on employee (and organizational) performance.

The Importance of Policy

Most organizations establish policies in order to

- clarify exactly what results or goals are sought by an organization;
- provide operational guidance for handling common problems (variations) encountered during the work;
- ensure that organizational activities across all functions of an organization are consistent with strategic plans.

When Should Organizational Policy Be Used as an HPE Strategy?

HPE practitioners should direct attention to formulating, clarifying, or communicating organizational policy in the following circumstances:

- Strategic plans change.

- Employee performance problems are directly traceable to nonexistent, vague, ambiguous, or outdated policy.
- Employees or managers complain about the lack of policy or point to lack of coordination across the organization as a possible cause of a human performance gap.
- Different functions in an organization are not effectively coordinating their efforts, prompting such symptoms as cross-departmental finger pointing, blaming, and turf battles.

Organizational policy should be one guiding force for enhancing human performance because it puts the organization on the record as preferring certain approaches over others and making clear exactly how important issues should be addressed.

Formulating, Clarifying, and Communicating Policies and Procedures

There is no one right way to formulate or clarify policies and procedures. Often the best clue is the corporate culture and a look at how decisions are usually made. Are they made at the top and imposed down? Are they made at the bottom and communicated up? Are they made in the middle and moved up and down from there? Is the corporate culture top-down (authoritarian and mechanistic) or bottom-up (empowering and organic)? Are only some issues addressed at higher, middle, or bottom levels and other issues left to be addressed elsewhere?

Once it is clear that a new policy or procedure is needed or that an old policy or procedure needs to be updated, there are several ways to go about the process. One approach is to assign one individual, such as an HPE practitioner, to draft a policy and related procedures and circulate them among other staff for modifications and approvals. Another approach is to select a task force, committee, or cross-functional team to draft the policy and procedure and then circulate it for modifications and approvals.

Some organizations have their own policy and procedure format and expect any draft policy and procedure statement to be consistent with that format. Other organizations do not rely on a consistent format. As a rule, however, a policy should state its purpose and a guiding philosophy, clarifying the results desired and why they are desired. The procedure should describe exactly how the policy should be implemented. Some procedures are written chronologically (to indicate who should do what in what order); some are written in playscript technique to clarify, much as in a theatrical production, who should be doing what and when; some are written in other ways. The sample policy and procedure on succession planning in Exhibit 11-1 can be used as a model for developing other policies and procedures.

Exhibit 11-1. A Sample Succession Planning Policy

Purpose

To ensure replacements for key job incumbents in executive, management, technical, and professional positions in the organization. This policy covers middle management positions and above in [*name of organization*].

Desired Results

The desired results of the succession planning program include the following:

- Identify high-potential employees capable of rapid advancement to positions of higher responsibility than those they presently occupy.
- Ensure the systematic and long-term development of individuals to replace key job incumbents as need arises due to deaths, disabilities, retirements, and other unexpected losses.
- Provide a continuous flow of talented people to meet the organization's management needs.
- Meet the organization's need to exercise social responsibility by providing for the advancement of protected labor groups inside the organization.

Procedures

The succession planning program will be carried out as follows:

1. In January of each year, the MD director will arrange a meeting with the CEO to review results from the previous year's succession planning efforts and to plan for the present year's process.
2. In February, top managers will attend a meeting coordinated by the MD director in which:
    a. the CEO will emphasize the importance of succession planning and review the previous year's results;
    b. the MD director will distribute forms and establish due dates for their completion and return;
    c. the MD director will review the results of a computerized analysis to pinpoint areas of the organization in which predictable turnover, resulting from retirements or other changes, will lead to special needs for management talent;
    d. the results of a computerized analysis will be reviewed to demonstrate how successful the organization has been in attracting protected labor groups into high-level positions and to plot strategies for improving affirmative action practices.

Exhibit 11-1 (concluded)

3. In April, the forms will be completed and returned to the MD director. If necessary, a follow-up meeting will be held.
4. Throughout the year, the MD director will periodically visit top managers to review progress in developing identified successors throughout their areas of responsibility.
5. As need arises, the database will be accessed as a source of possible successors in the organization.

Policy and procedure clarification begins when a problem with a policy or procedure is detected, when a new strategic plan is introduced, when employees say that they do not understand an existing policy or procedure, or when employees signal that they were never informed of a policy or procedure. Clarification may be approached as a communication issue or as a training issue. Policies and procedures should be treated in training and communicated through other means as well.

Communicating policies and procedures is critically important. Many methods may be used, including the following:

- policy and/or procedure manuals
- written or electronic memorandum reminders
- staff meetings
- training or orientation sessions

The organization may have up-to-date policies and procedures that are not being communicated. Upon the acceptance of a policy or procedure, the HPE practitioner or a task force should consider how to communicate the policy or procedure, and a communication plan should be established to ensure that employees are informed of policies or procedures.

Problems with Using Organizational Policies and Procedures as an HPE Strategy

In many organizations, written policies and procedures are viewed with scorn and are regarded as trappings of bureaucracy. Nobody pays much attention to them. Indeed, some entrepreneurs boast that their organizations have no written policies or procedures and that employees are told to "apply the golden rule" when they encounter problems. In other settings, employees who encounter problems rarely drop what they are doing to read a policy or procedure manual; they usually turn to a coworker and ask what to do. Most policies and procedures are informal, despite the obvious problems that can lead to.

To address these issues, policies and procedures should usually be kept to a minimum and be directed to only the most important matters. They should also be frequently reviewed, updated, and communicated.

Enhancing Organizational Design

Organizational design is critically important to establishing a high-performance work environment. The reason: People have to know who is responsible for doing what—and why—to function effectively. Organizational design establishes the authority and responsibility relationships that are so critical to successful performance. To achieve high performance, managers or employees must do more than "try their best." They must have a sense of responsibility for what they do. The organization's design establishes responsibility—and accountability.

What Is Organizational Design?

Organizational design means arranging divisions or functions, work groups, teams, and jobs in power and authority relationships that are consistent with—or at least do not interfere with—strategic goals and desired results. *Organizational structure* refers to the reporting relationships of the organization, the arrangement of who reports to whom. *Organizational redesign* is the process of changing relationships between organizational units or jobs to achieve more harmonious balances among them. Organizational redesign is common in the wake of radical changes such as downsizings or mergers. Redesigns without careful forethought are often unsuccessful.

Why Is Organizational Design Important?

Few contemporary observers dispute that organizational design is one of the most important decisions that can be made in an organization. Deciding who reports to whom and what functions or operations fit together can be critical in meeting customer needs, ensuring effective work flow, developing potential talent, and preserving organizational resources.

Research on organizational design has revealed that there is no one best way to organize and that different approaches to organizing are not equally effective.[1] Classic (and still relevant) studies of organizational design were conducted by Tom Burns and G. M. Stalker,[2] Joan Woodward,[3] Alfred Chandler,[4] Richard Hall,[5] and Paul R. Lawrence and Jay W. Lorsch.[6] Burns and Stalker examined 20 British and Scottish organizations and concluded that any organizational design can be effective, depending on the external environment in which the organization operates. Mechanistic organizations are effective in stable external environments; organic organizations are effective in dynamic environments. Woodward, having studied 100 British organizations, concluded that structure and effectiveness are related only when production technology is controlled. Chandler, credited as the founder of strategic planning, looked at 70 U.S. industrial giants and argued that the choice of structure should follow (rather than precede) choice of strategy. Chandler found that successful organizations operating in a single industry tended to retain a top-down structure, while successful organizations operating in several industries at once tended to decentralize geographically.

Hall found that functions within organizations vary in the same way as organizations themselves; successful functions that deal with a dynamic environment tend to structure themselves organically, while functions that deal with a stable environment structure themselves in a top-down, mechanistic way. His findings are important for making organizational design decisions within divisions, departments, work groups, or teams.

Lawrence and Lorsch examined structure in light of uncertainty and concluded that different organizational designs should be used within functions or even within jobs, depending on the uncertainty of task outcomes. The uncertainty of a task (defined as "the difference between the amount of information required to perform the task and the amount of information already possessed by the organization") is a key issue in making decisions about how to organize the work.[7]

When Should Organizational Design Be a Focus of Attention for HPE Strategy?

Attention needs to be directed to organizational design whenever an organization, division, department, work unit, or team undergoes major change from inside or outside. If the external environment becomes more unstable because it is becoming more competitive or if the internal environment becomes more unstable due to changing work methods or relationships with other departments or work operations, reassessing organizational design is warranted.

Organizational design problems are possible sources of human performance problems under the following conditions:

- "Turf battles" across work units or teams, departments, or divisions are apparent.
- Managers or employees complain that their organizational units are not the only ones involved in a work process, method, activity, or responsibility.
- Overlapping or duplicative duties, titles, or responsibilities are evident on organization charts.
- Customer complaints are traceable to unclear or duplicative efforts by different units or teams, departments, or divisions.

What Choices Exist in Organizational Design?

The basic tenets of organizational design have remained largely unchanged since the days of Frederick W. Taylor early in the 20th century. However, increasing attention is being devoted to fluid designs, partly because of the widespread view that the external environments of organizations are becoming more dynamic as a result of fierce global competition.

There are several possible choices for organizational design. They include the following:

- entrepreneurial design
- functional design
- divisional design
- project design
- matrix design
- team design
- virtual design

In the *entrepreneurial design* (see Exhibit 11-2), one manager or business owner functions as the leader, and employees are added to deal with increasing workload and task differences. Entrepreneurial designs are curious in that many business owners operate in an authoritarian manner. However, work is not specialized, and many employees share the same or different tasks; everyone pitches in to do everything. The entrepreneurial design is appropriate in small organizations with 50 or fewer employees.

Exhibit 11-2. The Entrepreneurial Design

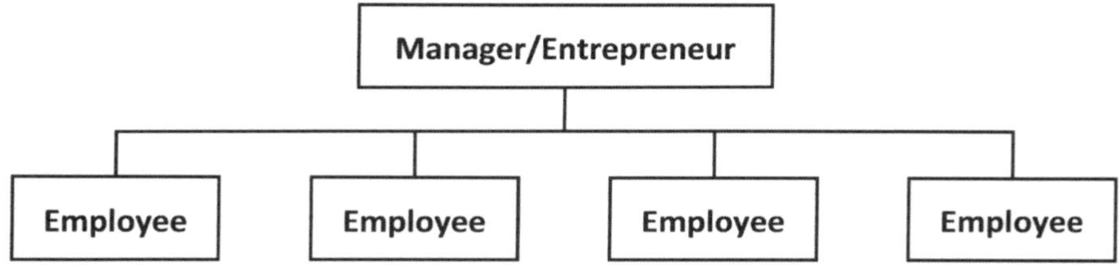

In the *functional design* (see Exhibit 11-3), the workload is divided among different functions or areas of responsibility. One top manager oversees the organization. Managers are also appointed to oversee such discrete functions as production/operations, finance, sales and marketing, and personnel. (Other functions are possible.) The functional design is appropriate in stable environments or as a transitional phase for entrepreneurial companies positioning themselves for explosive growth.

Exhibit 11-3. The Functional Design

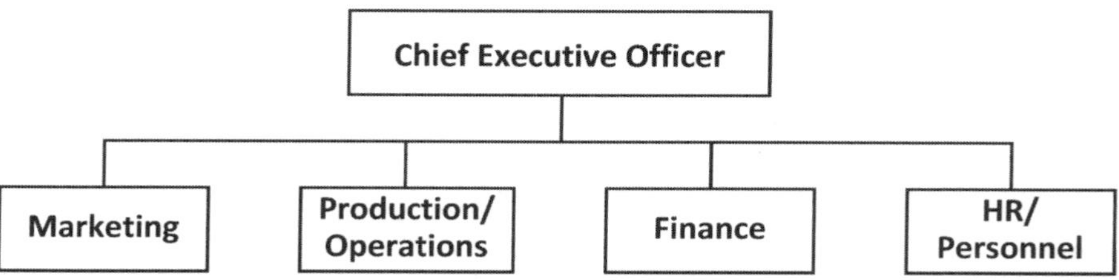

In the *divisional design* (see Exhibit 11-4), functions are usually maintained, but another layer of management or task specialization is added to oversee activities in special markets, geographical areas, or product/service lines. For instance, a global organization that manufactures perfume may add a layer of management or task specialization to handle sales on different continents.

Exhibit 11-4. The Divisional Design

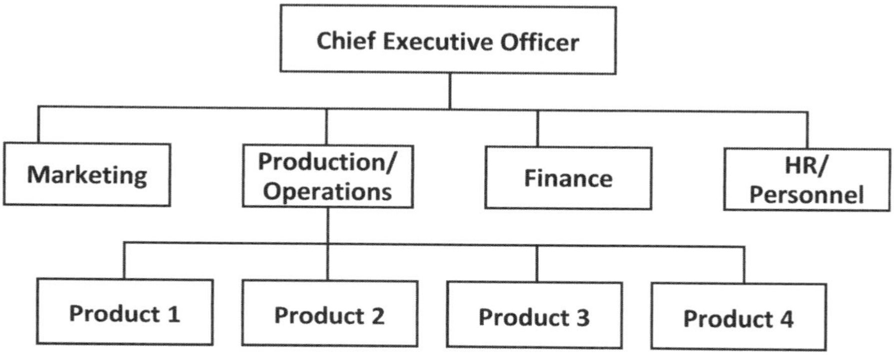

Chief Executive Officer
Marketing
Production/ Operations
Finance
HR/ Personnel
Product 1
Product 2
Product 3
Product 4

The *project structure* (see Exhibit 11-5) adds a layer of management or task specialization below divisions and functions. *Projects* are temporary activities that require special handling, such as new-product launches, new industrial plant designs, or new service lines. A project manager oversees the temporary activity within the framework of existing divisions and functions. However, the project manager is usually subordinated to divisional or functional managers.

Exhibit 11-5. The Project Structure Design

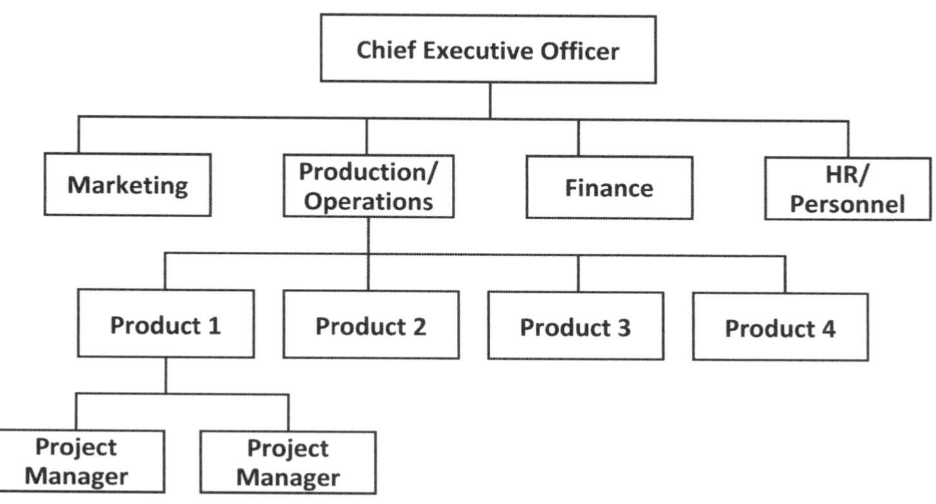

The *matrix management design* (see Exhibit 11-6) adds complexity to design. All features of a project structure are maintained, with only one important exception: the project manager is elevated to a status equal to a division manager. That means that workers may have two immediate supervisors, one for a project and one for a division. The idea is to encourage cross-functional sharing to expedite prompt, effective responses to customer needs or requests.

Exhibit 11-6. The Matrix Management Design

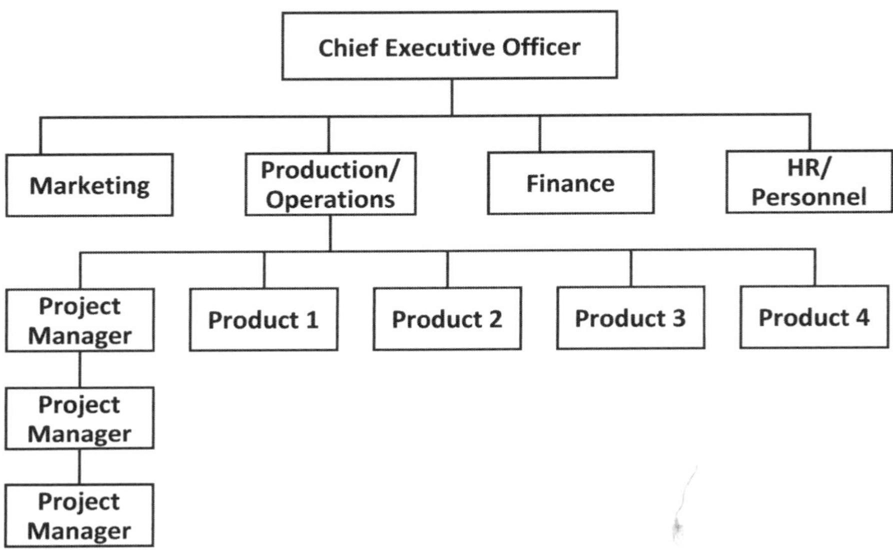

The *team structure* (see Exhibit 11-7) is similar to the project and matrix structures and often overlaps with them. Teams may be temporary or permanent. They may be restricted to one division or function, or they may operate across functions, divisions, or project assignments. Teams have gained immense popularity in recent years, since they provide flexibility and broad sharing across jobs. They also encourage necessary inter-dependency across organizational boundaries.

Exhibit 11-7. The Team Structure Design

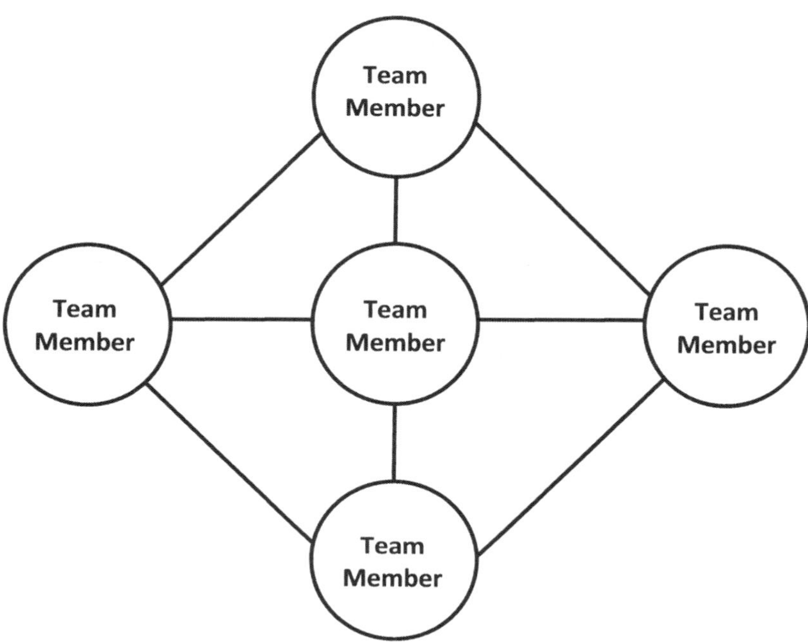

According to a survey of 4,500 teams in more than 500 organizations by the Wilson Learning Corporation, it is *collaboration* rather than *teamwork* that enables companies to turn a limited team process into a positive driving force. The most frequently mentioned organizational barriers to effective team performance are unfair rewards and compensation; unsupportive personnel and human resource development systems; ineffective information systems; lack of top management commitment; incompatible organizational alignment; negative personal mind-sets among team members, incompatible individual abilities, and characteristics; and various team membership factors. The survey revealed that most corporations utilize six types of teams: (1) functional;(2) continuous improvement; (3) product; (4) project; (5) management; and (6) problem-solving. When asked how they evaluate the effectiveness of collaboration, 84 percent of respondents said they used task outcomes, 53 percent mentioned group process, and 41 percent cited team member satisfaction.

The *virtual design* (see Exhibit 11-8) is most radical of all but appears to be the organizational structure of the future. The organization chooses to outsource its work or relies heavily on external vendors, temporary employees, or others brought inside to cope with peak workloads or specialized assignments. Only a skeleton crew is employed full time, and its members may function more as contract managers overseeing an army of temporary help than as individual contributors. One advantage of this design is its tremendous flexibility. It also helps the organization hold down costly employee benefits. A disadvantage is that insufficient time, money, or effort may be devoted to cultivating a long-term base of experience, and institutional memory and organizational learning may be sacrificed on the altar of expediency.

Exhibit 11-8. The Virtual Design

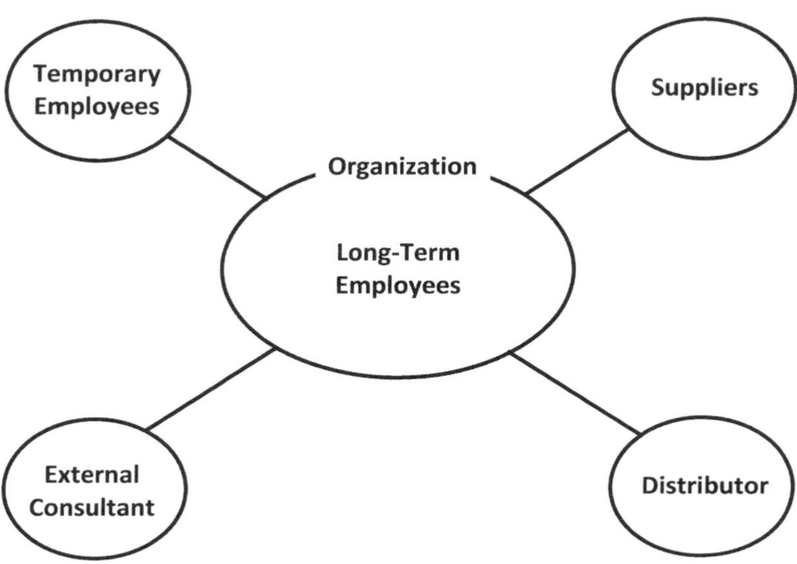

Recent attention to organizational design is focused on workflows across jobs, teams, departments, and divisions. The aim is to go beyond organization charts and paper-and-pencil depictions of reporting relationships (so-called formal design) to examine the actual, daily processes and interrelationships of work units as they meet customer needs, manufacture products, or deliver services. Keys to such examinations are analyses of the inputs, transformation processes, and outputs of each function, division, project team, work team, or job. Often such examinations require *organizational maps,* depictions of where and how the work flows, and an analysis of necessary improvements. An organizational map is like a flowchart that depicts the movement of work through each work area, how each work area processes it, and how it then moves on to other areas.

How Can Organizational Design Be Used as an HPE Strategy?

In most cases, HPE practitioners acting alone are unable to affect organizational design. The reason is that most major decisions about organizational design are reserved for top managers, middle managers, and supervisors or teams for their respective areas of responsibility. Changing organizational design requires management and employee involvement.

The need for organizational redesign may become apparent to HPE practitioners as they lead or coordinate troubleshooting or planning activities. Information about existing organizational design problems or issues should be fed back to key decision makers.

If HPE practitioners can make recommendations about changes in organizational design leading to a reduction of duplicative efforts, they should do so. If the problem is endemic to the entire organization, an external consultant should be hired to provide unbiased advice to key decision makers. Divisional, departmental, and team or work-unit design issues can usually be addressed inside the organization, and HPE practitioners can facilitate such efforts.

To address organizational design problems, consider these questions:

- What structural or design defects appear to exist?
- What evidence suggests that the defects are leading to "turf battles," duplicative efforts, or other unproductive activities?
- How have other organizations arranged their responsibilities around similar work products or processes to avoid duplication of effort or missing areas of responsibilities?
- How well could the design of other organizations be adapted to this organization?
- Who should be involved in decision making about organizational design, and how can they be convinced that a problem exists?
- How can a shift in organizational design be made in a way that minimizes disruptions? What HPE strategies may have to be combined with organizational redesign to achieve a smooth transition from an existing to a desired organizational design?

Use the worksheet in Exhibit 11-9 to pose these questions to employees and managers when a problem with organizational design is suspected or when an apparent opportunity arises to enhance human performance through organizational redesign.

Exhibit 11-9. A Worksheet for Considering Organizational Redesign

Directions: Use this worksheet to structure your thinking about the impact of organizational design on division, department, work group or team, or individual performance. Consider each question and provide your answer in the space provided below the question. There are no right or wrong answers; however, in special situations, there may be some answers that are better than others.

1. What structural or design defects appear to exist?

   Answer:

2. What evidence suggests that the defects are leading to "turf battles," duplicative efforts, or other unproductive activities?

   Answer:

3. How have other organizations arranged their responsibilities around similar work products or processes to avoid duplication of effort or missing areas of responsibilities?

   Answer:

---

4. How well could the design of other organizations be adapted to this organization?

   Answer:

Exhibit 11-9 (concluded)

5. Who should be involved in decision making about organizational design and how can they be convinced that a problem exists?

   Answer:

6. How can a shift in organizational design be made in a way that minimized disruptions? What HPE strategies may have to be combined with organizational redesign to achieve a smooth transition from an existing to a desired organizational design?

   Answer:

What Problems Exist with Organizational Design as an HPE Strategy?

Organizational redesign is a high-stakes endeavor. Mistakes made in redesign—especially when reorganization occurs on a grand scale—may translate directly into monumental problems with customer service, workflow, and turnover.

Several problems can occur when organizational redesign is used as an HPE strategy:

1. It is easy for managers, employees, and HPE practitioners to overlook the systemic consequences of an isolated organizational redesign decision; changes in design may lead to problems in other areas of organizational performance. It is therefore imperative to consider during redesign who is likely to be affected by the change, and in what ways. An effort can then be made to prevent any unwanted side effects.

2. Organizational redesign is rarely a standalone effect. Other HPE strategies should be combined with it. Once people are clear about their responsibilities, it is difficult to change that understanding. A change in organizational design may require frequent informational sessions and training to help people understand what they should be doing, what results they should be achieving, and why the change is worthwhile. The organization may also need to review the way it rewards performance to ensure that rewards match new responsibilities.

Chapter 12
Implementing Human Performance Enhancement (HPE) Strategies to Address Work Environment Problems or Opportunities

Some HPE strategies are designed to solve performance problems, to improve the way the work is performed or organized, to support workers who carry out the work, or to capitalize on improvement opportunities at the work level. HPE strategies of this kind include the following:

- redesigning jobs or work tasks
- improving information flow about work-related issues
- improving feedback
- improving on-the-job and off-the-job training
- using structured practice
- improving equipment and tools
- using job or performance aids
- improving reward systems

HPE strategies directed to the work area of the performance model (see Exhibit 2-2) lend themselves to real-time, work-related HPE. Taken individually or collectively, they can exert tremendous influence on the quality, quantity, cost, and timeliness of human performance.

Redesigning Jobs or Job Tasks

Job and task redesign directs attention to the work assignments at the level of individuals and/or their job titles. But what exactly are job redesign and task redesign? Why are they useful? When are they appropriate as HPE strategies? How is job redesign carried out? How is task redesign carried out? What problems can affect job or task redesign?

What Is Job and Task Redesign?

Job design is the process of establishing work duties, activities, responsibilities, and desired outcomes. Its purpose is to clarify, and communicate, the necessary work to be performed by an individual, team, or other group. Just as job design is related to organizational design, so job redesign is closely related to organizational redesign. Whereas organizational design establishes responsibilities by function, division, department, or work group, job design establishes responsibilities or activities by job title, position, or work.

A *job* is a set of work duties, responsibilities, activities, or desired outcomes. Many people may share the same job title. A *position*, on the other hand, refers to the duties, responsibilities, activities, or desired outcomes carried out by one person. Only one individual occupies a position, although he or she may bear a job title shared by many people.

Task design is more specific than job design. A *task* is a finite activity with an identifiable beginning, middle, and ending. An employee's role in carrying out a procedure of several steps may represent a task. *Task analysis* is the process of analyzing tasks to detect the underlying competencies, knowledge, skills, or attitudes necessary for people to complete the task successfully. Many approaches to task analysis have been identified,[1] but all call for examining what performers need to know and do to carry out each task step.

The trend in job and task design is to move away from rigid definitions of what people may (or may not) do based on written job descriptions and to move toward flexible descriptions of work centered on doing whatever is necessary to meet or exceed customer needs or expectations. That trend has prompted experimentation with teams in which many people share common goals and interdependent responsibilities. The same trend has prompted employers to experiment with part-time workers, job sharing among several workers, task sharing across several workers, and teams composed of representatives of the manufacturer, customers, suppliers, and distributors.

Why Is Job and Task Redesign Useful?

A job is the meeting point between organizational requirements and individual capabilities. Individuals perform only when they accept responsibility for duties, activities, or desired results. Clarifying job duties—or changing them—is thus one way to improve human performance. This does not necessarily require training or other HPE strategies, although other strategies will be required if changes in job design prompt employees to accept responsibilities for activities or results for which they have not previously had to perform or for which they are not currently rewarded.

When Are Job Redesign and Task Redesign Appropriate as HPE Strategies?

Job redesign can be used as an HPE strategy whenever

- work duties, tasks, responsibilities, or customer requirements are not being consistently met because responsibility is unclear;
- the organization has been reorganized or restructured;
- work processes have been reengineered;

- dramatic change has been imposed on the organization because of radical transformations in activities with suppliers, distributors, customers, or other key stakeholder groups.

In addition, job or task redesign may be necessary if the organization has introduced other HPE strategies, such as changes in reward or incentive systems or changes in the equipment or tools that employees use.

How Is Job Redesign Carried Out?

Over the years, much has been written about job redesign.[2] There is a difference between really changing work responsibilities, duties, activities, or desired outcomes and simply clarifying what people are expected to do in their jobs. Some people are not sure what they are responsible for; as a result, they do not perform to expectations. (Supervisors and their workers may agree on as little as 50 percent of the workers' job responsibilities.)

To clarify existing job responsibilities, HPE practitioners should use traditional or nontraditional approaches to job analysis. Job analysis should be understood to mean the process of discovering the work activities and desired work results of a job or type of work. Job analysis may require job incumbents and their supervisors and/or coworkers each to prepare written job descriptions or to write out responses to a structured interview questionnaire about what job incumbents are doing on a daily basis. The outcome of the job analysis process (summarized in Exhibit 12-1) is usually a job description. Many job descriptions are published in *The Dictionary of Occupational Titles*, a U.S. government publication that can be found in many public libraries. *The Dictionary of Occupational Titles* is being replaced by the impressive O*NET OnLine (see http://online.onetcenter.org/).

Although a job description describes what workers are doing or what results workers are achieving, it does not necessarily indicate what workers should be doing or what results they should be achieving. To determine that, it may be necessary to form a project team composed of exemplary job incumbents, their immediate organizational superiors, and representatives of other affected groups. The project team should investigate how the job incumbents' work duties should be changed to meet customer needs or expectations better, achieve the organization's strategic goals, or conform to requirements stemming from new responsibilities allocated in a newly restructured or redesigned organization.

Exhibit 12-1. Steps in the Job Analysis Process

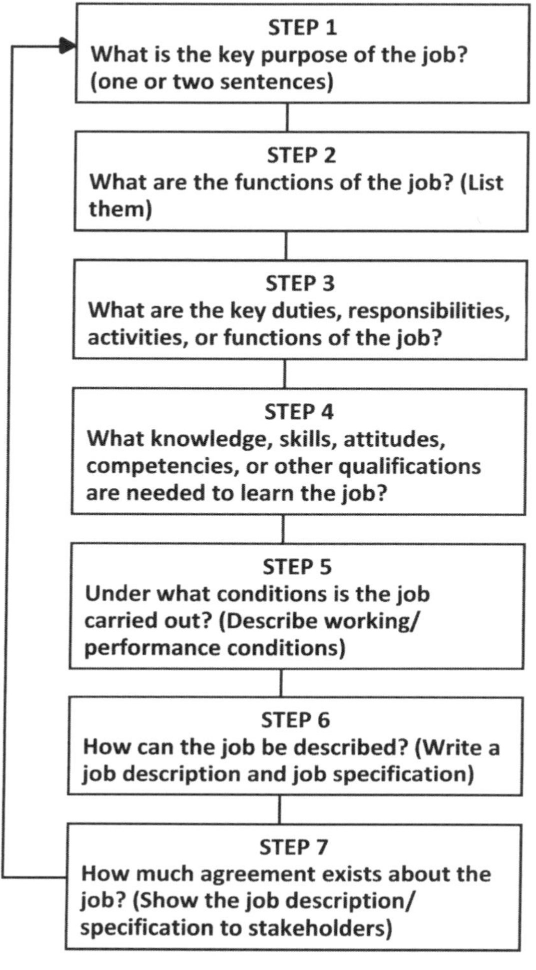

STEP 1
What is the key purpose of the job? (one or two sentences)
STEP 2
What are the functions of the job? (List them)
STEP 3
What are the key duties, responsibilities, activities, or functions of the job?
STEP 4
What knowledge, skills, attitudes, competencies, or other qualifications are needed to learn the job?
STEP 5
Under what conditions is the job carried out? (Describe working/ performance conditions)
STEP 6
How can the job be described? (Write a job description and job specification)
STEP 7
How much agreement exists about the job? (Show the job description/ specification to stakeholders)

A good general approach is to follow this four-step process:

1. The project team is formed.
2. Team members investigate changes affecting the organization, customers, and the work. As part of this step, they may wish to benchmark the same job title in other companies.
3. Team members feed the information back to their peers.
4. Team members prepare a proposed job description that lists new work duties attuned to customer needs or organizational requirements; circulate it among exemplary job incumbents and their immediate organizational superiors; and prepare a flexible action plan to add, subtract, or modify the duties, responsibilities, work activities, or desired results of job incumbents.

Team members should also work with HPE practitioners to identify compatible HPE strategies to support job redesign, such as changes in selection, training, reward/incentive, and feedback practices. Such an approach has been successfully used in transforming directive supervisors into supportive team leaders.

How Is Task Redesign Carried Out?

Task redesign can be carried out in the same fashion as job redesign, by a team comprising representatives of everyone who carries out a task. If that group is large, only exemplary performers should be chosen. The group constructs a flowchart that depicts the way the task is currently carried out by writing each step on an 8½" x 11" sheet of paper and using the sheets to construct a chart of the steps on a large blank wall. Team members then come up with ideas about how to streamline the procedure or task by combining it, dropping it, or modifying it to achieve a more efficient or effective flow of activities. They also suggest ways to make the change, providing information and training to those who are currently carrying out the task or procedure. Customers or other stakeholders can be involved in this process.

What Problems Can Affect Job or Task Redesign?

Job and task redesign are imperfect HPE strategies. Seldom can they be carried out in isolation from organizational redesign because changes in one job or task affect other jobs or tasks. For this reason, then, it is advisable to assess the possible consequences of any job redesign before making it and to involve other teams or groups that may be affected.

Improving Information Flow about Work-Related Issues

"Why didn't you tell me that?" is a common—and plaintive—question in many work settings. It expresses the bewilderment of an employee or manager who stumbles on a change of which he or she was previously unaware. "Poor communication"—meaning lack of information on which to base decisions or actions—is a commonly cited cause of performance problems.[3] Providing the information necessary for workers to perform their jobs effectively was cited by training professionals in my 2004 survey as a most commonly used and significant HPE strategy.[4]

But what is information flow? When should information flow be a focus of attention for enhancing human performance? How should information flow be improved? What problem affects efforts to improve information flow?

What Is Information Flow?

Information flow refers to quantity and quality of work-related information that flows into, up, down, across, and laterally in organizational settings. It is closely related to *organizational communication*, defined as "the process of creating and exchanging messages within a network of interdependent relationships to cope with environmental uncertainty."[5]

When Should Information Flow Be a Focus of Attention for Enhancing Human Performance?

Improving information flow may be an effective HPE strategy in these circumstances:

- Employees complain that they do not receive sufficient information about their jobs and organizations.
- Management does not follow up on employee messages.
- Messages are sent too early or too late to be used.
- The grapevine supplements the void created by management's lack of openness, candor, or visibility.
- Impersonal channels are substituted for face-to-face contact.
- Employees are given no chance to offer suggestions about decisions affecting them.[6]

Information flow should also be examined when an unacceptable time lag exists between changes in customer, supplier, or distributor requirements and action taken by appropriate groups or individuals inside the organization.

How Can Information Flow Be Improved?

Good intentions are not enough to improve information flow. Management, employees, and HPE practitioners must be genuinely committed to the process.

One approach to improving information flow and organizational communication is to apply the *communication audit*, which compares existing to desired information flow.[7] A communication audit may focus on an entire organization or any part of it. The aim of a communication audit is to assess current organizational communication practices, desirable improvements to those practices, and the impact of those practices. Improving communication can be an HPE strategy aimed at improving the timeliness and specificity of information flow.

To conduct an audit, HPE practitioners can follow these steps:

1. Identify the organization's implicit (or explicit) communication policy. Decide what information decision makers are to provide to employees, customers, and other stakeholders.
2. Assess how well employees and other stakeholders believe that information is flowing within the organization by using written questionnaires, face-to-face interviews, team meetings, focus groups, observation methods, and other approaches (see Exhibit 12-2).

3. When the results are in, feed them back to stakeholders, establish action plans to improve information flow, and create methods of monitoring and measuring improvements in information flow. As part of this process, ask employees and other stakeholders to devise strategies to improve communication at all levels throughout the organization.

Exhibit 12-2. Sample Questions to Assess the Quality and Timeliness of Information Flow

Directions: Use this questionnaire to collect information about the quality and timeliness of information flow in an organization. Give this questionnaire to employees. Ask them to respond honestly and anonymously. Ask them also to forward the completed questionnaire to an identified individual. When the questionnaires are in, compile the results. Then feed them back to decision makers and employees. Ask them to suggest ways to improve information flow in the organization.

1. How well do you receive information that you need to do your job? Do you feel the information you receive is adequate or inadequate? Why? Explain.

2. How specific is the information that you receive? Is the information too general to be useful? Explain.

3. What could be done, in your opinion, to improve the flow of information you need to receive to perform effectively? Provide suggestions for action.

What Problem Affects Efforts to Improve Information Flow?

One key problem affecting HPE strategies centered on improving information flow is managers' and other decision makers' tendency to blame poor communication or lack of information for many human performance problems. They use the issue, as they sometimes use lack of training, as a catchall for many (or all) ills afflicting the organization. However, performance problems are not always attributable to poor communication, nor is improving the timely and specific flow of information the panacea for every illness.

To address this problem, HPE practitioners should work with managers, employees, and other stakeholders to distinguish genuine communication problems from other problems. A good place to begin is with two key questions:

1. Who needs information about a change to perform?
2. For what reason(s) might people wish to deliberately conceal or distort information?

The answer to the first question is not always apparent to everyone in an organization. To answer it, it will be necessary to improve employee awareness about who does what. The second question focuses on motivations. Information flow is psychological more than logical; people will provide, conceal, or distort information in their own self-interest. To improve the timely and specific flow of information, then, it is necessary to address disincentives for communicating, incentives for not communicating, and incentives for communicating.

Improving Job Feedback Methods

Feedback is closely related to information about work. Indeed, feedback is a special form of information. Yet lack of feedback on work consequences and lack of timely feedback were cited as the most often encountered and most significant human performance problems faced by training and development professionals in a year 2004 survey.[8]

What is feedback? When should it be a focal point for attention for enhancing human performance? How should feedback be improved? What problems can affect efforts to improve job feedback?

What Is Feedback?

As Thomas Gilbert has pointed out, "[M]ore than half the problems of human competence can be traced to inadequate data. Such an easily correctable defect would not exist if people were more aware of it and its consequences."[9] *Feedback* refers to messages as they are understood. It exists only in the larger context of a communication-performance model, which may be called a *feedback system* that consists of all elements contributing to information provided back to a performer. A feedback system, like David K. Berlo's classic communication model,[10] includes important elements such as a sender, receiver, channel, message, noise, and medium (see Exhibit 12-3). A *sender* is the performer who directs information, takes action, and achieves results. The *receiver* is the recipient of the information or the beneficiary of action or results. The *message* is the information, action, or behavior sent. The *medium* is the mode of transmission; the *channel* is the specified band of the medium by which the message is sent; *noise* is any distraction that impedes message transmission.

Exhibit 12-3. A Communication Model Highlighting Feedback

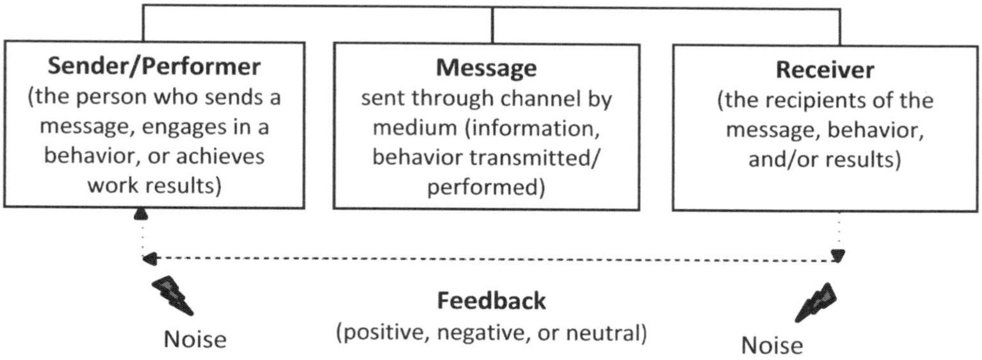

Generally, *feedback* refers to information that flows back to the sender/performer because of a message he or she has sent or because of an action or behavior in which he or she was engaged. It can be positive, negative, or neutral. *Positive feedback* is praise; *negative feedback* is criticism (constructive or destructive); *neutral feedback* is purely informational. Feedback regulates individual—and, indeed, group—performance in a self-regulating communication-performance system.

When Should Feedback Be a Focus of Attention for Enhancing Human Performance?

As noted in a classic treatment of feedback by David Nadler, "[F]eedback can create changes in the behavior of individuals, groups, or organizations because it both energizes (that is, motivates) and directs behavior."[11] Attending to feedback as an HPE strategy may be appropriate in the following circumstances:

- Employees and other stakeholders complain that they are not receiving information about how internal or external customers, suppliers, or distributors are responding to their behavior or the results of their work.
- There is evidence, substantiated by multiple sources, that mistakes could have been avoided (or opportunities seized) if performers had received more timely or specific feedback about the results of their actions.

How Should Feedback Be Improved?

To improve the quality, specificity, and timeliness of feedback, HPE practitioners can establish or improve methods that link sender-performers to receiver-recipients. To do this, they can follow this eight-step model (outlined in Exhibit 12-4):

1. **Clarify the purpose of the feedback system to be installed or improved.** Will the focus be on upward, downward, lateral, positive, negative, or neutral feedback? What groups will be affected, and why have they been targeted for improvement? What results are to be gained? What will be the value of the feedback improvement process to the organization's strategy and customer service goals?
2. **Select and train facilitators on ways to improve the timeliness and specificity of feedback to individuals, teams, or groups.** This approach can be most useful in successfully installing a new approach to feedback throughout an organization.
3. **Brief managers and other stakeholders on the goals of the effort.** What results are sought? How do they help meet business needs? Of what value are they to the managers, employees, and other key stakeholders? What can managers do to ensure that the HPE strategy is implemented successfully? If necessary, train managers on new and more effective approaches to providing performance feedback to their employees.
4. **Orient employees to the effort.** Tell them the goals to be achieved. Show how those goals relate to the needs of the business, the stakeholders, and the employees themselves. Provide them with skills-oriented training as necessary on ways that they can seek feedback and provide effective feedback to coworkers, managers, and other stakeholders.
5. **Prepare and circulate a feedback instrument to collect employee and other stakeholder perceptions about the quality of feedback available to performers.**
6. **Feed the results of the instrument back to teams, individuals, or others who are the focal points of the HPE strategy.**
7. **Work with each team or individual to establish an action plan to improve the timeliness and specificity of feedback given and received.**
8. **Ask those involved to assess how well they feel it has helped to improve feedback in the organization.**[12]

Exhibit 12-4. A Model for Improving Feedback

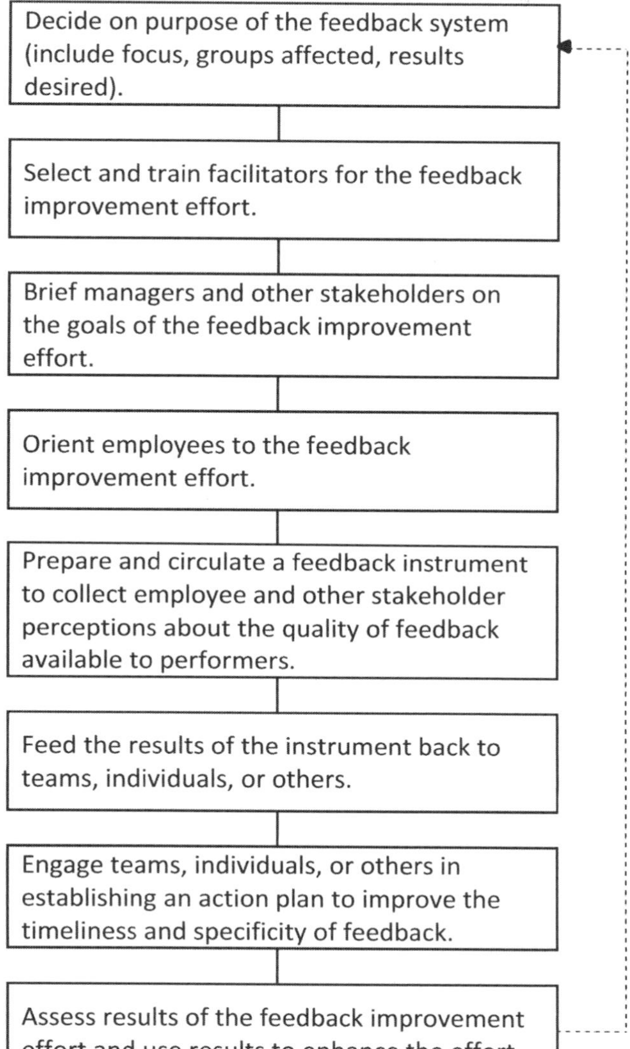

What Problems Can Affect Efforts to Improve Job Feedback?

Although much has been written about feedback and feedback systems,[13] less has been done to improve them than one might think when their importance is considered. One reason is that managers and employees are not always too sure *how* to improve feedback. Another reason is that managers and employees have trouble defining the idea clearly so that others understand what they mean by feedback. A third reason is that some people confuse timely, specific feedback with the annual employee performance appraisal ritual. Annual appraisals, while representing one form of feedback, are neither timely nor specific.

To overcome these problems, HPE practitioners should lead the way to define feedback, ensure that feedback improvement and measurement approaches are incorporated in the organization's communication policy, and draw attention to the many methods of improving timely, specific feedback. They can do this by making it a practice to collect customer, supplier, and distributor information regularly and feed it back to performers; providing training on feedback as appropriate; and finding ways to encourage interaction between groups inside and outside the organization.

Improving On-the-Job and Off-the-Job Training

When training and development professionals think of a solution to a human performance problem, training is (not surprisingly) the first thing that usually enters their minds. Traditional training methods have long been governed by the Instructional Systems Design (ISD) approach.[14] New models of ISD have been emerging in recent years to keep pace with growing, technologically oriented instructional support options, the declining half-life of knowledge, and the growing popularity of performance support systems.

What exactly are on-the-job and off-the-job training? When should they be used? How can on-the-job and off-the-job training methods be improved? What problems can affect training as a method of enhancing human performance?

What Are On-the-Job Training and Off-the-Job Training?

Training that occurs in the workplace and during the work day is called *on-the-job training* (OJT); training that occurs off-site and off-line is called *off-the-job training* (OFJT). One of the most frequently used but least publicized forms of training, OJT prompts employer expenditures three to six times greater than those for OFJT.[15]

Both OJT and OFJT can be unplanned or planned. *Unplanned OJT* often amounts to nothing more than "following Joe around the plant" or "sitting by Nellie." *Planned OJT*, on the other hand, helps learner-performers reduce the unproductive breaking-in period that typically follows new employee selection, transfer, or promotion. Increased attention has been directed to OJT in recent years because it is a real-time change strategy. *Unplanned OFJT* includes in-service training in which employees "huddle" with their supervisors or coworkers to address common problems. *Planned OFJT*, like planned OJT, has been carefully prepared to maximize the time employees spend away from their jobs. It is most appropriate when many workers share a common training need.

When Should OJT and OFJT Be Used?

Not every human performance problem lends itself to a training solution. Training should be used to solve human performance problems only when workers lack the competencies to perform. It should not be used when workers lack motivation, appropriate tools or equipment, or appropriate supervision, or when other issues are affecting performance. Training is the HPE strategy of last resort because rigorously designed and delivered training is expensive.

Training should be used when workers lack knowledge to perform *and*

- appropriate resources are available to design, deliver, and follow up the training;
- alternative HPE strategies will not address the underlying causes of human performance problems or capitalize on human performance enhancement opportunities.

Planned OJT is appropriate when the conditions just listed can be met *and*

- daily work distractions can be minimized;
- training on the work site will not pose health, safety, or productivity problems for other employees;
- benefits can be derived from offering training in real time and in the work setting.

Off-the-job training, on the other hand, is appropriate when many employees share a common training need and when sufficient expertise and resources are available to design and deliver the training.

How Can On-the-Job and Off-the-Job Training Methods Be Improved?

A seven-step model may be followed when planning and delivering OJT or OFJT (see Exhibit 12-5).

1. **Analyze the workers, work requirements, and work environment.**[16] Who are the learners, and what do they know about the issues on which the training will focus? What are the requirements for demonstrating successful performance, and how are they measured? Under what conditions will the workers be asked to perform? Be sure to separate training from nontraining needs.
2. **Conduct a needs assessment.** A needs assessment determines only the *training* needs of the targeted learners. It specifies the difference between what is happening and what should be happening as it relates to the required competencies of the targeted participants.
3. **Specify and sequence the instructional objectives governing the training.** *Instructional objectives* are derived directly from the results of the training needs assessment.[17] While training needs suggest performance deficiencies or opportunities, instructional objectives suggest ways to meet the training needs and should clarify the desired outcomes of training.

4. **Make, buy, or modify instructional materials to meet the instructional objectives and thereby meet the training needs.** At this point, HPE practitioners should decide how to deliver the training and what materials are necessary to meet the objectives. Possible choices for delivery include selecting external consultants, using internal training and development professionals, relying on a combination of internal training and development professionals and external consultants, offering on-the-job training, or developing media-based instruction to be delivered by videotape, audiotape, or computer-based support. Additional choices include selecting and purchasing off-the-shelf training materials from commercial publishers or vendors, purchasing and modifying off-the-shelf training materials, locating internal training materials already in use within the organization, and preparing internal training materials.
5. **Test training materials before widespread delivery.** This is called *formative evaluation*.[18] Its aim is to improve training materials by trying them out first on a small group and then revising them.
6. **Deliver training to the targeted audience.** Appropriate delivery options depend, of course, on the medium (or media) chosen for delivery. Many training and development professionals are experimenting with *distance education*, which involves the application of many instructional media over many sites. Examples of distance education technology include videoteleconference, audioteleconference, electronic mail, and programmed print instruction.
7. **Conduct summative evaluation.** This is a follow-up evaluation to find out how well the training has been applied by learners on their jobs and what organizational outcomes or return-on-investment resulted from the training.[19] The key to success in summative evaluation is establishing a *transfer-of-training strategy* to ensure that what the targeted learners master is applied on their jobs.[20] There are more than one hundred possible transfer-of-training strategies.[21] (The worksheet in Exhibit 12-6 can help you structure your thinking about ways that transfer of training can be improved.) The results of summative evaluation should be fed back into future analyses of workers, work requirements, and the work environment and into future training efforts to create continuous training (CT) improvement.

Exhibit 12-5. A Seven-Step Model to Guide Training Design, Delivery, and Evaluation

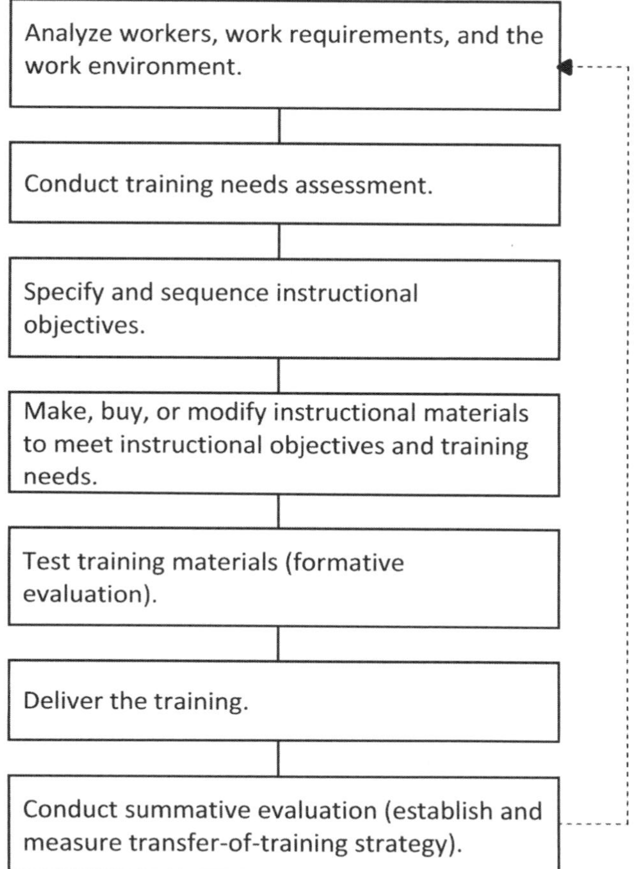
Analyze workers, work requirements, and the work environment.
Conduct training needs assessment.
Specify and sequence instructional objectives.
Make, buy, or modify instructional materials to meet instructional objectives and training needs.
Test training materials (formative evaluation).
Deliver the training.
Conduct summative evaluation (establish and measure transfer-of-training strategy).

Exhibit 12-6. A Worksheet to Improve Transfer-of-Training

Directions: Use this worksheet to structure your thinking about ways to maximize the effective transfer of training. Answer the questions appearing below. Ask employees and their immediate organizational superiors to answer these questions before and after an employee participates in off-the-job training. There are no right or wrong answers.

1. Training represents an investment made by the organization. Why is the employee being sent to training? What *measurable* job-related results are needed from the training experience? Try to be as precise as possible in your answer, since measurable criteria are the best means by which to demonstrate on-the-job returns resulting from off-the-job training investments.

2. How do you feel that the participant in this training course can prove on-the-job improvements?

3. What is the responsibility of the immediate supervisor of the participant in ensuring that the participant applies on the job what he or she learned in training? What is the best way you could recommend that be conducted?

4. What is the participant's responsibility in ensuring that he or she applies on the job what he or she learned in off-the-job training? How should his or her improvement be measured?

Some differences may exist between the model for OJT and that for OFJT.[22] Terminology may also differ somewhat, depending on the group targeted for training. For instance, OJT is more often associated with nonexempt than with exempt employees, although the same principles will work.[23]

What Problems Can Affect Training as a Method of Enhancing Human Performance?

Training is increasingly becoming the HPE strategy of last resort. Interest has been growing in OJT more than in OFJT. OJT is commanding renewed interest because it is a real-time change strategy and because in OJT, supervisors and coworkers take active roles in training, reducing transfer-of-training problems. They all have a stake in the performer's success, and they are better positioned than OFJT and development professionals to hold the performers accountable on their jobs for what they learned during the training.

In recent years, attention has also been shifting from training to learning.[24] What should be the role of learners in identifying, designing, and carrying out their own learning? If learners could be fully empowered to identify what they need to learn—and if they could be equipped with the learning-to-learn strategies they need to undertake learning successfully on their own—many researchers believe that a tremendous leap in human performance enhancement could be made.

Improving Structured Practice

Structured practice is similar to near-the-job training (NJT). Unlike OFJT and OJT, structured practice is conducted in an area next to the work site. Structured practice can encompass the following:

- Employees learning a new computer software program are given an opportunity to practice it in a company learning center.
- Employees who are being trained on a machine used on an assembly line are given hands-on practice with an identical machine in an area next to the assembly line so that mistakes will not lead to scrap products or wasted materials.
- A manager is asked to role play a disciplinary interview while a trained observer looks on.

When should structured practice be used to enhance human performance? How should it be used? What problems can affect the use of structured practice as an HPE strategy?

When Should Structured Practice Be Used?

HPE practitioners can use structured practice instead of training or other HPE strategies when performers already know what to do but have infrequent occasions to apply what they know. Pairing structured practice with planned OJT or OFJT gives learners an opportunity to apply what they learn and ensures that they can effectively do what they have been trained to do.

How Should Structured Practice Be Used?

Using structured practice effectively requires following the same basic steps that are used in planning OJT or OFJT: establishing instructional objectives to be achieved by learners and scheduling the structured practice, allowing regular access to it. If possible, a facilitator can be assigned to ensure that individuals are given *planned* practice.

What Problems Can Affect the Use of Structured Practice?

Two key problems afflict structured practice. First, it may be chosen for the wrong reasons. It should not be substituted for training; rather, it should be used as a standalone method only when learners already know what to do but have forgotten how to do it because of infrequent practice. Second, structured practice may suffer from being unplanned. HPE practitioners should caution managers to avoid limiting access to structured practice to downtime only, since that usually leads to inconsistent opportunities for practice among many learners.

Improving Equipment and Tools

Equipment surrounds the performer; *tools* are used in daily work. Without appropriate and available equipment and tools, performers cannot work competently. Imagine a pilot trying to fly without a plane or an accountant trying to function without a calculator, and you can easily see how important equipment and tools are to achieving desired results.

When should improvements in equipment and tools be applied to enhance human performance? How should they be used to lead to those enhancements? What key problem can affect the use of equipment and tools for enhancing human performance?

When Should Improvements in Equipment and Tools Be Used to Enhance Human Performance?

Improving equipment and tools is an appropriate HPE strategy when employees are complaining that their equipment or tools are outdated, unavailable, or inappropriate to their needs; when evidence suggests that superior advantage can be gained over competitors through investments in state-of-the-art equipment or tools; or when such investments can improve an organization's safety record (thereby demonstrating commitment to employees and legal compliance to regulators), ensure a match between human and machine requirements, or make reasonable accommodation for the mentally, physically, or learning disabled.

How Should Equipment and Tools Be Used to Lead to Enhancements in Human Performance?

The methods for enhancing human performance by improving equipment and tools are similar to those used for improving feedback. HPE practitioners should identify performance problems stemming from inadequate, unavailable, or inappropriate equipment and tools by asking employees and other stakeholders, feeding the results back to decision makers and others, and establishing action plans to improve the adequacy, availability, and appropriateness of equipment and tools. If necessary, they can double check employee perceptions by observing the equipment and tools in use.

What Key Problem Can Affect the Use of Equipment and Tools?

Perhaps the greatest problem confronting HPE practitioners who undertake an HPE strategy geared to improve the use of equipment and tools is management's unwillingness (or occasional inability) to invest in the necessary equipment and tools to do the work. Government agencies and some private-sector companies occasionally freeze purchases of equipment and tools. Yet employees are expected to continue production unabated—or even realize improvements—despite the inadequate equipment and tools they are given.

In such cases, HPE practitioners should undertake studies to find out whether investments in new equipment or tools will yield a payoff. If they lack the skill to undertake such studies, they should request assistance from production management and accounting professionals. It may be possible to show that investments in equipment and tools will yield returns far greater than the initial investments. Such studies may also underscore the fallacy of across-the-board freezes on purchasing.

Using Job or Performance Aids

A *job aid* is designed to help workers do their jobs and may be applied on or off the job. A *performance aid* is similar to a job aid, except that it is used in real time and on the job. According to the human performance technologist Joe Harless, "[I]nside every fat training course there is a thin job aid crying to get out."[25]

When should job or performance aids be used? How should they be designed and used? What problems can affect the use of job and performance aids for enhancing human performance?

When Should Job or Performance Aids Be Used?

Job or performance aids are particularly useful when employees need real-time assistance to help them perform. Examples of effective job or performance aids include procedure manuals, context-sensitive help on computer systems, labels or signs, reminder cards, brief informational brochures, and checklists. Particularly lending themselves to job or performance aids are work methods that are infrequently performed (so that people sometimes forget what to do), that rely on a worker's imperfect memory, and that do not pose health or safety hazards.

How Should Job or Performance Aids Be Designed and Used?

Job and performance aids represent such a broad array of possible performance support tools that there is no universal way to design and use them. However, if work procedures can be broken down using task analysis, then aids such as checklists can be designed around them, using the format depicted in Exhibit 12-7. Such checklists can then be conveyed to workers in procedure manuals, in company employee newsletters, and over electronic mail. They can guide workers through infrequently used, but important, procedures as the need arises. They can also supplement training, providing workers with useful aids that they can apply on the job to help them transfer what they learned in training sessions.

Exhibit 12-7. A Format for a Procedure-Based Checklist

Have you… (In the space below, list the procedures in the exact order in which they are to be conducted.)	**Yes** ☒	**No** ☒	**Notes** ☒
	☐	☐	☐
	☐	☐	☐
	☐	☐	☐
	☐	☐	☐
	☐	☐	☐
	☐	☐	☐

What Problems Can Affect the Use of Job and Performance Aids for Enhancing Human Performance?

Job or performance aids should not be used when they will date quickly, when reliance on them will undercut the credibility of performers, or when the information required to act is too detailed or complex to lend itself to abbreviation.

Improving Reward Systems

People will do what they are rewarded for doing. They will also avoid doing what they are punished for doing. They may—or may not—do what they are neither rewarded nor punished for doing. Despite the obvious common sense underlying these dicta, decision makers have for many years persisted in ignoring these simple facts of organizational life. Some managers staunchly (and wrongly) maintain that people perform merely to keep their jobs; others believe organizational loyalty always outweighs mercenary motives involving personal profit or loss. Such thinking belies human nature and shows naïveté both about human performance and good management practice.

What is a reward, and what is an incentive? When should rewards and incentives be applied to enhance human performance? How should they be designed and used? What problems can affect the use of reward and incentive systems for enhancing human performance?

What Is a Reward, and What Is an Incentive?

An incentive *precedes* performance and induces performers to seek an expected result. A reward, in contrast, *follows* performance and reinforces the results.

In many respects, an incentive and reward system resembles a feedback system (see Exhibit 12-8). Just as a feedback system is based on a loop of information in which information flows back to the performer after a behavior or result, an incentive and reward system is based on a loop of reinforcements and their results. That is especially appropriate because the best-known feedback system in many organizations—the employee performance appraisal process—is usually linked in some way to the incentive and reward system (compensation). *If workers value the rewards they expect to achieve and if they believe that the work environment will permit them to realize those rewards through their own efforts, then expectations and incentives will motivate desired behavior and/or results.* This key principle underlies so-called *expectancy theory*,[26] one of the best-known and most widely researched views of motivation.

Exhibit 12-8. Expectancy Theory Applied to Incentives and Rewards

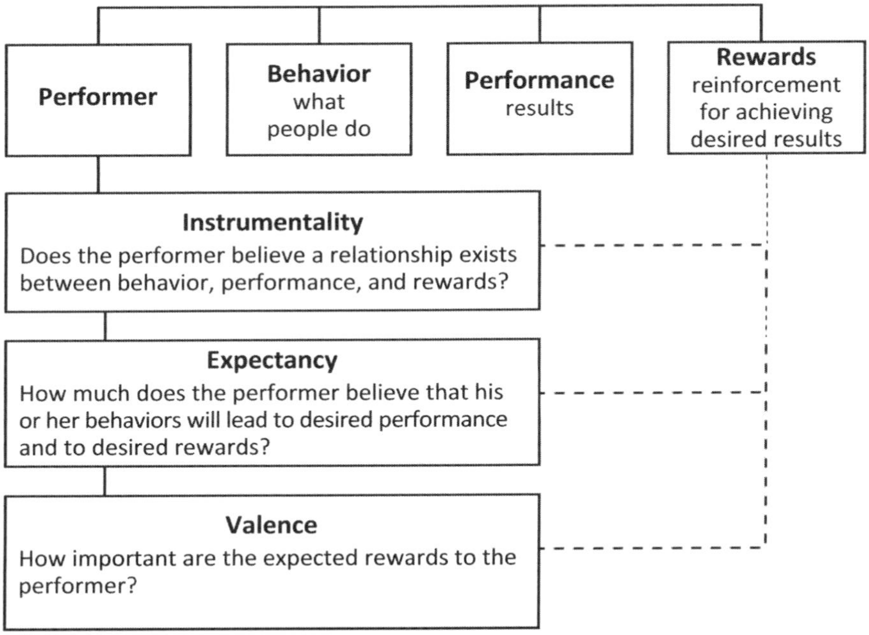

Performer	Behavior what people do	Performance results	Rewards reinforcement for achieving desired results

Instrumentality
Does the performer believe a relationship exists between behavior, performance, and rewards?

Expectancy
How much does the performer believe that his or her behaviors will lead to desired performance and to desired rewards?

Valence
How important are the expected rewards to the performer?

When Should Rewards and Incentives Be Applied?

Improving the organization's incentive and reward system may be appropriate in these circumstances:

- Rewards are unclear or are not defined.
- The range of existing rewards is unclear.
- The time lag between behavior or performance and reward is too long (rewards are usually more motivating when they follow results as quickly as possible).
- Nobody is sure how to measure behavior or results to form the basis for allocating rewards.
- Questions are raised about the fairness of the way rewards are allocated.
- Authority and responsibility for providing incentives or allocating rewards are unclear.
- Employees as a group or individuals do not value the rewards available (a problem with valence, as shown in Exhibit 12-8).
- Employees as a group or individuals do not believe there is a logical relationship between their behaviors or results and the rewards they will receive (a problem with instrumentality, as shown in Exhibit 12-8).

- Employees are not rewarded or are punished for behaving or performing as desired.
- There are no rewards.
- A mismatch exists between the size, quality, or value of the rewards and the level of effort necessary to achieve them.

How Should Incentives and Rewards Be Designed and Used?

When analyzing reward systems, HPE practitioners must first identify the existing incentive and reward system and define what is currently happening. How are people currently being provided with incentives and rewards? What complaints exist about the way incentives and rewards are allocated? How much truth exists to those complaints? Do employees and other stakeholders believe that there is an effective match between desired results (performance), the instrumentality and expectancy of desired rewards, and the valence accorded to the rewards?

HPE practitioners must next turn to desired results. What should be happening? What performance or accomplishment is sought? The goals of the incentive and reward system should be compared to strategic goals and objectives. What does the organization seek to achieve? Do the goals center on increased production, improved quality, reduced time to achieve results, or increased customer satisfaction? At what level is it desirable to provide incentives—at the individual, team or work unit, departmental, divisional, or organizational levels? Why?

Third, HPE practitioners need to examine measurement methods. How is the organization presently measuring performance and allocating rewards? How effective and efficient are those measurement methods? How equitably and consistently are they applied?

Fourth, the timeliness of rewards is also evaluated. How much time elapses from the demonstration of desired performance and the reinforcement that rewards provide? What side effects, if any, have resulted from long time lapses? How much turnover, absenteeism, or other negative side effects have resulted from them, if any?

HPE practitioners should, finally, evaluate possible improvement efforts. In what ways could the organization encourage a better match between desired results and incentives or rewards? How could improvements be made? HPE practitioners and decision makers should think beyond simple and traditional employee compensation programs to consider alternative and nonfinancial reward systems as well as innovative compensation practices such as team-based pay, gainsharing, broadbanding, knowledge-based pay, and competency-based pay.

The worksheet in Exhibit 12-9 can help stimulate dialogue among employees, decision makers, and stakeholders about desirable approaches to incentive and reward systems.

Exhibit 12-9. A Worksheet for Stimulating Dialogue about Incentive and Reward Practices as an HPE Strategy

Directions: Use this worksheet to stimulate dialogue among employees, decision makers, and stakeholders about desirable ways to enhance human performance by improving the organization's incentive and reward practices. For each question appearing in the left column, ask respondents to answer briefly in the space at right. (There are no right or wrong answers in any absolute sense.) Collect the results, feed them back to respondents, and then ask them to suggest some ways to enhance human performance by improving the organization's incentive and reward practices.

QUESTION	ANSWER
1. What is the current incentive and reward system? In other words... • What is currently happening? • How are people currently being provided with incentives and rewards? • What complaints exist about the way incentives and rewards are allocated? How true are those complaints? • How well do employees and other stakeholders perceive there to be an effective match between desired results (performance), the instrumentality and expectancy of desired rewards, and the valence accorded to the rewards?	
2. What should be happening with the incentive and reward system? • What performance or accomplishment is sought? • How clearly are the goals of the incentive and reward system listed? • How well do the goals of the incentives and reward system match up to the organization's strategic plan? strategic goals and objectives? • At what level is it desirable to provide incentives—at the individual, team or work unit, departmental, divisional, or organizational levels? Why?	

Exhibit 12-9 (concluded)

QUESTION	ANSWER
3. How is the organization presently measuring performance and allocating rewards? How effective and efficient are those measurement methods? How fairly and equitably are they applied?	
4. How much time elapses from the demonstration of desired performance and the reinforcement that rewards provide? • What side effects, if any, have resulted from long time lapses? How much turnover, absenteeism, and other negative side effects have resulted from them, if any?	
5. In what ways could the organization encourage a better match between desired results and incentive rewards?	

What Problems Can Affect the Use of Reward and Incentive Systems?

Many problems afflict incentive and reward systems in today's organizations. They may be generally categorized as problems with expectancy, instrumentality, and valence.

Problems with expectancy and instrumentality stem from employee experience. Individuals see what happens to others. If they see that desired performance yields rewards, then they will perceive that their own efforts will pay off. On the other hand, if they see that desired performance is not rewarded or is punished, they will act accordingly. Perceptions of truth are as important as, if not more important than, verifiable truth.

Problems with valence stem from a common misperception that all employees prize financial or money rewards more than anything. That is not always true. It is important for HPE practitioners to help decision makers clarify what rewards are most important to individuals, teams, and other targeted groups. More than one thousand ways to reward employees have been identified, and they should be considered.[27] Some cost nothing but can yield dramatic improvements in employee productivity.

Chapter 13
Implementing Human Performance Enhancement (HPE) Strategies to Address Worker Problems or Opportunities

HPE strategies can solve performance problems or capitalize on performance improvement at the worker level by improving the match between the individual and the work. HPE strategies of this kind include

- identifying and building individual competencies;
- improving employee selection methods;
- applying progressive discipline.

These HPE strategies can be short term or long term in their focus or consequences.

Identifying and Building Worker Competencies

Competency identification has emerged as an important topic in HPE in recent years. But what is a competency? When is competency identification appropriate as an HPE strategy? How are competencies assessed? What are some problems with competency identification?

What Is a Competency?

A *competency* is perhaps best understood as the underlying characteristics of successful performers.[1] It can include bodies of knowledge, skills, traits, abilities, attitudes, or beliefs. In short, a competency is anything that distinguishes an exemplary performer from an average or below-average performer.

Competency identification discovers the underlying competencies of successful performers.[2] The result is a *competency model*, which describes the competencies of a job category, work team, department, division, or organization.

Competency identification has captured attention because it has greater flexibility and descriptive power than other methods of skill assessment, such as traditional task analysis, in its ability to distinguish between the characteristics of exemplary performers and average ones.[3] Focused on individuals rather than on the work they do, competencies get at such hard-to-define qualities as feelings, attitudes, and decision-making strategies—qualities that are becoming more important as work becomes less physical and more dependent on intellectual skills and as the workforce shifts from manufacturing (with its focus on tangible work products) to service (with its focus on intangible service). Competencies can be future-oriented in a way that is different from that of alternative approaches to describing work or workers.

When Is Competency Identification Appropriate as an HPE Strategy?

Competency identification as a strategy for HPE can be used in these circumstances:

- There is a need to integrate organizational strategic goals and individual characteristics.
- Clarifying the underlying characteristics of successful performers is desirable to direct attention to the hard-to-define qualities that are the underpinnings of success in a corporate culture.
- Nobody in the organization is sure what characteristics are—or should be—most prized or cultivated.
- HPE practitioners or other stakeholders see value in integrating all facets of HPE around identifiable characteristics.

How Are Competencies Identified?

Many methods may be used to conduct competency identification. However, the basic steps resemble those in any research investigation. These steps are depicted schematically in Exhibit 13-1.

To conduct competency identification, follow these steps:

1. **Clarify the problem to solve or the issue to be studied.** In competency identification, then, the issue is this: Why is a competency identification worth doing? What prompted it? Who wants it, and why do they want it?
2. **Articulate the questions to be answered or the objectives to be achieved.** Part of this step is establishing the study's parameters. Will the entire organization be assessed? Will only one division, department, work team or work group, or job category be the focus?
3. **Collect available information about the question to be answered or the objectives to be achieved for the focal group under investigation.** What information already exists, inside and outside the organization, about the job category and the people in that job category? Is it possible to obtain information about the job or the people in it from job descriptions, job evaluation studies conducted for the purpose of establishing compensation levels, or earlier competency studies conducted in the organization or outside it? In other words, where can information be obtained, and what light does it shed (if any) on the underlying competencies of successful performers in one corporate culture?

Exhibit 13-1. Key Steps in Conducting a Competency Identification

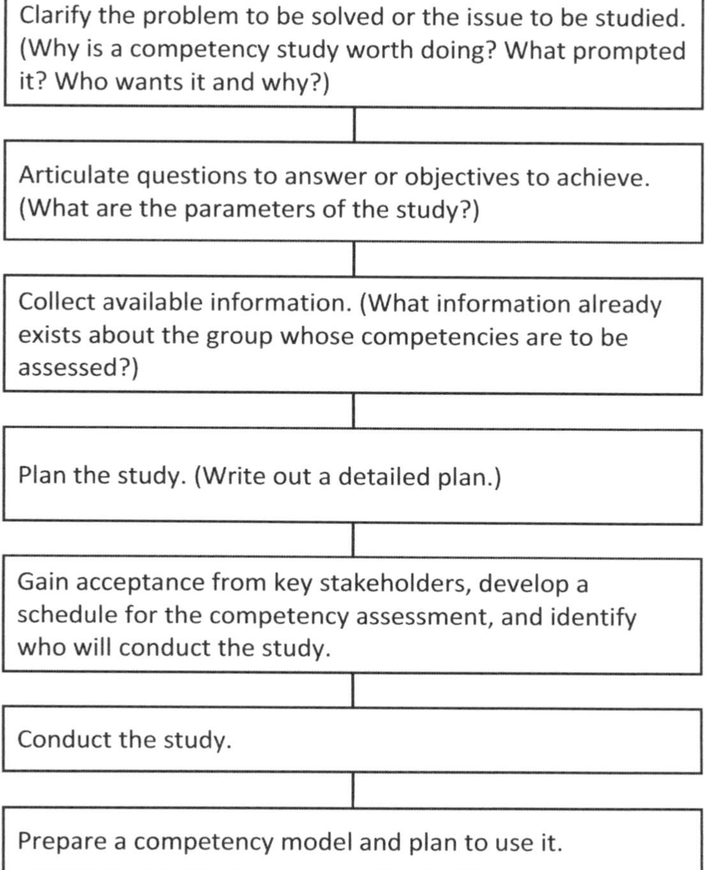
Clarify the problem to be solved or the issue to be studied. (Why is a competency study worth doing? What prompted it? Who wants it and why?)
Articulate questions to answer or objectives to achieve. (What are the parameters of the study?)
Collect available information. (What information already exists about the group whose competencies are to be assessed?)
Plan the study. (Write out a detailed plan.)
Gain acceptance from key stakeholders, develop a schedule for the competency assessment, and identify who will conduct the study.
Conduct the study.
Prepare a competency model and plan to use it.

4. **Plan the study.** Write out a detailed description of the purpose, the questions or issues to be investigated, targeted groups or individuals, sample selection methods, data collection methods, and data analysis methods. In short, put on paper why the competency identification is worth conducting, what results are sought from it, for what group those results are intended, who will use the results, how the results will be used, how the subjects of the study will be selected, how the identification study will be conducted, how the results will be analyzed and interpreted, how the results will be reported, and how they will be used.
5. **Gain acceptance for the plan from key stakeholders, develop a schedule for conducting the competency identification, and identify who will conduct the study.** At this point, it is usually wise to circulate the plan among stakeholders for comment and modification. This helps build support and lets people know about the study. It also builds realistic study expectations. One approach is

to ask external consultants to visit the organization to present their ideas about conducting the identification study. When key stakeholders attend such presentations, they learn about competency identification and begin to decide how they would like to see the identification effort carried out.

6. **Conduct the study itself.** This may involve sending mail (or electronic mail) questionnaires to the targeted exemplary performers who are to serve as study subjects. They may also be interviewed face-to-face, by phone, or by videoteleconference. Most competency identification studies rely on a method called *behavioral events interviewing*.[4] The aim of this method is to isolate the characteristics of exemplary performers in the group targeted for study. For instance, exemplary senior executives would be interviewed in the development of an executive competency model. A sample behavioral events interview questionnaire that can be sent to participants is provided in Exhibit 13-2.

Exhibit 13-2. A Sample Behavioral Events Interview Questionnaire (To Be Mailed/Emailed)

Directions: The HPE specialist should send copies of the following questionnaire to identify exemplary performers in the organization. The results can then be subjected to content analysis as a starting point for developing a list of common themes or competencies underlying the events.

1. What is the most difficult work situation that you have ever encountered in your career? (*Describe what happened, who was involved, and when it happened. Do not provide names, although you may supply job titles.*)

2. Why do you consider this situation the most difficult one you have ever encountered?

An alternative approach to conducting competency identification, called *Rapid Results Assessment*,[5] relies on a group format. Exemplary performers and one or more of their exemplary organizational superiors are assembled in a large room for one or two days. During that time, three facilitators help the group. One facilitator prompts participants to list as many daily activities or responsibilities as possible. A second facilitator writes those activities, responsibilities, or behaviors on 8½" x 11" sheets of paper with a broad-tip marker. A third facilitator posts them on the wall with masking tape. Participants are thus able to see what they have identified. Such group meetings usually begin with identifying and then sequencing observable behaviors, activities, duties, or responsibilities. These are placed on a *Rapid Results Assessment Chart*, which can be refined after the group meetings by eliminating overlapping duties. (A draft chart still requiring refinement is depicted in Exhibit 13-3 on the following page.) Follow-up questionnaires after the meetings help to identify the underlying competencies that allow exemplary performers to carry out those activities, responsibilities, or behaviors.

7. **Prepare a competency model and plan how to use it.** At this point, the model is described to stakeholders. A competency model may be used to integrate all facets of human resources, such as recruiting, selecting, orienting, training, cross-training, retraining, developing, transferring, promoting, and compensating employees.

What Are Some Problems with Using Competency Identification?

There are three key problems with using competency identification as an HPE strategy.

First, definitions of competencies and competency identification vary considerably. It is important to clarify the meanings of these terms early in a competency identification effort. Otherwise, a competency identification may be counterproductive in the same way as a false argument in which people needlessly quarrel over different underlying issues.

Second, approaches to competency identification run the gamut from the quick and dirty to the rigorous, valid, and reliable. Managers sometimes demand rigorous results without allocating sufficient time for a thorough study. In fact, however, quick-and-dirty competency identifications may actually do more harm than good because they can be misleading. To conduct a rigorous study, most organizations have to invest considerable time, money, and staff. Key questions to consider are these:

- What is the reason for conducting the competency identification effort?
- How much rigor is necessary, and why?
- How quickly are the results needed, and why?
- Who will use the results of the competency identification study, and how will those results be used?

Exhibit 13-3. A Draft Rapid Results Assessment Chart

Staff Management													
Expand understanding of the org. through brown bags, etc.	Interview potential staff.	Improve visibility of dept.	Participate in org. committees outside of project activities.	Say something complimentary to staff.	Serve as resource person to staff.	Inform staff of changes that affect them.	Organize informal team-building activities.	Identify local and national expertise.	Recruit competent staff.	Interpret human resources policies for staff.	Facilitate planning meetings with staff.	Prepare and update job descriptions.	Be sensitive to, and rectify, inequities.
Demonstrate consideration and appreciation for employees.	Give and receive constructive feedback.	Resolve staff-related interpersonal problems.	Serve as mediator between staff.	Collaborate with staff and solicit input.	Prioritize staff duties and deadlines.	Assign responsibilities and delegate tasks to appropriate people.	Meet with staff to ensure they are achieving deadlines.	Prioritize project work and manage time effectively.	Provide orientation to new staff.	Conduct training needs assessment.	Ensure that staff have the tools and skills to do the job.	Deliver training sessions.	Empower staff.
Coach and mentor staff.	Consider organizational and individual needs in decision making.	Update professional skills as job changes.	Write performance appraisals.	Promote and facilitate career management with staff.	Set quality performance standards.								
Project Planning													
Monitor and ensure that there are no environmental or safety hazards.	Define project goals.	Define short-term and long-term plans.	Design pilot activities and projects.	Prepare a project baseline.	Conduct cost-benefit analysis.	Monitor and scan for political changes.	Understand holistic view of projects (portfolio).	Foresee security problems and act accordingly.	Design projects.	Establish timelines for projects.	Establish monitoring and evaluation strategy.	Market the project to the local population and/or participants.	Develop a common vision among project staff.

Exhibit 13-3 (continued)

Project Coordination													
Monitor complimentary letters.	Maintain telephone relationships with project sponsors.	Write letters to explain problem resolution.	Write to and communicate with others in a clear, concise, and timely manner.	Contact local administration.	Network with other organization projects.	Communicate with staff and supervisors on project progress.	Clear schedules to deal with emergencies.	Avoid duplication of efforts.	Assess inventory and plan for the future.	Communicate effectively with vendors.	Consult with subject matter experts.		Organize and supervise external consultants.
	Read project-specific publications.	Consult with technical people to see if materials are appropriate.	Control misinformation and reduce rumor mongering.	Make decisions with counterparts.	Anticipate and solve problems and loopholes.	Finesse political issues that might impact project.							
Project Management													
Prepare and assist in technical meetings.	Go on field visits.	Monitor and adjust timelines.	Monitor progress on deadlines.	Expose the project to technical information as appropriate.	Update project log book.	Update logical framework.	Communicate information about project.	Prepare donor reports.	Benchmark with internal and external partners.	Prepare midterms and/or final project evaluations.	Design and edit technical and promotional documents for publication.	Automate and improve components of a process.	Streamline processes.
Console angry people over the phone.	Assess training needs of counterparts and/or participants.	Deliver training sessions for participants.	Keep commodity losses below 5%.	Monitor projects against targets.	Participate in project audits.	Monitor project participant satisfaction.	Prepare participants for project closure or phase-over.	Project closure.					

Exhibit 13-3 (concluded)

Administration and Finance													
Make decisions on materials to buy.	Determine the need for and generate purchase order requests.	Approve expenses and sign checks.	Clarify expectations to vendors.	Negotiate vendor contracts.	Discuss report format with supervisor.	Establish and maintain accounting records.	Analyze and reconcile accounts.	Assess whether an action requires legal consultation.	Review, approve, sign, and forward vendor invoices.	Negotiate diplomatic relations with tenants.	Document department policies.	Consolidate accounting data.	Manage grant compliance.
Understand financial reports.	Create policies and procedures.	Foresee budgetary problems.	Provide feedback to internal customers on costs.	Prepare financial reports.	Monitor budgets.	Review overseas financial reports.	Investigate thefts and losses.	Negotiate and review contracts.	Respond to queries regarding financial reports.				
Representation													
Assist regional fundraisers.	Present a good image of the organization overseas.	Attend formal receptions to represent the organization.	Participate in project-related activities outside the organization.	Accompany on field visits.	Design and make recommendations to visitors.	Represent the organization to government.	Represent project to press.						
Attitude (Part II: To be listed separate from the RRA chart)													
Manage stress.	Maintain confidentiality.	Saying "no" to tasks you can't handle.	Take responsibility on a daily basis.	Learn local language.	Continue to be educated by receiving information from peers.	Manage your supervisor.	Listen without bias to staff.	Learn to deal with different personalities.	List the tasks for the next day.	Efficiently use computer software programs.	Use intuition as well as analysis.	Know how the work fits into the bigger picture.	Model good performance.
Work with staff to uphold quality.	Make mental notes on how to do better.	Prioritize work.	Understand and respect local culture.	Reflect on self-improvement.	Know your shortcomings.	Be accessible to staff.	Maintain a sense of humor.	Know when to ask for help.	Balance work/personal life issues.		Develop skills by keeping up-to-date.		

Internal HPE practitioners are frequently unable to perform rigorous competency identification studies on their own and require expert external consulting assistance, mainly because the process is too time consuming to do right.

The third problem with competency identification is that some managers view it with suspicion. Some managers wonder how they can cultivate such seemingly vague competencies as "customer service ability" or "intellectual flexibility" when these characteristics are described in ways that cannot be easily measured. To overcome this problem, HPE practitioners usually have to lead an organizational effort to go beyond mere competency identification and focus attention on ways of measuring what the competencies are and how they are demonstrated. Like competency identification itself, such an effort may involve balancing the speed and rigor of various approaches.

Improving Employee Selection Methods

Employee selection is the process of choosing employees to do the work. While competency identification helps ensure a match between work and individual, selection is a first step to make that match a reality. Why is selection important? When is employee selection an appropriate focus for an HPE strategy? How are employee selection methods improved? What problems can affect employee selection? This part of the chapter addresses these questions.

Why Is Employee Selection Important?

Employee selection is important for one major reason: it is cheaper and faster to pick people who can perform right away than it is to train them. Everyone wants to pick a winner. However, it is not always clear *who* a winner is or *what competencies* are required of an individual by an organization. In recent years, employee selection has become more complicated due to increasing use of contingent workers and consultants and a simultaneous increase in outsourcing.

Errors in employee selection are costly and time consuming to correct.[6] Correcting a selection error may mean transferring or terminating a worker or changing the worker's responsibilities. Stressful to the manager, correcting a selection error can also demoralize the misplaced worker and his or her coworkers. It also requires the manager to spend unexpected time on recruiting, selecting, and training a replacement or restructuring the way the work is performed.

When Is Employee Selection an Appropriate Focus for an HPE Strategy?

Selecting good performers is never an optional HPE strategy, as some others are. However, special attention should be directed to employee selection methods when the organization makes a radical change in strategy, when a pattern develops in which individuals chosen for work assignments or positions are unable to be trained for them because they lack obvious prequalifications, and when the organization increases its use of contingent workers. Changes in strategy, of course, may produce changes in the desired results of work activities; an inability to be trained, without a protected disability, usually suggests that the selection process is not adequately separating those who meet requirements from those who are lacking. Contingent workers bear little loyalty to their short-term employer and pose special selection challenges.

How Can Employee Selection Methods Be Improved?

To improve employee selection, begin by examining how the organization analyzes work and recruits people. Audit the process. Direct initial attention to questions such as these:

- How are the needs for positions or assignments identified and justified?
- What information about the work must be provided by the organization and by the immediate supervisor?
- Who acts on that information?
- How does he or she act on the information?
- How is information about work vacancies communicated?
- How widely and how effectively is that information communicated?
- From what sources is the organization currently attracting talent? What percentage of new hires is coming from internal sources? External sources? Are some recruitment sources (such as certain schools or companies) predominant?
- How often and how widely are flexible staffing methods used? How well are they used? How are temporary employees selected? How are participants recruited and selected for job sharing, flextime, flexplace, or other versatile staffing methods?
- How much have existing recruitment and selection methods encouraged diversity in the organization?

As a next step, research errors made in selection. What evidence exists about the frequency and location of such errors? To find out, examine personnel records to determine how many people have been transferred, terminated, or demoted. (Realize that not all mismatches are identified easily, since some individuals may resign instead of being terminated for cause.) Like a good detective, an HPE practitioner should interview some or all the managers of former employees to gather additional information about the reasons for these personnel actions.

Then examine existing employee selection policies, procedures, and practices. How has the organization stated that the process should work? To answer that question, flowchart procedures and then collect information about actual practices by shadowing job applicants and interviewing managers about how decisions are made to hire, transfer, or promote. Document what is actually happening.

Frequently, employee selection can be improved by taking these steps:

- training interviewers
- introducing multiple steps and raters in the selection process
- clarifying the meaning of existing selection policies and practices
- broadening recruitment strategies so that qualified applicants are more likely to learn of vacancies

Use the worksheet in Exhibit 13-4 to guide a selection audit.

Exhibit 13-4. A Worksheet to Guide an Audit of Employee Selection Practices

Directions: Use this worksheet as a starting point for examining employee selection practices in an organization. For each question appearing in the left column, collect information about the issue within the organization and then answer the question in the space to the right. Also use the space at right to take notes about possible areas for improvement.

QUESTION	ANSWER or NOTES
How are the needs for positions or assignments identified and justified?	
What information about the work must be provided by the organization and by the immediate supervisor?	
Who acts on that information?	
How does he or she act on the information?	
How is this information about work vacancies communicated?	
How widely and how effectively is that information communicated?	

Exhibit 13-4 (concluded)

QUESTION	ANSWER or NOTES
From what sources is the organization presently attracting talent? What percentage of new hires is coming from internal sources? external sources? Are some recruitment sources (such as certain schools or companies) predominant?	
How often and how widely are flexible staffing methods used? How are temporary employees selected? How are participants recruited and selected for job sharing, flextime, flexplace, or other flexible staffing methods? How often is offshoring used?	
How much have existing recruitment and selection methods served to encourage diversity in the organization?	
What evidence exists about the frequency and location of selection errors?	
Is it possible to improve selection methods by any of the following methods:	
• training interviewers?	
• introducing multiple steps and raters in the decision-making process?	
• communicating and training on selection policies and practices?	
• broadening strategies for recruitment so that qualified applicants are more likely to learn of vacancies?	
• providing feedback to unsuccessful applicants about ways they could improve their knowledge or skills so that they would be more likely to be accepted in the future?	

What Problems Can Affect Employee Selection?

Recruiting and selecting individuals for jobs or assignments is an inexact science. Managers and employee teams must often rely on intuition as much as on facts. However, many common problems can affect the selection process, including the following:

- unwillingness by managers to devote time to the recruitment or selection process
- lack of clarity about what results will be sought from the work or worker
- failure to convert *work* requirements into their related *worker* requirements before the recruitment or selection process begins
- failure to clarify the criteria that must be met by a successful applicant before the selection process begins

To address these problems, HPE practitioners should spearhead efforts to improve the organization's selection process for both jobs and for short-term assignments and conduct training on selection methods. Diversity programs can build awareness of the need to respect differences and make selection decisions accordingly.

Applying Progressive Discipline

Discipline refers to worker compliance with existing policies, procedures, work rules, and other requirements. While recruitment and selection ideally ensure that individuals are initially assigned to jobs or work assignments for which they are well suited, progressive discipline holds people accountable for doing what they are supposed to be doing and achieving the results they are supposed to be achieving.

What is progressive discipline? When is progressive discipline an appropriate focus for HPE strategy? How can progressive disciplinary methods be improved? What problems can hamper the application of progressive discipline as an HPE strategy?

What Is Progressive Discipline?

Progressive discipline is the process of holding individuals accountable, within the constraints of the work environment, for the results they are to achieve. It is *progressive* because individuals are subjected to increasingly severe actions over time if their behavior or work results do not improve.

Discipline may be positive or negative. *Positive discipline* is the basis for individual accountability. It provides people with the information, resources, and other support mechanisms they need to perform and includes informing them of work rules and company policies. Positive discipline establishes the framework for accountability by enabling people to achieve optimum performance and to avoid behaviors, problems, situations, or performance that will lead to negative discipline. *Negative discipline* imposes penalties on individuals who deliberately depart from work rules, company policies, codes of conduct, or desired work results. In a progressive disciplinary system, the penalties become more severe over time if the behavior or performance does not improve.

When Is Progressive Discipline an Appropriate Focus for HPE Strategy?

Positive discipline can be used with all employees to establish a framework for accountability. Inform people what work rules exist, what will happen if the rules are violated, and why they are important. Also inform them about what desired job performance standards exist, what will happen if the standards are not met, how they were established, and why they are important. Often a good employee orientation program can become a basis for establishing individual accountability by informing individuals of work rules and worker responsibilities.

Use negative discipline only when all of the following conditions are met:

- Work rules are deliberately violated without extenuating circumstances.
- Employees fail to achieve minimum job performance standards in a reasonable time, even though they are trained on what to do and how to do it.
- Sufficient evidence exists to identify the perpetrator.
- The perpetrator is or was aware of the work rule(s).
- The perpetrator is or was aware of the consequences of violating the work rule(s).

Examples of appropriate occasions for imposing negative discipline include excessive absenteeism, tardiness, insubordination, theft, horseplay, and sabotage.

Negative discipline may also be applied to employees who, although given adequate training and resources, choose not to achieve reasonable work results.

The important point to remember is that it is fair to hold individuals accountable for their own actions, but it is unfair to hold them accountable for matters beyond their control. Negative discipline should therefore be avoided when management has failed to do the following:

- establish work rules
- communicate work rules
- explain the reasons underlying work rules
- establish job performance standards or work expectations
- communicate the job performance standards or work expectations
- consistently apply work rules or job performance standards

Managers, like employees, should be held accountable for their action—or inaction. If managers themselves violate work rules, they should receive the same disciplinary treatment to which other workers are subject. After all, management must model compliance with work rules and job performance standards if they are to maintain the credibility essential to leadership.

How Can Progressive Disciplinary Methods Be Improved?

Often it is wise to form a project team consisting of relevant stakeholders to establish disciplinary procedures. A project team charged with reviewing disciplinary practices may consist of representatives from line (operating) management, the human resources function, and the legal function. If the organization is team based and if teams carry out member discipline, then team representatives should be included. If the organization is unionized, then an HPE strategy must be pursued within the framework of existing collective bargaining agreements.

To improve progressive disciplinary processes, a project team can audit current policy and practice, beginning by directing attention to questions such as these:

- Does a progressive disciplinary policy exist, and is it clearly understood?
- Has the disciplinary policy been communicated to managers, supervisors, and employees?
- Do procedures exist that are associated with the policy?
- Are the procedures well understood?
- Are employees routinely informed of work rules or job performance standards early in their employment with the organization or early in their assignments?
- Are employees informed about the consequences of violating work rules or failing to achieve job performance standards?
- Is it clear who should hold employees accountable?
- Have those to whom employees are accountable been trained to apply disciplinary policy consistently and follow procedures?

Find out about the most common disciplinary problems by interviewing team members, supervisors, managers, and others who deal with large groups of employees on a daily basis. Pose questions such as these:

- What are the most common employee behavior problems you encounter?
- What are the most difficult employee behavior problems you encounter?
- How are you handling those problems?
- What recommendations would you make to solve the problems?

Then examine personnel records to find out why employees are being documented and how those problems are resolved.

Last, review existing progressive disciplinary policies and procedures. How should the disciplinary process work? Answer that question, in part, by flowcharting existing disciplinary procedures.

Part Five: Evaluating Results

CHAPTER 1: Why Training Is Not Enough

CHAPTER 2: What Is Human Performance Enhancement (HPE)?

CHAPTER 3: Transforming a Training Department into a Human Performance Enhancement (HPE) Department

CHAPTER 4: Analyzing *What Is* Happening

CHAPTER 5: Envisioning *What Should Be* Happening

CHAPTER 6: Clarifying Present and Future Performance Gaps

CHAPTER 7: Determining the Importance of Performance Gaps

CHAPTER 8: Identifying the Underlying Causes of Performance Gaps

CHAPTER 9: Selecting Human Performance Enhancement (HPE) Strategies

CHAPTER 10: Implementing Human Performance Enhancement (HPE) Strategies to Address Organizational Environment Problems or Opportunities

CHAPTER 11: Implementing Human Performance Enhancement (HPE) Strategies to Address Work Problems or Opportunities

CHAPTER 12: Implementing Human Performance Enhancement (HPE) Strategies to Address Work Environment Problems or Opportunities

CHAPTER 13: Implementing Human Performance Enhancement (HPE) Strategies to Address Worker Problems or Opportunities

CHAPTER 14: Evaluating Human Performance Enhancement (HPE) Strategies

Chapter 14
Evaluating Human Performance Enhancement (HPE) Strategies

Evaluating training continues to be a timely issue. Top managers are no longer willing to sponsor training for training's sake or to take training's value on faith. They demand accountability. They are also demanding evidence that training produces change that translates into bottom-line results.[1]

The same concern surrounds other HPE strategies. Canny HPE practitioners plan to field evaluative questions from the time they initiate HPE strategies. They also work to show the value of their efforts even when nobody demands it. The wisest HPE practitioners establish a framework for accountability during the selection and implementation of HPE strategies and ensure the personal involvement of key decision makers in choosing bottom-line measures to demonstrate the value of their efforts. It is, after all, far easier to secure acceptance of measurement criteria before the implementation of an HPE strategy rather than after. Establishing desired results before a change effort also provides measurable goals for which to strive.

What is evaluation? How do HPE strategy evaluation methods resemble training evaluation methods? How do they differ? What competencies should HPE practitioners possess to enact the role of HPE evaluator? This final chapter addresses these important questions.

What Is Evaluation?

Evaluation is the process of placing value.[2] A *value,* in turn, is a "belief about what is good or bad, important or unimportant."[3] Indeed, "values beget attitudes, which specify behavior. The values of those who hold power fundamentally shape the character of an organization."[4]

Evaluating HPE strategy is the process of placing value on results. It can occur before, during, or after HPE strategy implementation. Timing is thus an issue in evaluation. *Forecasting* is the process of predicting the results of an HPE strategy; it precedes implementation.[5] *Formative evaluation* occurs at the end of a small-scale tryout (pilot) of the HPE strategy.[6] *Concurrent evaluation* occurs during implementation of the HPE strategy, and *summative evaluation* occurs after the implementation.[7]

Evaluation is carried out for four reasons:

1. It yields information about *what changes* resulted from HPE strategy.
2. It provides information about *how much change* resulted from HPE strategy.

3. It suggests *what value* can be placed on the change that occurred.
4. It suggests *how much value* can be assigned to those changes.[8]

How Do HPE Strategy Evaluation Methods Resemble Training Evaluation Methods?

In the most general sense, HPE evaluation resembles training evaluation. After all, training is an HPE strategy. It may therefore be useful to frame this discussion by reviewing training evaluation methods.

Levels of Training Evaluation

Donald Kirkpatrick is generally credited with developing a key conceptual model to govern training evaluation.[9] His model, which has been widely adopted since 1960, remains a convenient and easily understandable way to think about evaluation in general. Kirkpatrick's model describes four levels of evaluation: participant reaction, participant learning, participant on-the-job behavior, and organizational results.

Participant reaction is the lowest level on Kirkpatrick's hierarchy. It addresses this key question: *How much did participants like the training experience?* Approaches to measuring participant reactions include end-of-course attitude questionnaires and questionnaires sent to participants following the training experience (an example of an open-ended questionnaire is shown in Exhibit 14-1). Training and development professionals can also measure participant reactions by conducting follow-up surveys of participants by telephone, electronic mail, or focus group.

Evaluating training by measuring participant reactions is easy, fast, and inexpensive. Unfortunately, the results do not necessarily satisfy top managers or others who assess the bottom-line impact of training or calculate the return on training investments because the results focus on participant likes and dislikes rather than on the training's job-related or organizationally related impact. Participants may "like" useless but entertaining training and "dislike" boring but useful training.

Participant learning occupies the second level on Kirkpatrick's hierarchy. It addresses this key question: *How much did participants learn from the training experience?* Attempts to measure participant learning have traditionally been less common than attempts to measure participant reactions. Approaches to measuring learning include paper-and-pencil tests and on-the-job performance demonstrations. Training and development professionals can also measure participant learning by administering oral questions to participants after the training is delivered.

Measuring participant learning establishes accountability for the training and development professionals who designed and delivered the training. However, many adults do not enjoy test taking. They may experience test anxiety or wonder what employment decisions may be made on the basis of the test results. Test anxiety is particularly acute among employees of organizations that have recently undergone downsizing, where employees fear that tests may factor into decisions about who will be laid off. Nor are

Exhibit 14-1. A Sample Participant Evaluation

Directions: Complete the following evaluation at the end of the training session. Circle the number at the right that most closely approximates your feelings about the statement in the left column. Use the following scale:

5 = Strongly Agree
4 = Agree
3 = Neither Agree nor Disagree
2 = Disagree
1 = Strongly Disagree

There are no right or wrong answers in any absolute sense. Mark your response quickly, since your first reaction is most likely to reflect your genuine feelings.

	Strongly Agree	Agree	Neither Agree nor Disagree	Disagree	Strongly Disagree
1. This training course had a clearly defined purpose.	5	4	3	2	1
2. This training course had clearly defined objectives.	5	4	3	2	1
3. The structure of this training course was clear from the outset.	5	4	3	2	1
4. This training course was clearly related to my job.	5	4	3	2	1
5. I feel that I learned much in this training course.	5	4	3	2	1
6. I will apply what I learned back on my job.	5	4	3	2	1
7. I am confident that my coworkers will support the on-the-job application of what I learned in this training course.	5	4	3	2	1
8. I am confident that my supervisor will support the on-the-job application of what I learned in this training course.	5	4	3	2	1

9. What were the chief benefits of this training course?

10. What areas need improvement in this training course?

11. If I were asked to prove how this training would improve my job performance in measurable ways, I would suggest:

tests more useful than participant reactions in satisfying the desire of top managers to calculate the financial return on training investments; the results focus on participant learning, but, unfortunately, participants may "learn" from useless training.

Participant on-the-job behavior occupies the third level on Kirkpatrick's hierarchy. It addresses this key question: *How much did participants change their behavior on the job because of a training experience?* Attempts to measure participant on-the-job behavioral change have traditionally been even less frequent than attempts to measure participant learning. Approaches to measuring on-the-job behavioral change include follow-up questionnaires sent to participants; their organizational subordinates; their organizational superiors; and customers, suppliers, and distributors. Training and development professionals can also measure on-the-job behavioral change through unobtrusive measures such as examinations of participants' performance appraisals or of work results.

Evaluating training by measuring participant on-the-job behavioral change has the advantage of establishing a basis of accountability for the participants. It may show that changes begun in training (because of new learning) have carried over to the job. However, establishing a definitive correlation between training and job behavior change has long been problematic, since many variables besides training influence how individuals behave on their jobs. The amount of support they receive from coworkers and immediate organizational superiors may significantly influence changes begun in training. Unfortunately, well-designed training may end up yielding no change on the job because conditions in any of the four performance quadrants do not support that change. On the other hand, ill-designed training may yield significant change if working conditions support it.

The fourth and highest level of Kirkpatrick's hierarchy is organizational results. It addresses this key question: *How much did training affect the organization?* Measuring the organizational results of training means determining the financial returns on training investments. How well did the training translate into a favorable ratio of outputs to inputs? What measurable gains in the bottom line were realized by the organization as a result of the training?

Assessing the organizational results of training has traditionally been the least commonly used method of training evaluation. One reason is that it is usually time consuming and expensive to do. A second reason is that there are no foolproof approaches—although many training and development professionals continue to seek a quick-and-dirty (and bulletproof) approach to it. A third reason is that, even when evidence of organizational results from training can be offered, it may not be convincing to skeptical decision makers and stakeholders; there is an important difference between *accumulating evidence* and *rendering unquestionable proof.* Decision makers may disbelieve the evidence submitted, particularly when it comes from self-interested training and development professionals who conceived and evaluated the training effort.

Approaches to measuring organizational results vary. One approach is to specify, before training is conducted, exactly what measurable on-the-job and organizational results are sought. Key decision makers should have a part in such an effort, which may be undertaken by a project team. Of particular importance are the measurable instructional objectives of the training effort, since they provide a clear statement of the desired results. These can be enhanced to include desired and measurable organizational changes that should eventually result from the training.

Evaluating training by measuring organizational results offers the advantage of establishing a basis of accountability for the organization. It can also reveal where future investments may have a significant payoff. However, these advantages should be weighed against the time, money, and effort involved in measuring the return. That does not come inexpensively or effortlessly.

The Four Levels of HPE Strategy Evaluation

Kirkpatrick's evaluation model lends itself to HPE strategy evaluation with only minor modifications in keeping with a new focus on performance enhancement and on change. The refitted levels might be called Rothwell's four levels for evaluating HPE strategy:

- **Level 1:** Worker satisfaction with the HPE strategy
- **Level 2:** Work results of the HPE strategy
- **Level 3:** Work environment results of the HPE strategy
- **Level 4:** Organizational results of the HPE strategy

These levels are tied to the four concentric circles that make up the four performance quadrants discussed throughout this book (see Exhibit 14-2). They tie evaluation to the intended results of the HPE strategy and to the four levels of performance.

Level 1 focuses on worker satisfaction with the HPE strategy. Like the Kirkpatrick model, it addresses this question: *How well do the participants like the change strategy?* Since HPE can use many methods, the question can refer to one or more strategies, including organized efforts to improve feedback, rewards and incentives, selection policies, organizational policies and procedures, job aids, and employee training efforts. As in collecting information about participant satisfaction following training, Level 1 measurement methods rely on satisfaction questionnaires, focus groups, or other methods that have been well developed in measuring customer satisfaction. The disadvantage of focusing on worker satisfaction is that, as with training evaluations, workers may "like" or "dislike" HPE strategies for the wrong reasons. Since the aim of an HPE strategy is to enhance human performance, any criterion for assessing satisfaction other than its impact on performance is usually inappropriate. The best approach is to confine questions about worker satisfaction to perceptions about how well an HPE strategy contributed to human performance enhancement.

Level 2 focuses on work results. Like Kirkpatrick's level 3, it directs attention to this question: *How well did the HPE strategy achieve measurable performance improvement at the work level?* As in Level 1, Level 2 involves measuring more than one category of HPE strategy. If more than one HPE strategy is being evaluated, it will usually be necessary to aggregate the results. To complicate matters, many variables may influence HPE strategies at the work level. Probably the best that can be hoped for is to achieve a "best

Exhibit 14-2. Levels of HPE Strategy Evaluation

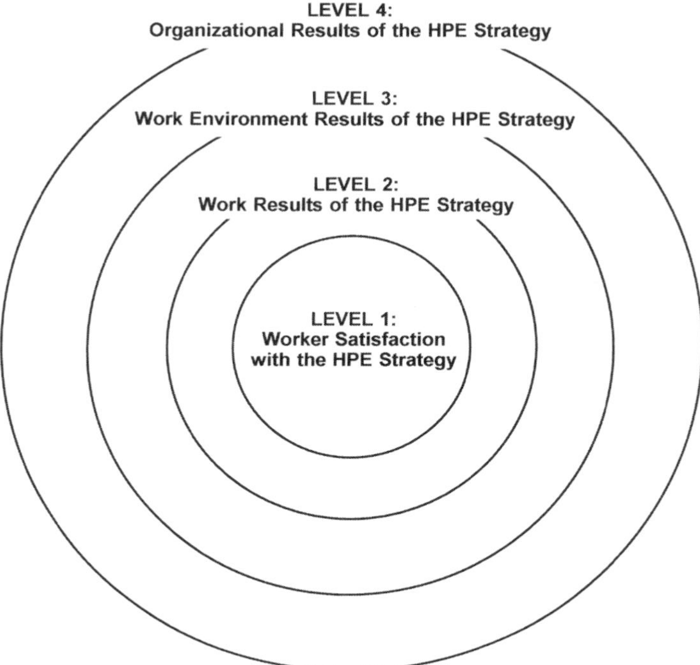

guess" approximation of productivity improvements resulting from the HPE strategy at the work level.

Level 3 evaluation focuses on work environment results of the HPE strategy. This level is akin to Kirkpatrick's Level 4. It directs attention to this question: *How well did the HPE strategy achieve measurable performance improvement for the organization?* The aim is to calculate a return on the overall investment in the HPE strategy, even if the strategy involved using multiple change levers, such as job aids, selection improvement efforts, feedback improvement efforts, training, or reward or incentive improvement efforts. Another aim is to assess how much the HPE strategy helped the organization implement its corporate strategy and thus achieve organizational strategic goals.

Level 4 evaluation focuses on organizational environment results of the HPE strategy. This level has no counterpart in Kirkpatrick's hierarchy. It directs attention to this question: *How well did the HPE strategy achieve measurable performance improvement at the competitive level?* The aim is to calculate how much the HPE strategy helped the organization improve customer service, achieve a competitive edge, anticipate external environmental change, and beat competitors to the punch. This level is immensely difficult to quantify, but it can be evaluated through success stories or other means.[10]

How Do HPE Strategy Evaluation Methods Differ from Training Evaluation Methods?

As might be gleaned from the preceding section, a key difference exists between HPE strategy evaluation and training evaluation. Training evaluation, as described by Kirkpatrick's model, focuses on *planned learning* and its impact on participants, job behaviors, and organizational results. HPE strategy evaluation, as described by my model, focuses on *planned HPE and change.* My model is thus inherently directed to measuring bottom-line results as well as strategic impact.

What Step-by-Step Models Can Guide HPE Evaluation Strategy?

Models are useful, and they can also be fun. They help conceptualize what to do and how to do it. A step-by-step model to guide HPE evaluation strategy may be helpful to HPE practitioners faced with conducting HPE evaluation.

A key point should be emphasized, however: *It is advisable to establish performance goals to guide an HPE strategy before it is implemented.* Decisions about implementing or foregoing an HPE strategy (or combination of strategies) should be made *before* action is taken.

There are several reasons for this advice. Such a practice is economical, focusing the organization's resources on those areas in which the greatest gains are likely to be made. In addition, specifying desired results in advance establishes accountability for HPE practitioners and builds ownership between key stakeholders and decision makers in achieving results. Ownership is more difficult to create after training is conducted, selection methods have been changed, or any other HPE strategy has already been undertaken.

That is not to say that it is impossible to conduct concurrent or after-the-fact evaluation. What follows are three different models for evaluating HPE strategy. The first model should be used before an HPE strategy is implemented, the second model should be used during implementation, and the third model should be used when the HPE strategy has been in place long enough to judge outcomes.

Model 1: Forecasting the Results of HPE Strategy

Forecasting the results of an HPE strategy is done at the time a strategy or combination of strategies is selected and before the strategy is implemented (see Exhibit 14-3).

Exhibit 14-3. A Model for Forecasting the Results of HPE Strategy

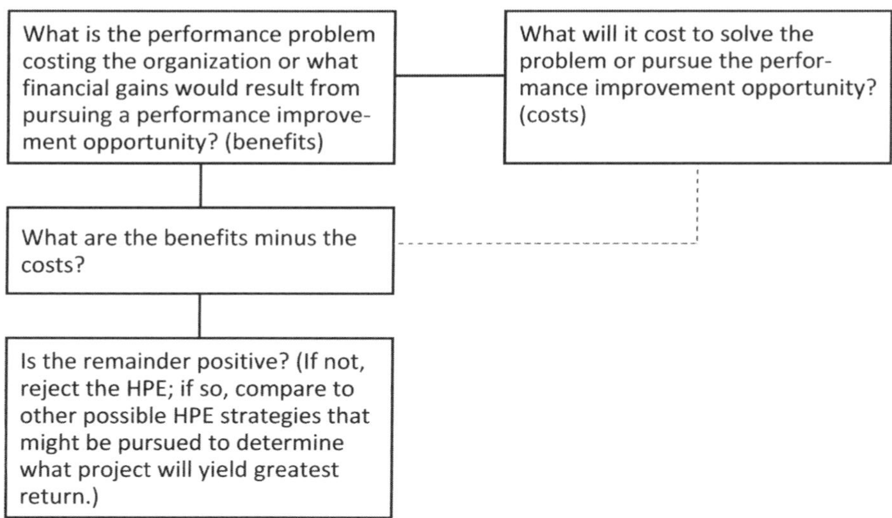

If the HPE strategy is undertaken to solve a human performance problem, estimate what that problem is costing the organization. Base the estimate on the consequences of the problem, such as lost business, lost production, or scrap. If that is not clear, ask decision makers how they know that a problem exists. Their answer will shed light on what to measure. Then estimate what it will cost the organization to solve the problem. Include costs associated with clarifying the problem, identifying possible HPE strategies, and implementing the HPE strategies. Compare the costs of solving the problem to the expected benefits. Take action only if the cost-benefit ratio shows that estimated benefits will outweigh estimated costs. To identify the costs and benefits associated with the HPE strategy, interview line managers, employees, customers, distributors, suppliers, or other key groups that may have the necessary information. Use an interview guide like the one in Exhibit 14-4 as a starting point to surface the costs and benefits associated with the HPE strategy.

An alternative strategy is to form a task force of stakeholders and ask them to identify measurable objectives to be achieved by the end of the HPE strategy. Those objectives should be expressed as increased units of production, measurable improvements on customer satisfaction surveys, or other results acceptable to task force members. Use the interview guide in Exhibit 14-4 to clarify measurable results with the members of the task force before the HPE strategy is undertaken. Then communicate those results beyond the task force so that other decision makers have the opportunity to comment and accept ownership in the measures.

Exhibit 14-4. An Interview Guide for Surfacing the Costs and Benefits of HPE Strategy

Directions: Select individuals inside and outside the organization who are familiar with the human performance problem to be solved or the human performance enhancement opportunity to be pursued. Pose the following questions to them.

1. What is the problem to be solved, or what is the opportunity to be pursued? (*Describe it.*)

2. What is the problem costing the organization, or what benefits could be realized by pursuing a human performance enhancement? Indicate how it can be *measured* in financial terms. What information is available about the actual costs or benefits of the problem or opportunity? Where was that information obtained and how reliable is it?

3. What will it cost to solve the problem or pursue the human performance enhancement opportunity? (You may wish to suggest some possible ways to solve the problem or pursue the opportunity. Then estimate the costs for analyzing the problem/opportunity, implementing an HPE strategy, and evaluating results.)

4. What is the estimated difference between benefits (item 2) and costs (item 3)? Subtract item 3 from item 2.

5. Is the remainder expressed in item 4 negative? If so, reject the project. If it is positive, consider the project. However, compare the expected return from this project to other possible projects that the organization may be considering. Prioritize them on the basis of expected rate or return.

Model 2: Conducting Concurrent Evaluation of HPE Strategy

Think of concurrent evaluation as a continuous improvement effort. Use the model in Exhibit 14-5 to guide the evaluation process as the HPE strategy is implemented.

Exhibit 14-5. A Model for Conducting Concurrent Evaluation of HPE Strategy

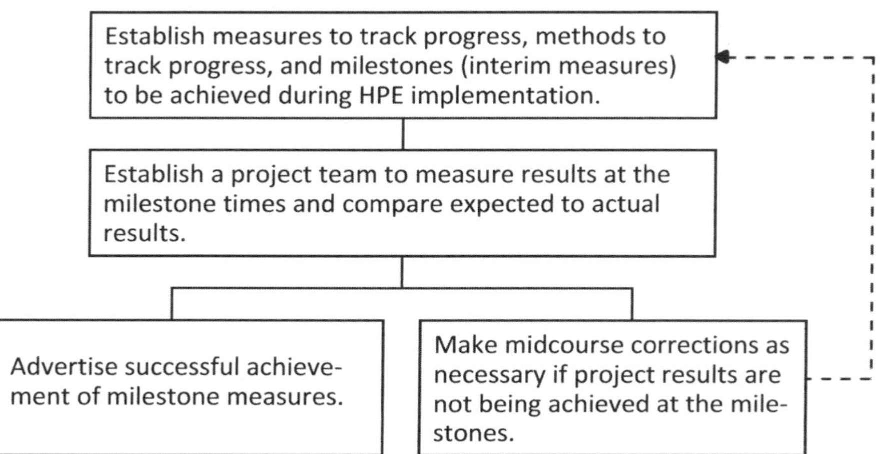

As a first step, establish methods to track measurable financial results as they are realized. If possible, establish *milestones*—that is, interim points during the HPE strategy implementation to measure progress toward an ultimate goal of financial savings and gains. A milestone, for instance, might be on-the-job cost savings or productivity gains realized following the delivery of three of five training sessions or six months after a new reward program has been implemented. Nonfinancial measures, such as improvements in customer satisfaction ratings during HPE strategy implementation, can also be used. Specify in the milestones *how* the results will be measured and exactly what the results should be. The desired results should have been established during the selection of the HPE strategy and expressed as measurable results to be achieved. This process is akin to establishing organizational strategic objectives and tracking progress against them.

Ask stakeholders to help establish the milestones, the desirable points in time at which to measure results, and the measurement methods to use. If possible, form a standing task force or review committee to receive progress reports during implementation. Use the task force as a quality improvement team to help make program corrections when the results of the HPE strategy do not match expectations.

Model 3: Evaluating Outcomes of HPE Strategy

Evaluate outcomes by comparing the measurable objectives established before implementation to the results achieved after the strategy has been in place for a reasonable time. It is difficult to establish a definitive "end" for an HPE strategy, since it may have a long duration. Use the model depicted in Exhibit 14-6 to guide the evaluation process.

Exhibit 14-6. A Model for Evaluating the Outcomes of HPE Strategy

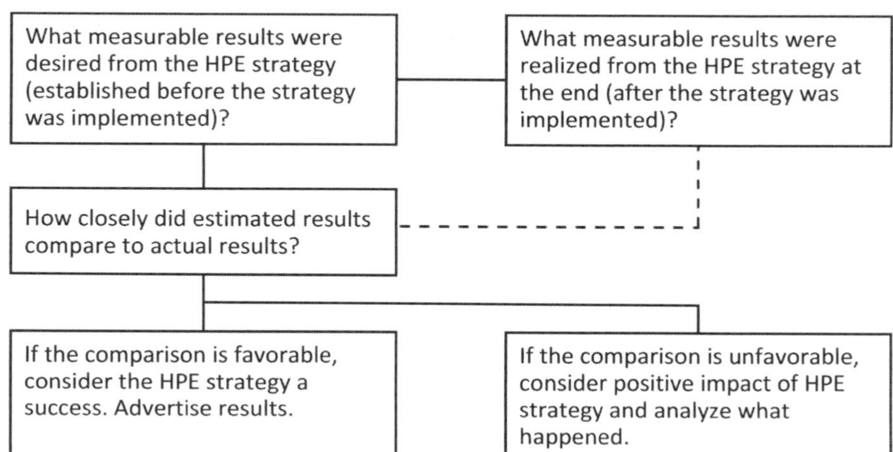

If the HPE strategy is intended to be semi-permanent, as may be the case with a safety training program, a job aid, or a salary bonus program, then a summative evaluation may be necessary only when a major change affects the strategic goals and objectives of the organization. In practical terms, an HPE strategy may not be evaluated for final outcomes for several years. (However, concurrent evaluation should continue even when final outcomes are not evaluated.) Decision makers may request final outcome evaluations of training, but they only rarely make such requests for other HPE strategies.

Evaluating the outcomes of HPE strategy should be a straightforward process, provided that measurable objectives were established before implementation and the results were tracked during implementation. If objectives were not established before implementation, which is too often the case, it will be necessary to clarify afterward what measurable results were achieved. Then evidence of results should be solicited from participants, such as those who attended training sessions, users of jobs aids, stakeholders in reward and incentive systems, or stakeholders of a selection effort. One approach is to solicit "success" and "failure" stories from participants/users about the HPE strategy and its results. The stories may suggest appropriate measures to apply to the HPE strategy. They may also provide evidence of measurable results. Exhibit 14-7 provides a questionnaire designed to solicit such stories.

Exhibit 14-7. A Questionnaire to Surface Success and Failure Stories about the Outcomes of HPE Strategy

Directions: Use this approach to collect information about the results of any HPE strategy after it has been implemented. Select participants or stakeholders in the HPE strategy. Then pose the questions below to the stakeholders through interview or questionnaire. Later, compile an overall summary report to indicate success cases. If you wish, go back to the stakeholders or participants to verify financial savings or benefits claimed.

1. Since participating in (name the HPE strategy, such as an effort to improve feedback to individuals, provide job-related training, or match rewards and incentives to desired results), describe one situation in which you have been personally involved that dramatized the impact of the change in a positive or negative way.

   Describe the situation here:

2. What happened as a result of the situation? In other words, what were the consequences of the situation?

   Describe the consequences here:

3. How would you characterize the situation? Was it positive (it helped the organization improve performance) or negative (it failed to help the organization improve performance)?

   Circle one: **POSITIVE** **NEGATIVE**

   Explain why you believe the situation or its consequences were positive or negative.

4. If you were asked to place a price tag on the consequences of this situation, what would it be? Estimate the financial gain/loss to the organization in *this situation only*. Be sure to provide a brief explanation of how you computed the return/loss.

What Research Has Been Done on Evaluating HPE, and What Has It Shown?

Much has been written about evaluating HPE interventions,[11] but little data-based research is publicly available about it. (That is not to say that there is none. The best research is available only to those who work with leading consulting firms, which periodically survey their own members and then provide the results only to those who participated in the survey and in the services of the consulting firm.)

But bear in mind that measurement is key to the mindset of HPE. It is best to determine the cost of a performance problem and its likely benefits before selecting an intervention. Indeed, HPE interventions should be regarded as investments. For that reason, their relative value should be assessed before they are selected.

The Competencies of the HPE Evaluator

When filling the role of HPE evaluator (see Appendix I), the HPE practitioner evaluates results before, during, and after HPE strategy implementation. Although it is only one of ten roles for the HPE practitioner, it is by no means the least important; evaluation results should be cycled back as a driver for continuous performance improvement (CPI). To carry out the role, HPE practitioners need four key competencies:

- **Ability to evaluate or coordinate evaluation of human performance enhancement strategies, integrating evaluation processes with organizational strategy evaluation.** This competency links HPE strategy evaluation to organizational strategy evaluation. When displaying this competency, HPE practitioners report the outcomes of HPE strategy to key decision makers in bottom-line terms related to the organization's strategic goals and objectives. Making the connection between HPE and organizational strategy may require HPE practitioners to work with the organization's key decision makers and strategists.
- **Ability to evaluate, or coordinate evaluation of, human performance enhancement strategies, integrating evaluation processes with corporate culture, structure, and politics.** It is not enough to tie HPE strategy to organizational strategy. Within the organization, HPE professionals must integrate HPE evaluation strategy with corporate culture, structure, and politics. Recall that *corporate culture* refers to the unspoken assumptions about what works and what does not work. It stems from the collective institutional experience of the organization and its members, and it is an aftereffect of organizational learning. *Structure* refers to reporting relationships; *politics* refers to the exercise of power in the organization. Competent HPE professionals should be aware of the unique corporate culture in which they work and the implications of reporting relationships and politics on perceptions of HPE strategy evaluation results. What activities or results are particularly prized in the organization? How are results best presented? Whose opinions have greatest import, and why? Such

issues should be considered when planning, implementing, and evaluating HPE strategy and presenting the results.

- **Ability to evaluate, or coordinate evaluation of, human performance enhancement strategies, integrating evaluation processes with work processes and work methods.** Evaluating HPE strategy is most effective when evaluation results shed light on new ways to approach the work. For this reason, HPE practitioners can communicate the results of HPE strategy evaluation to workers in terms tied to their work. That may require continuing dialogue with workers about the impact of HPE strategy on what they do, how they do it, and what results they obtain.
- **Ability to evaluate, or coordinate the evaluation of, human performance enhancement strategies, giving each worker a say in evaluation processes and in feeding results back into future human performance enhancement strategies.** The results of HPE strategy evaluation should be presented to each worker. Feedback at the individual level is a powerful HPE strategy in its own right, and evaluation results can be used in practical terms to stimulate ideas about performance enhancement. Moreover, workers should be involved and empowered when HPE strategies are directed at them. Depending on what HPE strategy is evaluated, approaches to involving workers may differ. However, one approach is to establish a standing task force composed of workers from many organizational levels and charge them with finding ways to communicate and feed back the results of HPE strategy evaluation to all workers in the organization.

Epilogue: What Is the Future of HPE?

This book has been a manual for transforming the training department into a human performance enhancement department. Although written primarily for training and development professionals, the book can also be useful to—and applied by—operating managers working to improve human performance and to standing committees formed to address HPE in an organization.

Operating managers bear the lion's share of responsibility for creating a high-performance workplace. Increasingly, operating managers are directly responsible for selecting, implementing, and evaluating HPE strategy on their own. It is time for them—as well as trainers-turned-HPE practitioners—to carry the message of this book into the trenches and onto the firing line of today's fast-paced organizations.

But what does the future of HPE hold in store? While trends are difficult to predict with certainty, consider three trends that may affect HPE:

1. Technology will facilitate the process.
2. Operating managers will increasingly expect it of training and development professionals.
3. HPE will focus beyond mere organizational measures to consider other impacts—on individuals, families, communities, and others.

First, technology will facilitate the process. Software already exists to facilitate decision making in HPE. Indeed, HPE consultants should check out ADVISOR P.I.™ (see http://www.bnhexpertsoft.com/english/products/advpi/overview.htm). According to the website, the software "is a decision support tool. It conducts a needs analysis of a performance deficiency (gap) and recommends the most cost-effective solutions. Solutions considered by ADVISOR P.I. include training, job aids, job/process/ organization re-design, new/ improved incentive system, polices/procedures, tools, hiring practices, communication plan and others. ADVISOR P.I. is based on the published work of several experts in the field of Human Performance Technology. It uses a systematic process for improving performance in the workplace." The author predicts that more such software will become available, offering support for anyone who wishes to apply the HPE mindset to human problems in workplace settings.

Second, operating managers will increasingly expect it of training and development professionals. While operating managers may still inappropriately request training, more operating managers are growing more savvy about the range of strategies available to solve human performance problems. Hence, they know that training is not always a preferred, or even cost-effective, performance enhancement strategy. They are increasingly likely to request alternative solutions—and even forecasts of the costs and benefits of various HPE strategies before they are implemented.

Third and finally, the author predicts that HPE will begin to focus beyond mere organizational measures to consider other impacts—on individuals, families, communities, and others. While cost-benefit and ROI may be important to stakeholders, stockholders, and managers, these groups are not the only ones involved in—or standing to benefit from—HPE interventions. Increasingly, individuals will ask how performance intervention strategies will impact them, affecting their work-life balance. Moreover, increased sensitivity to ethical issues will drive HPE practitioners to consider the broader impact of their efforts on communities and other groups affected by intervention strategies.

Still, the future is bright for those who are poised to take advantage of it. Enjoy it.

Appendix I.

Core Competencies for Human Performance Enhancement (HPE) Practitioners

Core Competencies for Human Performance Enhancement Practitioners

Steps in the New HPE Model	Role Name for HPE Practitioners	Corresponding HPE Core Competencies			
		Organizational Environment (*World Outside the Organization)*	Work Environment (*World Inside the Organization*)	Work (*Transformation Processes*)	Worker (*People Performing the Work*)
[1] Analyze what is happening	Auditor	• Ability to examine needs and expectations of customers, suppliers, distributors, and stakeholders.	• Ability to formulate, assess, and convert organizational plans to HPE efforts. • Ability to key improvement efforts to organizational mission and strategy • Ability to identify organizational strengths and weaknesses	• Ability to examine workflow within and between depart-ments • Ability to detect bottlenecks in work processing	• Ability to assess the competencies of workers • Ability to assess workforce supply
[2] Envision what should be happening	Visionary	• Ability to identify customer needs and expectations • Ability to detect threats and opportunities in the organizational environment	• Ability to modify criteria of high-performance work organizations to one corporate culture • Ability to identify employee needs and expectations	• Ability to clarify ways to improve workflow to achieve break-through productivity increases	• Ability to forecast future competencies • Ability to assess workforce needs

Core Competencies for Human Performance Enhancement Practitioners (continued)

[2] Envision what should be happening (concluded)		• Ability to locate world-class benchmarks of organizational performance			
[3] Clarify present and future gaps	Gap Assessor	• Ability to compare *what is* and *what should be* in the organization's interactions with the external environment	• Ability to compare *what is* and *what should be* in the organization's internal operations	• Ability to compare *what is* and *what should be* in work processing	• Ability to compare the difference between *what is* and *what should be* at the individual level • Ability to detect mismatch between individual and job in which she or he is placed
[4] Determine the present and future importance of the gaps	Human Performance Enhancement Facilitator	• Ability to determine the importance of gaps between *what is* and *what should be* in the organization's interactions with the external environment	• Ability to determine the importance of gaps between *what is* and *what should be* within the organization	• Ability to determine the importance of gaps between *what is* and *what should be* in work processing	• Ability to determine the importance of gaps between what the worker can do and what the worker should be able to do

Core Competencies for Human Performance Enhancement Practitioners (continued)

[5] Identify the underlying cause(s) of gaps	Strategic Troubleshooter	• Ability to isolate strategic mismatches in the organization's interactions with the external environment • Ability to benchmark other organizations in the industry or "best-in-class" organizations	• Ability to isolate large-scale and small-scale cause(s) of gaps within the organization	• Ability to troubleshoot the cause(s) of gaps in the work or workflow	• Ability to troubleshoot the cause(s) of performance gaps between worker and other performance environments
[6] Select performance enhancement strategies, individually or collectively, that close the gap(s) by addressing their cause(s)	Human Performance Enhancement Methods Specialist	• Ability to identify possible human performance enhancement strategies • Ability to benchmark/compare the application of HPE strategies in other organizations and in one corporate culture	• Ability to excite enthusiasm among others about planning and implementing HPE strategies on an organizational scale • Ability to involve and empower others in the process of selecting HPE strategies on an organizational scale	• Ability to excite enthusiasm among others about planning and implementing HPE strategies specific to work methods or processes • Ability to involve and empower others in the process of selecting HPE strategies linked to the work	• Ability to identify and apply HPE strategies at the level of the individual worker • Ability to involve and empower the worker in the process of selecting HPE strategies linked to the individual

Core Competencies for Human Performance Enhancement Practitioners (continued)

[7] Assess the likely outcomes of implementation to minimize negative side effects and maximize results	Forecaster of Consequences	• Ability to forecast the *likely consequences* of HPE strategies as they may eventually affect relations with customers, suppliers, distributors, and other external stakeholders	• Ability to forecast the *likely consequences* of HPE strategies as they may eventually affect intergroup and intragroup relations inside the organization	• Ability to forecast the *likely consequences* of HPE strategies as they may eventually affect work methods and processes	• Ability to forecast the *likely consequences* of HPE strategies as they may eventually affect individuals and their performance
[8] Establish an action plan for the implementation of the performance enhancement strategies	Action Plan Facilitator	• Ability to prepare and coordinate the preparation of action plans for HPE, integrating them with organizational strategic plans	• Ability to prepare and coordinate the preparation of action plans for HPE, integrating them with organizational culture, structure, and politics	• Ability to prepare and coordinate the preparation of action plans for HPE, integrating them with work processes and methods	• Ability to prepare and coordinate the preparation of action plans for HPE, giving each worker a say in decisions and actions affecting her or him

Core Competencies for Human Performance Enhancement Practitioners (concluded)

[9] Implement the performance enhancement strategies	Human Performance Enhancement Implementor	• Ability to implement or coordinate implementation of HPE strategies, integrating them with organizational strategic plans	• Ability to implement or coordinate implementation of HPE strategies, integrating them with organizational culture, structure, and politics	• Ability to implement or coordinate implementation of HPE strategies, integrating them with work processes and work methods	• Ability to implement or coordinate implementation of HPE strategies, giving each worker a say in decisions and actions affecting her or him
[10] Evaluate results during and after implementation, feeding information back into step 1	Human Performance Enhancement Evaluator	• Ability to evaluate or coordinate evaluation of HPE strategies, integrating evaluation processes with organizational strategy evaluation	• Ability to evaluate or coordinate evaluation of HPE strategies, integrating evaluation processes with corporate culture, structure, and politics	• Ability to evaluate or coordinate evaluation of HPE strategies, integrating evaluation processes with work processes and work methods	• Ability to evaluate or coordinate evaluation of HPE strategies, giving each worker a say in evaluation processes and in feeding results back into future HPE strategies

Appendix II.

Assessing Human Performance Enhancement Competencies

A Data Collection Instrument

William J. Rothwell, Ph.D.
President
Rothwell & Associates

Instructions: *Competency Assessment* identifies the characteristics underlying the successful performance of exemplary workers. It can be past, present, or future-oriented.

One way to transform the traditional training and development department into a human performance enhancement (HPE) function is to establish an organization-specific HPE competency model and then build the competencies of the training and development staff until staff competencies match the HPE competencies.

Use this instrument to identify the HPE competencies critical to future success in your organization and then rate yourself against them. In the left column on the following pages, you will find statements describing HPE competencies. In the center column, *rate by circling a number how important you believe that competency is to future success in your job category in your organization.* Use the following scale:

1 = Not at all important
2 = Little importance
3 = Some importance
4 = Much importance
5 = Very much importance

Then, in the right-hand column, rate by *circling a number indicating how competent you believe yourself to be in that competency area at present.* Use the following scale:

1 = Not at all competent
2 = Little competence
3 = Some competence
4 = Much competence
5 = Very much competence

As you complete each role category on the instrument, compile a subtotal for the center and right columns and place the score in the appropriate box on each page. When you finish the entire instrument, copy your scores from each box to the appropriate totals at the end of the instrument. Then return the completed instrument to a designated survey administrator for scoring. The results of this study will be used to assess HPE competencies in this organization. Your participation is essential.

Competency Assessment

Directions: Rate the future importance of each competency and your present competency level of each of the HPE competencies for your job category in the organization.

Auditor (*Identifies what **is** happening*)

Human Performance Enhancement (HPE) Competency	Future Importance					Present Competence				
	Not At All=1	Little = 2	Some = 3	Much = 4	Very Much=5	Not At All=1	Little = 2	Some = 3	Much = 4	Very Much=5
1) Ability to examine needs and expectations of customers, suppliers, distributors, and stake-holders	1	2	3	4	5	1	2	3	4	5
2) Ability to formulate, assess, and convert organizational plans into HPE efforts or strategies	1	2	3	4	5	1	2	3	4	5
3) Ability to key improvement efforts to organizational mission and strategies	1	2	3	4	5	1	2	3	4	5
4) Ability to identify organizational strengths and weaknesses	1	2	3	4	5	1	2	3	4	5
5) Ability to examine work-flow within and between departments	1	2	3	4	5	1	2	3	4	5
6) Ability to detect bottle-necks in work processing	1	2	3	4	5	1	2	3	4	5
7) Ability to assess present competency levels	1	2	3	4	5	1	2	3	4	5
8) Ability to assess work-force supply	1	2	3	4	5	1	2	3	4	5
Competency Scores by Role:	**Future Importance Score:**					**Present Competency Score:**				

Competency Assessment (continued)

Visionary (*Identifies what **should be** happening*)

Human Performance Enhancement (HPE) Competency	Future Importance					Present Competence				
	Not At All=1	Little = 2	Some = 3	Much = 4	Very Much=5	Not At All=1	Little = 2	Some = 3	Much = 4	Very Much=5
9) Ability to identify customer needs and expectations	1	2	3	4	5	1	2	3	4	5
10) Ability to detect threats and opportunities in the organizational environment	1	2	3	4	5	1	2	3	4	5
11) Ability to locate world-class benchmarks of organizational performance	1	2	3	4	5	1	2	3	4	5
12) Ability to modify criteria of high-performance work (HPW) organizations to one corporate culture	1	2	3	4	5	1	2	3	4	5
13) Ability to identify employee needs and expectations	1	2	3	4	5	1	2	3	4	5
14) Ability to clarify ways to improve workflow to achieve break-through productivity increases	1	2	3	4	5	1	2	3	4	5
15) Ability to forecast future competency needs	1	2	3	4	5	1	2	3	4	5
16) Ability to assess work-force needs for the organization	1	2	3	4	5	1	2	3	4	5
Competency Scores by Role:	**Future Importance Score:**					**Present Competency Score:**				

Competency Assessment (continued)

Gap Assessor (*Clarifies present and future performance gaps*)

Human Performance Enhancement (HPE) Competency	**Future Importance**					**Present Competence**				
	Not At All=1	**Little = 2**	**Some = 3**	**Much = 4**	**Very Much=5**	**Not At All=1**	**Little = 2**	**Some = 3**	**Much = 4**	**Very Much=5**
17) Ability to compare *what is* and *what should be* in the organization's interactions with the external environment	1	2	3	4	5	1	2	3	4	5
18) Ability to compare *what is* and *what should be* in the organization's internal environment	1	2	3	4	5	1	2	3	4	5
19) Ability to compare *what is* and *what should be* in work processing	1	2	3	4	5	1	2	3	4	5
20) Ability to compare the difference between *what is* and *what should be* at the individual level	1	2	3	4	5	1	2	3	4	5
21) Ability to detect mis-match(es) between individual and the job in which she or he is placed	1	2	3	4	5	1	2	3	4	5
Competency Scores by Role:	**Future Importance Score:**					**Present Competency Score:**				

Competency Assessment (continued)

Human Performance Enhancement Facilitator

(Determines the present and future importance of performance gaps)

Human Performance Enhancement (HPE) Competency	Future Importance					Present Competence				
	Not At All=1	Little = 2	Some = 3	Much = 4	Very Much=5	Not At All=1	Little = 2	Some = 3	Much = 4	Very Much=5
22) Ability to determine the importance of gaps between *what is* and *what should be* in the organization's interactions with the external environment	1	2	3	4	5	1	2	3	4	5
23) Ability to determine the importance of gaps between *what is* and *what should be* within the organization	1	2	3	4	5	1	2	3	4	5
24) Ability to determine the importance of gaps between *what is* and *what should be* in work processing	1	2	3	4	5	1	2	3	4	5
25) Ability to determine the importance of gaps between what the worker *can do* and what the worker *should be able to do*	1	2	3	4	5	1	2	3	4	5
Competency Scores by Role:	**Future Importance Score:**					**Present Competency Score:**				

Competency Assessment (continued)

Strategic Troubleshooter (*Identifies the underlying causes of performance gaps*)

Human Performance Enhancement (HPE) Competency	Future Importance					Present Competence				
	Not At All=1	Little = 2	Some = 3	Much = 4	Very Much=5	Not At All=1	Little = 2	Some = 3	Much = 4	Very Much=5
26) Ability to isolate strategic mismatches in the organization's interactions with the external environment	1	2	3	4	5	1	2	3	4	5
27) Ability to benchmark with other organizations in the industry or best-in-class organizations	1	2	3	4	5	1	2	3	4	5
28) Ability to isolate large-scale and small-scale cause(s) of gaps within the organization	1	2	3	4	5	1	2	3	4	5
29) Ability to troubleshoot the cause(s) of gaps in the work or workflow	1	2	3	4	5	1	2	3	4	5
30) Ability to troubleshoot the cause(s) of performance gaps between worker and other performance environments (work level, work environment level, and organizational environment level)	1	2	3	4	5	1	2	3	4	5
Competency Scores by Role:	**Future Importance Score:**					**Present Competency Score:**				

Competency Assessment (continued)

Human Performance Enhancement Methods Specialist

(Selects HPE strategies, individually or collectively, to close performance gap(s) by addressing their underlying causes)

Human Performance Enhancement (HPE) Competency	Future Importance					Present Competence				
	Not At All=1	Little = 2	Some = 3	Much = 4	Very Much=5	Not At All=1	Little = 2	Some = 3	Much = 4	Very Much=5
31) Ability to identify possible HPE strategies	1	2	3	4	5	1	2	3	4	5
32) Ability to benchmark/ compare the application of HPE strategies in other organizations and in one corporate culture	1	2	3	4	5	1	2	3	4	5
33) Ability to excite enthusiasm among others about planning and implementing HPE strategies on an organizational scale	1	2	3	4	5	1	2	3	4	5
34) Ability to involve and empower others in the process of selecting HPE strategies on an organizational scale	1	2	3	4	5	1	2	3	4	5
35) Ability to excite enthusiasm among others about planning and implementing HPE strategies specific to work methods or processes	1	2	3	4	5	1	2	3	4	5
36) Ability to involve and empower others in the process of selecting HPE strategies linked to the work	1	2	3	4	5	1	2	3	4	5
37) Ability to identify and apply HPE strategies at the level of the individual workers	1	2	3	4	5	1	2	3	4	5
38) Ability to involve and empower the worker in the process of selecting HPE strategies linked to the individual	1	2	3	4	5	1	2	3	4	5
Competency Scores by Role:	**Future Importance Score:**					**Present Competency Score:**				

Competency Assessment (continued)

Forecaster of Consequences (*Assesses the likely outcomes of implementation to minimize negative side effects and maximize results*)

Human Performance Enhancement (HPE) Competency	Future Importance					Present Competence				
	Not At All=1	Little = 2	Some = 3	Much = 4	Very Much=5	Not At All=1	Little = 2	Some = 3	Much = 4	Very Much=5
39) Ability to forecast the likely consequences of HPE strategies as they may eventually affect relations with customers, suppliers, distributors, and other external stakeholders	1	2	3	4	5	1	2	3	4	5
40) Ability to forecast the likely consequences of HPE strategies as they may eventually affect intergroup and intragroup relations and performance inside an organization	1	2	3	4	5	1	2	3	4	5
41) Ability to forecast the likely consequences of HPE strategies on work processes and methods	1	2	3	4	5	1	2	3	4	5
42) Ability to forecast the likely consequences of HPE strategies on individual workers	1	2	3	4	5	1	2	3	4	5
Competency Scores by Role:	**Future Importance Score:**					**Present Competency Score:**				

Competency Assessment (continued)

Action Plan Facilitator (*Assesses the likely outcomes of implementation to minimize negative side effects and maximize results*)

Human Performance Enhancement (HPE) Competency	Future Importance					Present Competence				
	Not At All=1	Little = 2	Some = 3	Much = 4	Very Much=5	Not At All=1	Little = 2	Some = 3	Much = 4	Very Much=5
43) Ability to prepare and coordinate the preparation of action plans for HPE strategy, integrating them with organizational strategic plans	1	2	3	4	5	1	2	3	4	5
44) Ability to prepare and coordinate the preparation of action plans for HPE strategy, integrating them with organizational culture, structure, and politics	1	2	3	4	5	1	2	3	4	5
45) Ability to prepare and coordinate the preparation of action plans for HPE strategy, integrating them with work processes and methods	1	2	3	4	5	1	2	3	4	5
46) Ability to prepare and coordinate the preparation of action plans for HPE strategy, giving each worker a say in decisions and actions affecting him or her	1	2	3	4	5	1	2	3	4	5
Competency Scores by Role:	**Future Importance Score:**					**Present Competency Score:**				

Competency Assessment (continued)

Human Performance Enhancement Implementor (*Implements HPE strategy*)

Human Performance Enhancement (HPE) Competency	Future Importance					Present Competence				
	Not At All=1	Little = 2	Some = 3	Much = 4	Very Much=5	Not At All=1	Little = 2	Some = 3	Much = 4	Very Much=5
47) Ability to implement or coordinate implementation of HPE strategies, integrating them with organizational culture, structure, and politics	1	2	3	4	5	1	2	3	4	5
48) Ability to implement or coordinate implementation of HPE strategies, integrating them with work processes and methods	1	2	3	4	5	1	2	3	4	5
49) Ability to implement or coordinate implementation of HPE strategies, giving each worker a say in decisions and actions affecting him or her	1	2	3	4	5	1	2	3	4	5
Competency Scores by Role:	**Future Importance Score:**					**Present Competency Score:**				

Competency Assessment (continued)

Human Performance Enhancement Evaluator (*Evaluates results before, during, and after implementation, feeding information back into step 1 of the model*)

Human Performance Enhancement (HPE) Competency	Future Importance					Present Competence				
	Not At All=1	Little = 2	Some = 3	Much = 4	Very Much=5	Not At All=1	Little = 2	Some = 3	Much = 4	Very Much=5
50) Ability to evaluate or coordinate evaluation of HPE strategies, integrating evaluating processes with organizational strategy evaluation	1	2	3	4	5	1	2	3	4	5
51) Ability to evaluate or coordinate evaluation of HPE strategies, integrating evaluation processes with corporate culture, structure, and politics	1	2	3	4	5	1	2	3	4	5
52) Ability to evaluate or coordinate evaluation of HPE strategies, integrating evaluation processes with work processes or work methods	1	2	3	4	5	1	2	3	4	5
53) Ability to evaluate or coordinate evaluation of HPE strategies, giving each worker a say in evaluation processes and in feeding results back into future HPE strategies	1	2	3	4	5	1	2	3	4	5
Competency Scores by Role:	**Future Importance Score:**					**Present Competency Score:**				

Competency Assessment (continued)

Scoring: After you have completed the instrument, copy your scores from each role area on the instrument into the appropriate columns below. When you finish, return the completed instrument to the survey administrator.

ROLE CATEGORY	SCORES	
	Future Importance	Present Competence
Auditor		
Visionary		
Change Agent		
Human Performance Enhancement Facilitator		
Strategic Troubleshooter		
Human Performance Enhancement Methods Specialist		
Forecaster of Consequences		
Action Plan Facilitator		
Human Performance Enhancement Implementor		
Human Performance Enhancement Evaluator		
TOTALS:		

Competency Assessment (concluded)

Action Planning: For each role listed in the left-hand column below, indicate in the right-hand column what development activities you believe you should pursue in order to build your competencies in each role of an HPE practitioner. There are no "right" or "wrong" answers. However, to be most beneficial, you should ask for the advice of your organizational superior, subordinates, or others who may be well-positioned to comment on the competencies that you should concentrate on building and methods of building them. Add paper as needed. If you wish to establish a formal individual development plan that clarifies your personal developmental objectives, methods of achieving them, and measures of accomplishment, do so on separate paper.

ROLE	POSSIBLE DEVELOPMENTAL ACTIVITIES
Auditor	
Visionary	
Change Agent	
Human Performance Enhancement Facilitator	
Strategic Troubleshooter	
Human Performance Enhancement Methods Specialist	
Forecaster of Consequences	
Action Plan Facilitator	
Human Performance Enhancement Implementor	
Human Performance Enhancement Evaluator	

Appendix III.

Worksheets for Analyzing and Enhancing Human Performance

Appendix III

A Worksheet for Enhancing Human Performance

Directions: Use this worksheet to help you structure your thinking about ways to enhance human performance. Use the worksheet to troubleshoot problems with human performance or explore opportunities for human performance improvement. Answer each question appearing below. If possible, ask several people to conduct the same analysis separately. When everyone is finished, compare notes. Add paper if necessary.

1. What *is* happening? (*Describe the current situation.*)

2. What *should be* happening? (*Describe the vision of the ideal present or future.)*

Worksheet for Enhancing Human Performance (continued)

3. What is the gap between what *is* happening and what *should be* happening? (*Describe the gap at present and in the future.*)

4. How important is the gap between *what is* happening and *what should be* happening? (*Describe what results are stemming from the gap at present. Then describe what results are likely to stem from the gap in the future if no action is taken to narrow or close it. If possible, assess the dollar cost to the organization.)*

5. What is the underlying cause (or what are the underlying causes) of the gap between what is happening and what should be happening? (*Describe whether the problem stems from lack of knowledge or skill or from a lack of appropriate environmental conditions necessary to support high performance. If there are multiple causes of the performance problem, describe each one and explain how it contributes to the gap.*)

Worksheet for Enhancing Human Performance (continued)

6. What human performance enhancement strategy or strategies could, individually or collectively, most effectively narrow or close the gap between what is happening and what should be happening by addressing the underlying cause(s) of the human performance problem? (*Consider such strategies as providing more information to perform, training, providing clearer feedback, improving the timely feedback to performers, providing job or performance aids, clarifying work responsibility, providing opportunities to practice, providing adequate tools for performance, clarifying organizational plans, clarifying organizational policy, using progressive discipline, providing equipment other than tools, providing equipment, addressing job insecurity, clarifying reporting relationships, changing reward systems, providing ergonomically-supportive equipment, transferring individuals ill-suited to their present jobs, terminating wrong hires, or other strategies that can be identified to be used individually or collectively.*)

   List possible strategies to use to address the HPE issue:

   Establish measurable performance improvement objectives:

Worksheet for Enhancing Human Performance (concluded)

7. What are the likely outcomes of implementing the HPE strategy? (*What negative side effects are likely to happen in the future if the HPE strategy is implemented? How could the negative side effects be minimized?*)

8. What flexible action plan could guide implementation of the HPE strategy while considering the possible negative side effects of implementation? (*Describe who should do what and when to achieve what measurable results.)*

9. How will the results of the HPE strategy be evaluated before, during, and after implementation? (*Explain who will do it, why they will do it, how they will do it, and what results are sought.*)

A Worksheet for Applying Thomas Gilbert's Behavioral Engineering Model

Directions: Use this worksheet to analyze any human performance enhancement problem or opportunity for improvement. For each type of behavior in the left column, describe the current behavior under the second column, the status of accomplishment in the third column, and whether the performance is worthy (or not) in the right column. Worthy performance means that it meets expectations. Accomplishment refers to outcomes. Use this tool to guide your analysis and to pinpoint areas for improvement.

Type of Behavior	**Behavior** For each type of behavior below, how is it demonstrated? Describe the answer to that question for each cell below.	**Accomplishment** For each type of behavior below, what are the outcomes versus desired outcomes?	**Worthy Performance?** For each type of behavior below, how well does the accomplishment meet expectations? Does it? Indicate "yes" or "no."
Information			
Tools			
Incentives			
Knowledge			
Capacity			
Motives/ Motivation			

A Worksheet to Guide Analysis

Rothwell's Model for HPE	Thomas Gilbert's Behavioral Areas					
	Information	Tools	Incentives	Knowledge	Capacity	Motives
Analyze what is happening	What information do people have?	What tools and equipment do people have?	How are people incented?	How much knowledge do workers possess?	How well are people matched to work require-ments?	How motivated are people to perform?

A Worksheet to Guide Analysis (continued)

Rothwell's Model for HPE	Thomas Gilbert's Behavioral Areas					
	Information	**Tools**	**Incentives**	**Knowledge**	**Capacity**	**Motives**
Envision what should be happening	What information do people need?	What tools and equipment do people need?	How could incentives be improved?	How much knowledge should workers possess?	How well could the match between people and work be improved?	How could motivation be improved?

A Worksheet to Guide Analysis (continued)

Rothwell's Model for HPE	Thomas Gilbert's Behavioral Areas					
	Information	Tools	Incentives	Knowledge	Capacity	Motives
Clarify present and future performance gaps (make measurable differences between what *is* happening and what *should be* happening)	What is the measurable gap between the two cells above on this column?	What is the measurable gap between the two cells above on this column?	What is the measurable gap between the two cells above on this column?	What is the measurable gap between the two cells above on this column?	What is the measurable gap between the two cells above on this column?	What is the measurable gap between the two cells above on this column?

A Worksheet to Guide Analysis (continued)

Rothwell's Model for HPE	Thomas Gilbert's Behavioral Areas					
	Information	Tools	Incentives	Knowledge	Capacity	Motives
Determine the importance of performance gaps	What are the stakeholders, and how much does each stakeholder care about the gaps?	What are the stakeholders, and how much does each stakeholder care about the gaps?	What are the stakeholders, and how much does each stakeholder care about the gaps?	What are the stakeholders, and how much does each stakeholder care about the gaps?	What are the stakeholders, and how much does each stakeholder care about the gaps?	What are the stakeholders, and how much does each stakeholder care about the gaps?

A Worksheet to Guide Analysis (continued)

Rothwell's Model for HPE	Thomas Gilbert's Behavioral Areas					
	Information	Tools	Incentives	Knowledge	Capacity	Motives
Identify the underlying causes of performance gaps	Why are there gaps?	Why are there gaps?	Why are there gaps?	Why are there gaps?	Why are there gaps?	Why are there gaps?

A Worksheet to Guide Analysis (continued)

Rothwell's Model for HPE	Thomas Gilbert's Behavioral Areas					
	Information	Tools	Incentives	Knowledge	Capacity	Motives
Select HPE Strategies	How can gaps be closed by addressing underlying causes in the past and in the future?	How can gaps be closed by addressing underlying causes in the past and in the future?	How can gaps be closed by addressing underlying causes in the past and in the future?	How can gaps be closed by addressing underlying causes in the past and in the future?	How can gaps be closed by addressing underlying causes in the past and in the future?	How can gaps be closed by addressing underlying causes in the past and in the future?

A Worksheet to Guide Analysis (continued)

Rothwell's Model for HPE	Thomas Gilbert's Behavioral Areas					
	Information	Tools	Incentives	Knowledge	Capacity	Motives
Implement HPE strategies to address organizational environment problems or opportunities	How can HPE interventions be implemented to address problems that affect the environment outside the organization?	How can HPE interventions be implemented to address problems that affect the environment outside the organization?	How can HPE interventions be implemented to address problems that affect the environment outside the organization?	How can HPE interventions be implemented to address problems that affect the environment outside the organization?	How can HPE interventions be implemented to address problems that affect the environment outside the organization?	How can HPE interventions be implemented to address problems that affect the environment outside the organization?

A Worksheet to Guide Analysis (continued)

Rothwell's Model for HPE	Thomas Gilbert's Behavioral Areas					
	Information	Tools	Incentives	Knowledge	Capacity	Motives
Implement HPE strategies to address work environment problems or opportunities	How can HPE interventions be implemented to address problems that affect the organization?	How can HPE interventions be implemented to address problems that affect the organization?	How can HPE interventions be implemented to address problems that affect the organization?	How can HPE interventions be implemented to address problems that affect the organization?	How can HPE interventions be implemented to address problems that affect the organization?	How can HPE interventions be implemented to address problems that affect the organization?

A Worksheet to Guide Analysis (continued)

Rothwell's Model for HPE	Thomas Gilbert's Behavioral Areas					
	Information	Tools	Incentives	Knowledge	Capacity	Motives
Implement HPE strategies to address work problems or opportunities	How can HPE interventions be implemented to address problems that affect the work that people do in the organization?	How can HPE interventions be implemented to address problems that affect the work that people do in the organization?	How can HPE interventions be implemented to address problems that affect the work that people do in the organization?	How can HPE interventions be implemented to address problems that affect the work that people do in the organization?	How can HPE interventions be implemented to address problems that affect the work that people do in the organization?	How can HPE interventions be implemented to address problems that affect the work that people do in the organization?

A Worksheet to Guide Analysis (continued)

Rothwell's Model for HPE	Thomas Gilbert's Behavioral Areas					
	Information	Tools	Incentives	Knowledge	Capacity	Motives
Implement HPE strategies to address problems or opportunities	How can HPE interventions be implemented to address problems that affect the workers that do the work in the organization?	How can HPE interventions be implemented to address problems that affect the workers that do the work in the organization?	How can HPE interventions be implemented to address problems that affect the workers that do the work in the organization?	How can HPE interventions be implemented to address problems that affect the workers that do the work in the organization?	How can HPE interventions be implemented to address problems that affect the workers that do the work in the organization?	How can HPE interventions be implemented to address problems that affect the workers that do the work in the organization?

A Worksheet to Guide Analysis (concluded)

Rothwell's Model for HPE	Thomas Gilbert's Behavioral Areas					
	Information	Tools	Incentives	Knowledge	Capacity	Motives
Evaluate HPE strategies	How can HPE strategies be evaluated? How do results compare to the goals of the HPE strategies?	How can HPE strategies be evaluated? How do results compare to the goals of the HPE strategies?	How can HPE strategies be evaluated? How do results compare to the goals of the HPE strategies?	How can HPE strategies be evaluated? How do results compare to the goals of the HPE strategies?	How can HPE strategies be evaluated? How do results compare to the goals of the HPE strategies?	How can HPE strategies be evaluated? How do results compare to the goals of the HPE strategies?

Appendix IV.

Proposal Preparation Worksheet

Proposal Preparation Worksheet

Directions: Use this worksheet to help develop a written proposal to decision makers for HPE strategy implementation. For each question appearing in the left column below, provide an answer in the right column. When you finish, write up a proposal for an HPE strategy. If possible, solicit ideas from interested stakeholders as you develop the proposal.

Questions for Developing a Written Proposal	Answers
1. What is the background? (*Describe what is happening, what should be happening, why that gap is important in costs to the organization, and possible underlying causes of the performance problem or improvement opportunity.*)	

Proposal Preparation Worksheet (continued)

Questions for Developing a Written Proposal	Answers
2. What HPE strategy would likely narrow or close the gap between what is happening and what should be happening? (*Provide a recommended solution strategy and a justification for it. Then describe specific, measurable performance enhancement objectives to be achieved by the end of the HPE strategy implementation process.*)	
3. How should the HPE strategy be implemented? (*Describe the steps to be taken, step-by-step, in the project/HPE strategy implementation process.*)	

Proposal Preparation Worksheet (continued)

Questions for Developing a Written Proposal	Answers
4. How long will it take to implement the HPE strategy? (*Provide a chart depicting the timeline of the project compared to steps in the project. A Gantt chart is good for this purpose.*)	
5. What will be the costs of implementing the HPE strategy? (*Provide a detailed project budget.*)	

Proposal Preparation Worksheet (concluded)

Questions for Developing a Written Proposal	Answers
6. What will be the likely benefits of the HPE strategy? (*Provide estimated and measurable improvements over time, expressing milestones at which points improvements can be measured, if possible.*)	

Endnotes

Chapter 1

1. See William J. Rothwell and H. C. Kazanas, *Mastering the Instructional Design Process: A Systematic Approach*, 4th ed. (San Francisco: Pfeiffer & Company, 2008).
2. Ibid.
3. See, for instance, Ibraiz Tarique, *Seven Trends in Corporate Training and Development: Strategies to Align Goals with Employee Needs* (No City: FT Press, 2014). See also: Society for Human Resource Management, *SHRM Workplace Forecast: The Top Workplace Trends According to HR Professionals* (Alexandria, VA: Society for Human Resource Management, 2013); and, Deloitte Consulting LLP and Bersin by Deloitte, *Global Human Capital Trends 2014: Engaging the 21st-Century Workforce* (No City: Deloitte, 2014).
4. Tom Peters, *Thriving on Chaos: A Handbook for a Management Revolution* (New York: Harper & Row, 1987), p. 55.
5. See, for instance, treatments on the strategic importance of time in S. Brown, *Speed: Facing Our Addiction to Fast and Faster—And Overcoming Our Fear of Slowing Down* (Berkeley, CA: Penguin, 2014); M. Patterson, *Accelerating Innovation* (New York: Van Nostrand Reinhold, 1993); P. Smith and D. Reinertsen, *Developing Products in Half the Time* (New York: Van Nostrand Reinhold, 1991); and S. Wheelwright and K. Clark, *Revolutionizing Product Development—Quantum Leaps in Speed, Efficiency and Quality* (New York: Free Press, 1992).
6. William J. Rothwell, *The Just-In-Time Training Assessment Instrument* (Amherst, MA: Human Resource Development Press, 1996).
7. William J. Rothwell and H. C. Kazanas, *Improving On-the-Job Training: How to Establish and Operate a Comprehensive OJT Program*, 2nd ed. (San Francisco: Pfeiffer & Company, 2004).
8. See William J. Rothwell, *The Self-Directed On-the-Job Learning Workshop* (Amherst, MA.: Human Resource Development Press, 1996).
9. W. Edwards Deming, *Out of the Crisis* (Cambridge, MA: Massachusetts Institute of Technology, 1986), p. 135.
10. See the following sources for more information about high-performance work organizations: E. Appelbaum and R. Batt, *The New American Workplace: Transforming Work Systems in the United States* (Ithaca, NY: ILR Press, 1994); L. J. Bassi, E. I. Gould, J. Kulik, J. Zornitsky, *Thinking Outside the Lines: High Performance Companies in Manufacturing and Services* (Cambridge, MA: ABT, 1993); P. Osterman, "How Common Is Workplace Transformation and Who Adopts It?" *Industrial and*

Labor Relations 47, no. 2 (1990): 173–188; Geary Rummler and A. Brache, *Improving Performance: How to Manage the White Space on the Organization Chart* (San Francisco: Jossey-Bass, 1990); J. A. Wallace III, "Participation's Effects on Performance and Satisfaction: A Reconsideration of the Research Evidence," *Academy of Management Review* 19; no. 2 (1994): 312–330. See also Anonymous, "Strategic Planning: Training's Role in Building a High-Performance Workplace," *IOMA's Report on Managing Training & Development* 3, no. 8 (2003): 7; Anonymous, "Innovative Workplaces and Their Workers," *Monthly Labor Review* 126, no. 5 (2003): 32; and, John Godard, "Beyond the High-Performance Paradigm? An Analysis of Variation in Canadian Managerial Perceptions of Reform Programme Effectiveness," *British Journal of Industrial Relations* 39, no. 1 (2001); 25. More recently see: Andrew Morgan and Sarah Anthony, "Creating a High-Performance Workplace: A Review of Issues and Opportunities," *Journal of Corporate Real Estate* 10, no. 1 (2008): 27–39 and Accenture, *The High-Performance Workforce Study* 2010 (No City: Accenture, 2010).

11. *The Road to High Performance Workplaces* (Washington, DC: Office of the American Workplace, U.S. Department of Labor, 1995).

12. William J. Rothwell and David D. Dubois, *The High Performance Workplace Organizational Assessment Package* (Amherst, MA: Human Resources Development Press, 1996).

13. William J. Rothwell, Jackie Stavros, Roland Sullivan and Arielle Stavros, *Practicing Organization Change and Development: A Guide for Consultants*, 3rd ed. (San Francisco: Pfeiffer & Co., 2010).

14. William J. Rothwell and H. C. Kazanas, "Participation: Key to Integrating Planning and Training?" *Performance and Instruction* 26, no. 9, 10 (1987): 27–31.

15. William J. Rothwell, *The Workplace Learner: How to Align Training Initiatives with Individual Learning Competencies* (New York: Amacom, 2002).

16. William J. Rothwell, *The Action Learning Guidebook* (San Francisco: Pfeiffer & Company, 1999).

17. Patricia McLagan, *The Models*, vol. 3 in *Models for HRD Practice* (Alexandria, VA: American Society for Training and Development, 1989), p. 77.

18. Ibid.

19. Ibid.

20. Ibid.

21. William Rothwell, W. (Ed.). *ASTD Models for Human Performance: Roles, Competencies, and Outputs*. 2nd ed. (Alexandria, VA: The American Society for Training and Development, 2000), p. 79.

22. Ibid.
23. Ibid.
24. Ibid.
25. William Rothwell and David Dubois (Eds.), *In Action: Improving Human Performance* (Alexandria, VA: The American Society for Training and Development, 1998).
26. George Piskurich and Ethan Sanders, *ASTD Models for Learning Technologies: Roles, Competencies, and Outputs* (Alexandria, VA.: The American Society for Training & Development, 1998).
27. William Rothwell, Ethan Sanders, and Jeffrey Soper, *ASTD Models for Workplace Learning and Performance: Roles, Competencies, and Outputs* (Alexandria, VA: The American Society for Training and Development, 1999). See also Patty Davis, Jennifer Naughton and William Rothwell, "New Roles and New Competencies for the Profession: Are You Ready for the Next Generation?" *T + D* (April 2004): 26–36.
28. Ibid., p. 43.
29. Ibid., pp. 53–56.
30. Dennis L. Gay and Thomas J. LaBonte, "Demystifying Performance: Getting Started," *T + D* 57, no. 7 (2003): 40–45.
31. Paul Bernthal, Karen Colteryahn, Patricia Davis, Jennifer Naughton, and William J. Rothwell, *Mapping the Future: Shaping New Workplace Learning and Performance Competencies*. Alexandria, VA: The American Society for Training and Development, 2004.
32. Ibid.
33. Ibid.
34. Ibid.
35. Justin Arneson, William J. Rothwell, and Jennifer Naughton, (2013). *ASTD Competency Study: The Training and Development Profession Revisited*. Alexandria, VA: ASTD Press, 2013.
36. Ibid.
37. Ibid.
38. Kimo Hemmes, Catherine Long, and Gordon Rowland, "Situating Learning of Human Performance Technology," *Performance Improvement Quarterly 11*, no. 3 (1998).
39. Richard F. Gerson, "The Emotional Side of Performance Improvement," *Performance Improvement Journal 39*, no. 8 (2000).

40. Ingrid J. Guerra, "Key Competencies Required of Performance Improvement Professionals," *Performance Improvement Quarterly 16*, no. 1 (2003). See also such websites as:
    http://myweb.fsu.edu/jklein/articles/Klein_Fox_2004.pdf
    http://skills.salary.com/Job/Human-Performance-Consultant
    www.atlantis-press.com/php/download_paper.php?id=2113

Chapter 2

1. Patricia McLagan, *The Models,* vol. 3 in *Models for HRD Practice* (Alexandria, VA: American Society for Training and Development, 1989), p. 77.
2. Ibid.
3. David D. Dubois and William J. Rothwell, *Competency-Based Human Resource Management* (Palo Alto, CA: Davies-Black Publishing, 2004).
4. William A. Deterline and Marc J. Rosenberg (Eds.), "Human Performance Technology: What It Is . . . How It Works," in *Workplace Productivity Performance Technology: Success Stories* (Washington, DC: National Society for Performance and Instruction, 1992), p. 3.
5. Ibid.
6. D. Ainsworth, "Performance Technology: A View from the Fo'c'sle," *NSPI Journal* (May 1979): 3–7.
7. Harold D. Stolovich, "Performance Technology: An Introduction," *NSPI Journal* 21, no. 3 (1982): 16 [ERIC Document No. EJ 265 933].
8. Ibid.
9. Dale Brethower and Peter-Cornelius Dams, "Systems Thinking (and Systems Doing)" *Performance Improvement,* (January 1999): 37–52.
10. Ethan Sanders, "What Is HPI? What Makes a Performance Consultant? How Can You Tell If You Already Are One?" in George Piskurich (Ed.), *HPI Essentials* (Alexandria, VA.: ASTD, 2002), pp. 1–10.
11. Roger M. Addison, "Performance Technology Landscape," *Performance Improvement* (February 2003): 13–15.
12. Ronald L. Jacobs, *Human Performance Technology: A Systems-Based Field for the Training and Development Profession* (Columbus, Ohio: ERIC Clearinghouse on Adult, Career, and Vocational Education, National Center for Research in Vocational Education, Ohio State University, 1987), p. 41.
13. Ibid.
14. Ibid.

15. Ibid.
16. Ibid.
17. Ibid.
18. Ibid.
19. Ibid.
20. William Rothwell and H. C. Kazanas, *The Strategic Development of Talent* (Amherst, MA: HRD Press, 2004).
21. Ronald L. Jacobs, *Human Performance Technology,* p. 41.
22. Thomas F. Gilbert, *Human Competence: Engineering Worthy Performance* [Tribute Edition]. (Washington, DC: International Society for Performance Improvement, 1996), p. 179.
23. Ronald L. Jacobs, *Human Performance Technology,* p. 41.
24. Ibid.
25. Donald Katz and Robert Kahn, *The Social Psychology of Organizations,* 2nd ed. (New York: Wiley, 1978).
26. Ronald L. Jacobs, *Human Performance Technology,* p. 41.
27. See the discussion in William J. Rothwell and H. C. Kazanas, *Mastering the Instructional Design Process: A Systematic Approach*, 4th ed. (San Francisco: Pfeiffer & Co., 2008).
28. Thomas F. Gilbert, *Human Competence,* p. 179.
29. Ibid.
30. Ibid.
31. Robert F. Mager and Peter Pipe, *Analyzing Performance Problems or You Really Oughta Wanna,* 2nd ed. (Belmont, CA: David S. Lake Publishers, 1984), p. 13. This work has since been revised, as has the model, and is now Robert F. Mager and Peter Pipe, *Analyzing Performance Problems or You Really Oughta Wanna,* 3rd ed. (Atlanta, GA: The Center for Effective Performance, 1997).
32. R. Mason and E. Mitroff, *Challenging Strategic Planning Assumptions: Theories, Cases, and Techniques* (New York: Wiley, 1981).
33. See, for instance, Richard F. Gerson and Robbie G. Gerson, *Positive Performance Improvement: A New Paradigm for Optimizing Your Workforce* (Boston: Nicholas Brealey, 2006).

34. David L. Cooperrider and Diana Whitney, *Appreciative Inquiry: A Positive Revolution in Change* (San Francisco: Berrett-Koehler, 2005); David L. Cooperrider, Diana Whitney, and Jackie Stavros, *Appreciative Inquiry Handbook: For Leaders of Change*, 2nd ed. (San Francisco: Berrett-Koehler, 2008).

35. C. K. Prahalad and Gary Hamel, "The Core Competence of the Corporation," *Harvard Business Review* (May–June 1990).

36. Ronald L. Jacobs, *Human Performance Technology*, p. 41.

37. Harold D. Stolovich, Erica J. Keeps, and Daniel Rodrigue, "Skills Sets for the Human Performance Technologist," *Performance Improvement Quarterly* 8, no. 2 (1995): 40–67.

38. James D. Klein, "Empirical Research on Performance Improvement," *Performance Improvement Quarterly* 15, no. 1 (2002): 99–110.

39. Carol M. Sanchez, "Performance Improvement in International Environments: Designing Individual Performance Interventions to Fit National Cultures," *Performance Improvement Quarterly* 13, no. 2 (2000): 56–70. See also Clare Elizabeth Carey, "International HPT: Rx for Culture Shock," *Performance Improvement Quarterly* 38, no. 5 (1999): 49–54 and Clare Elizabeth Carey, "Globalinks Revisited: Cross-Cultural Conditions Affecting HPT," *Performance Improvement* 37, no. 2 (1998): 8–13.

40. Ryan Watkins, Doug Leigh, and Roger Kaufman, "A Scientific Dialogue: A Performance Accomplishment Code of Professional Conduct," *Performance Improvement* 39, no. 4 (2000): 17–22. See also Janet Roehl, Sheila Murphy and Susan Burns, "Developing a Model for Ethical Dialogue and Decisionmaking," *Performance Improvement Journal 39*, no. 5 (2000): 9–12; Monica Lee, "On Codes of Ethics, The Individual and Performance," *Performance Improvement Quarterly 16*, no. 2 (2003); Jim Stewart, "The Ethics of PI: A Polemical Overview," *Performance Improvement Quarterly 16*, no. 2 (2003); and, Tim Hatcher, "Social Responsibility as an Ethical Imperative in Performance Improvement," *Performance Improvement Quarterly 16*, no. 2 (2003). An outstanding example of standards on ethics and integrity is Academy of Human Resource Development, *Standards on Ethics and Integrity* (San Jose, CA.: Academy of Human Resource Development, 1999). Download the standards from the AHRD website at http://www.ahrd.org/ahrd/publications/index.htm

41. Joe Willmore, "How to Give 'Em Performance When They Insist on Training," *T + D* 56, no. 5 (2002): 54–59.

Chapter 3

1. Joe Willmore, "The Seven (Actually Nine) Deadly Sins of New Performance Consultants," *T + D* 57, no. 8 (2003): 28–30; James B. Rieley and Ian Clarkson, "How Companies Shift Organizational Behaviors to Improve Performance," *Journal of Organizational Excellence* 20, no. 4 (2001): 45–52.
2. John Farrell, "The Sweet Sound of Success," *HRMagazine* 47, no. 10 (2002): 81–84.
3. Ruth Charchian and Stephen L. Cohen, "Playing a New Game as a Training Professional: It's Your Move," *Performance Improvement* 39, no. 7 (2000): 12–17.
4. "Candor or Camouflage? Saying 'No' When Training Won't Work," *Training Directors' Forum Newsletter* 15, no. 9 (1999): 1–3.
5. Jack Wolf, "Einstein's Theories Are Relative to Training," *Training and Development* 53, no. 5 (1999): 21–22.
6. See, for instance, Diane Dormant, "The ABCDs of Managing Change," in M. Smith, ed., *Introduction to Performance Technology* (Washington, DC: National Society for Performance and Instruction, 1986), pp. 238–256.
7. Edgar Schein, *Organizational Culture and Leadership: A Dynamic View* (San Francisco: Jossey-Bass, 1985).
8. C. Geertz, *The Interpretation of Cultures* (New York: Basic Books, 1973).
9. See, for instance, R. Bellingham, B. Cohen, M. Edwards, and J. Allen, "Corporate Culture Audit," in R. Bellingham, B. Cohen, M. Edwards, and J. Allen (Eds.), *The Corporate Culture Sourcebook* (Amherst, MA: Human Resource Development Press, 1990); Cynthia Solomon, *Culture Audits: Supporting Organizational Success* (Alexandria, VA: ASTD Press, 2004); and, Kim S. Cameron and Robert E. Quinn, *Diagnosing and Changing Organizational Culture: Based on the Competing Values Framework*, 3rd ed. (San Francisco: Jossey-Bass, 2011).

Chapter 4

1. See what has been written on analysis and on organizational diagnosis. Examples: Danny Langdon, "Should We Conduct Cause Analysis or Change-of-State Analysis?", *Performance Improvement* 42, no. 9 (2003): 8–13; Mark Munley, "From a Training Request to Performance Consulting," *Performance Improvement* 42, no. 7 (2003): 18–25; Jana L. Pershing, "Interviewing to Analyze & Assess Performance Improvement Initiatives," *Performance Improvement* 42, no. 6 (2003): 30–36; Ryan Watkins and John Wedman, "A Process for Aligning Performance Improvement Resources and Strategies," *Performance Improvement* 42, 7 (2003): 9–17. Also see: Clayton Alder, "Organizational Diagnosis," *Administrative Science Quarterly* 18, no. 1 (1973): 122–124; Achilles Armenakis and Steven Brown, "Organizational Culture: Assessment and Transformation," *Journal of Change Management* 11, no. 2 (2011):

305–328; Michael Beer, "Organizational Diagnosis,"*American Scientist* 62, no. 3 (1974): 372–373; Kenneth J. Benson, *Organizational Analysis: Critique and Innovation* (Thousand Oaks, CA: Sage Contemporary Social Science Issues, 1977); Richard M. Burton, *Strategic Organizational Diagnosis and Design: Developing Theory for Application* (No City: Kluwer Academic Publishers, 1998); Robert Chia and Kay Guan, "Organizational Analysis as Deconstructive Practice," *De Gruyter Studies in Organization* 77, no. 13 (1996): 245; Tito Conti, *Organizational Self-Assessment* (No City: Springer, 2012); Larry L. Cummings, "Organizational Analysis," *Administrative Science Quarterly* 15, no. 4 (1970): 500–502; Doru Curteanu, "Organizational Culture Diagnosis—A New Model," Manager *(București) 11, no. 1 (2010): 14;* Michael I. Harrison, *Diagnosing Organizations: Methods, Models, and Processes* (Thousand Oaks, CA: Sage, 2004); Michael I. Harrison & Arie Shirom, *Organizational Diagnosis and Assessment: Bridging Theory and Practice* (Thousand Oaks, CA: Sage, 1998); Ann Howard, *Diagnosis for Organizational Change: Methods and Models* (No City: Guilford Press, 1994); Nebojsa Janicijevic, "Business Processes in Organizational Diagnosis," *Management* 15, no. 2 (2010): 85–106; *John P. Kotter, Organizational Dynamics: Diagnosis and Intervention* (Englewood Cliffs, NJ: Prentice-Hall, 1978); Harry Levinson, Janice Molinari & Andrew G. Spohn, *Organizational Diagnosis* (Cambridge, MA: Harvard University Press, 1972); Anne F. Marrelli, "A Universal Performance Model for Human Performance Technology: The Time Has Come," *Performance Improvement* 50, no. 9 (2011): 6–12; Alan D. Meyer, Anne S. Tsui & C. R. Hinings, "Configurational Approaches to Organizational Analysis," *The Academy of Management Journal* 36, no. 6 (1993): 1175–1195; Jeffrey Pfeffer, "Organizational Diagnosis," *Contemporary Sociology* 2, no. 5 (1973): 516-517; M. I. Reed, *Redirections in Organizational Analysis* (No City: Social Science Paperbacks, 1985); Allan Schmid, "Organizational Diagnosis," Journal of Economic Issues 8, no. 4 (1974): 942–943; Craig Schneier, "Organizational Diagnosis," *Industrial and Labor Relations Review* 27, no. 2 (1974): 311; Marvin Weisbord, *Organizational Diagnosis: A Workbook of Theory and Practice* (New York: Basic Books, 1978); Stephen G. Willcocks, "Organizational Analysis," *Leadership and Organization Development Journal* 15, no. 1 (1994): 29–32.

2. Jack J. Phillips, *Return on Investment in Training and Performance Improvement Programs*, 2nd ed. (London: Routledge, 2011).
3. Glenn E. Baker, A. Grubbs, and Thomas Ahern, "Triangulation: Strengthening Your Best Guess," *Performance Improvement Quarterly* 3, no. 3 (1990): 27–35.
4. *The Road to High Performance Workplaces* (Washington, DC: Office of the American Workplace, U.S. Department of Labor, 1995).
5. Gregory S. Guest, Emily E. Namey, & Marilyn L. Mitchell, *Collecting Qualitative Data: A Field Manual for Applied Research* (Thousand Oaks, CA: Sage, 2012).
6. Many of these classic sources were also cited in Chapter 4, note 1 above.

Chapter 5

1. The classic article on the subject is C. K. Prahalad and Gary Hamel, "The Core Competence of the Corporation," *Harvard Business Review* (May–June 1990): 79–91.

2. Ernest J. McCormick, *Job Analysis: Methods and Applications* (New York: AMACOM, 1979), p. 79. See also Michael T. Brannick, Edward L. Levine and Frederick P Morgeson, *Job and Work Analysis: Methods, Research, and Applications for Human Resource Management*, 2nd ed. (Thousand Oaks, CA: Sage, 2009); Darin Hartley, *Job Analysis at the Speed of Reality* (Amherst, MA: HRD Press, 1999); and, Erich P. Prien, Leonard D. Goodstein, Jeanette Goodstein and Louis G. Gamble, Jr., *A Practical Guide to Job Analysis* (San Francisco: Pfeiffer, 2009).

3. Geary Rummler, "Linking Job Standards to Organization Performance Needs," in Judith W. Springer (Ed.), *Job Performance Standards and Measures* (Madison, WI: American Society for Training and Development, 1980), pp. 214–215, 218.

4. William J. Rothwell and H. C. Kazanas, *The Strategic Development of Talent* (Amherst, MA: Human Resource Development Press, 2004).

5. Ibid.

6. Ibid.

7. See Robert J. House, "A Path–Goal Theory of Leadership Effectiveness," *Administrative Science Quarterly* (September 1971): 321–339; Robert J. House and Terence R. Mitchell, "Path–Goal Theory of Leadership," *Journal of Contemporary Business* (Autumn 1974): 81–98.

8. Robert C. Camp, *Benchmarking: The Search for Industry Best Practices That Lead to Superior Performance* (Milwaukee, WI.: Quality Press, 1989), p. 12.

9. James A. Pershing (Ed.), *Handbook of Human Performance Technology*, 3rd ed. (San Francisco: Jossey-Bass, 2006).

10. Robert S. Kaplan and David P. Norton, *The Balanced Scorecard: Translating Strategy into Action* (Cambridge, MA: Harvard Business Press, 1996).

11. Meir Liraz, *How to Implement Management by Objectives in Your Business a Step by Step Guide to Implementing MBO* (No City: Liraz Publishing, 2013). One of the classics on this topic is George S. Odiorne, *Management by Objectives: A System of Managerial Leadership* (New York: Pitman, 1968).

12. See, for example, David Parmenter, *Key Performance Indicators (KPI): Developing, Implementing, and Using Winning KPIs*, 2nd ed (New York: Wiley, 2010).

13. William J. Rothwell, Jackie Stavros, Roland Sullivan, and Arielle Stavros (Eds.), *Practicing Organization Development: A Guide for Consultants*, 3rd ed. (San Diego: Pfeiffer & Co., 2010).

14. See, for instance, A. Parasuraman, Valarie A. Aeithaml, and Leonard L. Berry, *A Conceptual Model of Service Quality and Its Implications for Future Research* (Cambridge, MA: Marketing Science Institute, 1984); Leonard L. Berry, David R. Bennett, and Carter W. Brown, *Service Quality: A Profit Strategy for Financial Institutions* (Homewood, IL: Dow Jones-Irwin, 1989); Jan Carlson, *Customer Focus Research: Building Customer Loyalty as a Strategic Weapon* (Atlanta, GA: Touchstone Marketing Research, 1989).
15. William Rothwell and H. C. Kazanas. *Developing In-House Leadership and Management Development Programs: Their Creation, Management, and Continuous Improvement* (Westport, CT: Greenwood Publishing, 1999).
16. William J. Rothwell and H. C. Kazanas, *Planning and Managing Human Resources: Strategic Planning for Personnel Management,* 2nd ed. (Amherst, MA: Human Resource Development Press, 2003).

Chapter 6

1. Robert C. Camp, *Benchmarking: The Search for Industry Best Practices That Lead to Superior Performance* (Milwaukee, WI: Quality Press, 1989), p. 123. See also Rob Reider, *Benchmarking Strategies: A Tool for Profit Improvement* (New York: John Wiley & Sons, 1999).
2. See, as just one example, Richard F. Gerson and Robbie G. Gerson, *Positive Performance Improvement: A New Paradigm for Optimizing Your Workforce* (Boston: Nicholas Brealey, 2006).
3. Roland Sullivan, Linda Fairburn and William Rothwell, "The Whole System Transformation Conference: Fast Change for the 21st Century" (pp. 115–142). In S. Herman (Ed.), *Rewiring Organizations for the Networked Economy: Organizing, Managing, and Leading in the Information Age* (San Francisco: Jossey-Bass/Pfeiffer, 2002).
4. Marvin Weisbord, *Productive Workplaces: Organizing and Managing for Dignity, Meaning, and Community* (San Francisco: Jossey-Bass, 1980).

Chapter 7

1. See, for instance, Jac Fitz-Enz, *The New HR Analytics: Predicting the Economic Value of Your Company's Human Capital Investments* (New York: Amacom, 2010); Jac Fitz-Enz, *The ROI of Human Capital: Measuring the Economic Value of Employee Performance*, 2nd ed. (New York: Amacom, 2009); Jac Fitz-Enz & Barbara Davison, *How to Measure Human Resource Management*, 3rd ed. (New York: McGraw–Hill, 2001).
2. Benedict Ochs, *Linking Strategy, Objectives, and Results in the Design and Evaluation of Executive Development Programs: Perspectives of Fortune 25 CEOs* (Ph.D. diss., Pennsylvania State University, 1995).

3. Alfred Korzybski, *Science and Sanity: An Introduction to Non-Aristotelian Systems and General Semantics,* 3rd ed. (Garden City, NY: Country Life Publishing Corporation, 1948).

Chapter 8

1. See Robert F. Mager and Peter Pipe, *Analyzing Performance Problems or You Really Oughta Wanna,* 3rd ed. (Atlanta, GA: The Center for Effective Performance, 1997).
2. Thomas F. Gilbert, *Human Competence: Engineering Worthy Performance* [Tribute Edition]. (Washington, DC: International Society for Performance Improvement, 1996), p. 179.
3. Geary A. Rummler and Alan P. Brache, "Transforming Organizations Through Human Performance Technology," in Harold D. Stolovich and Erica J. Keeps (Eds.), *Handbook of Human Performance Technology: A Comprehensive Guide for Analyzing and Solving Performance Problems in Organizations* (San Francisco: Jossey-Bass, 1992), pp. 32–49.
4. See the classic description of that in George Odiorne, *Strategic Management of Human Resources: A Portfolio Approach* (San Francisco: Jossey–Bass, 1984).
5. William J. Rothwell and H. C. Kazanas, "Developing Management Employees to Cope with the Moving Target Effect," *Performance and Instruction* 32, no. 8 (1993): 1–5.
6. Michael Cohen, James March, and Johan Olsen, "A Garbage Can Model of Organizational Choice," *Administrative Science Quarterly* 17, no. 1 (1972): 1–25.
7. Richard A. Swanson, *Analysis for Improving Performance: Tools for Diagnosing and Documenting Workplace Expertise* (San Francisco: Berrett–Koehler, 1994). See also Paul R. Niven, *Balanced Scorecard Step-by-Step: Maximizing Performance and Maintaining Results* (New York: Wiley, 2002).

Chapter 9

1. See Robert F. Mager and Peter Pipe, *Analyzing Performance Problems or You Really Oughta Wanna,* 3rd ed. (Atlanta, GA: The Center for Effective Performance, 1997).
2. See William J. Rothwell and H. C. Kazanas, *Mastering the Instructional Design Process: A Systematic Approach*, 4th ed. (San Francisco: Pfeiffer & Company, 2008).
3. See George Bernard Meyer, *Job Performance Analysis Practices As Perceived by Members of the National Society for Performance and Instruction* (Ph.D. diss., Pennsylvania State University, 1995).
4. See, for instance, Danny G. Langdon, "Selecting Interventions" (pp. 15–25) in Danny G. Langdon, Kathleen S. Whiteside and Monica M. McKenna (Eds.), *Intervention Resource Guide: 50 Performance Improvement Tools* (San Francisco: Jossey-Bass,

1999) and Ethan Sanders and Sivasailam, "Thiagi" Thiagarajan, *Performance Intervention Maps* (Alexandria, VA: ASTD, 2006).

5. William J. Rothwell, *Identifying and Solving Human Performance Problems: A Survey* (unpublished survey results, Pennsylvania State University, 1995).
6. W. Edwards Deming, *Out of the Crisis* (Cambridge, MA: Massachusetts Institute of Technology, 1986).
7. William J. Rothwell, Jackie Stavros, Roland Sullivan, and Arielle Stavros, *Practicing Organization Change and Development: A Guide for Consultants*, 3rd ed. (San Francisco: Pfeiffer & Co., 2010).
8. James Kouzes and Barry Posner, *The Leadership Challenge: How to Get Extraordinary Things Done in Organizations* (San Francisco: Jossey-Bass, 1989).

Chapter 10

1. C. K. Prahalad and Gary Hamel, "The Core Competence of the Corporation," *Harvard Business Review* (May–June 1990).
2. See, for instance, W. Rothwell, *The Intervention Selector, Designer and Developer, and Implementor (*Alexandria, VA: The American Society for Training and Development, 2000).
3. William J. Rothwell and H. C. Kazanas, *The Strategic Development of Talent* (Amherst, MA: Human Resource Development Press, 2004).
4. Kathleen Whiteside, "Implementing Interventions" (pp. 26–33) in Danny G. Langdon, Kathleen S. Whiteside and Monica M. McKenna (Eds.), *Intervention Resource Guide: 50 Performance Improvement Tools* (San Francisco: Jossey-Bass, 1999).

Chapter 11

1. Jay Galbraith, *Designing Complex Organizations* (Reading, MA: Addison–Wesley, 1973), p. 2.
2. Tom Burns and G. M. Stalker, *The Management of Innovation* (London: Tavistock Publications, 1961). See also: Dave Gray, Sunni Brown, and James Macanufo, *Gamestorming: A Playbook for Innovators, Rulebreakers, and Changemakers* (Cambridge, MA: O'Reilly Media, 2010); Christian Terwiesch and Karl Ulrich, *Innovation Tournaments: Creating and Selecting Exceptional Opportunities* (Cambridge, MA: Harvard Business Review, 2009).
3. Joan Woodward, *Industrial Organization: Theory and Practice* (London: Oxford University Press, 1965).
4. Alfred Chandler, *Strategy and Structure* (Garden City, NY: Anchor Books, 1966).

5. Richard Hall, "Interorganizational Structure Variation," *Administrative Science Quarterly* (December 1962): 295–308.

6. Paul R. Lawrence and Jay W. Lorsch, *Organization and Environment* (Boston: Harvard Business School, Division of Research, 1967).

7. Jay Galbraith, *Designing Complex Organizations,* p. 5.

Chapter 12

1. See the classic treatment in Ernest J. McCormick, *Job Analysis: Methods and Applications* (New York: AMACOM, 1979). Also see Kenneth E. Carlisle, *Analyzing Jobs and Tasks* (Englewood Cliffs, NJ: Educational Technology Publications, 1986), Ron Zemke and Thomas Kramlinger, *Figuring Things Out: A Trainer's Guide to Need and Task Analysis* (Reading, MA: Addison-Wesley, 1982), and (for a more recent treatment) see Darin E. Hartley, *Job Analysis at the Speed of Reality* (Amherst, MA: Human Resource Development Press, 1999) and Michael T. Brannick and Edward L. Levine, *Job Analysis: Methods, Research, and Applications for Human Resource Management in the New Millennium* (Thousand Oaks, CA: Sage Publishing, 2002). For more on task analysis, see the classic: David H. Jonassen, Wallace H. Hannum, and Martin Tessmer, *Handbook of Task Analysis Procedures* (Westport, CT: Greenwood Publishing, 1989).

2. See, for instance, such classics as Louis E. Davis and James C. Taylor, *Design of Jobs,* 2nd ed. (Santa Monica, CA: Goodyear Publishing, 1979); J. Richard Hackman and Greg R. Oldham, *Work Redesign* (Reading, MA: Addison-Wesley, 1980); and Paul M. Muchinsky, *An Empirical Investigation into the Construct Redundancy of Job Evaluation and Job Redesign* (Ph.D. diss., Iowa State University, 1992). See also Toni Hupp, Craig Polak, and Odin Westgaard, *Designing Work Groups, Jobs, and Work Flow* (San Francisco: Jossey-Bass, 1995). See also an important article: Joseph E. McCann III and Marilyn Bruckner, "Resdesigning Work: Motivations, Challenges and Practices in 181 Companies," *Human Resource Planning 17,* no. 4 (1994): 23–41.

3. William J. Rothwell, *Identifying and Solving Human Performance Problems: A Survey* (unpublished survey results, Pennsylvania State University, 2004).

4. Ibid.

5. Gerald M. Goldhaber, *Organizational Communication,* 3rd ed. (Dubuque, IA: William C. Brown, 1983), p. 17.

6. Ibid., p. 8.

7. See Gerald Goldhaber and D. Rogers, *Auditing Organizational Communication Systems: The ICA Communication Audit* (Dubuque, Iowa: Kendall/Hunt, 1979). Though somewhat dated, the book is still the classic on the subject of the organizational communication audit. More recent treatments include Cal W. Downs and Allyson D. Adrian, *Assessing Organizational Communication: Strategic Communication Audits*

(New York: Guilford Press, 2004) and Owen Hargie and Dennis Tourish, *Handbook of Communication Audits for Organizations* (New York: Psychology Press, 2000). See also: Owen Hargie and Dennis Tourish, *Auditing Organizational Communication: A Handbook of Research, Theory and Practice* (London: Routledge, 2009).

8. William J. Rothwell, *Identifying and Solving Human Performance Problems.*

9. Thomas F. Gilbert, *Human Competence: Engineering Worthy Performance* [Tribute Edition] (Washington, DC: International Society for Performance Improvement, 1996), p. 179.

10. David K. Berlo, *The Process of Communication* (New York: Holt, Rinehart & Winston, 1960).

11. David Nadler, *Feedback and Organization Development: Using Data-Based Methods* (Reading, MA: Addison-Wesley, 1977), p. 67.

12. Karen Stoneman, Edward Bancroft, and Carole Halling, "Upward Feedback for Organizational Change," *Performance and Instruction, 34,* no. 7 (1995): 12–17.

13. See Ron Jacobs, *Effects of Feedback for Training and Development: Selected Research Abstracts* (Columbus: Ohio State University, 1988).

14. See William J. Rothwell and H. C. Kazanas, *Mastering the Instructional Design Process: A Systematic Approach*, 3rd ed. (San Francisco: Pfeiffer and Co., 2004).

15. William J. Rothwell and H. C. Kazanas, *Improving On-the-Job Training: How to Establish and Operate a Comprehensive OJT Program*, 2nd ed. (San Francisco: Pfeiffer & Co., 2004).

16. William J. Rothwell and H. C. Kazanas, *Mastering the Instructional Design Process.*

17. The classic treatment of instructional objectives is found in Robert F. Mager, *Preparing Instructional Objectives: A Critical Tool in the Development of Effective Instruction,* 3rd ed. (Atlanta: The Center for Effective Performance, 1997).

18. The classic definition of formative evaluation is found in B. Bloom, J. Hastings, and G. Madaus, *Handbook on Formative and Summative Evaluation of Student Learning* (New York: McGraw–Hill, 1971).

19. Ibid.

20. See Mary L. Broad and John W. Newstrom, *Transfer of Training: Action-Packed Strategies to Ensure High Payoff from Training Investments*, reprint edition (Reading, MA: Perseus Press, 2001).

21. The most practical article ever printed on this subject is Mary Broad, "Management Actions to Support Transfer of Training," *Training and Development Journal, 36,* no. 5 (1982): 124–131. While dated, that article lists more than one hundred transfer-of-training strategies.

22. Compare descriptions of on-the-job and off-the-job training design in William J. Rothwell and H. C. Kazanas, *Improving On-the-Job Training,* 2nd ed. and in William J. Rothwell and H. C. Kazanas, *Mastering the Instructional Design Process*, 3rd ed.

23. See William J. Rothwell and H. C. Kazanas, *Developing In-House Leadership and Management Development Programs: Their Creation, Management, and Continuous Improvement* (Westport, CT: Greenwood Publishing, 1999). Also see William J. Rothwell and Joseph Benkowski, *Building Effective Technical Training: How To Develop Hard Skills in Organizations* (San Francisco: Jossey-Bass/Pfeiffer, 2002) and William J. Rothwell, Wesley Donahue, and John Park, *Creating In-House Sales Training and Development Programs: A Competency-Based Approach to Building Sales Ability* (Westport, CT: Quorum Books, 2002).

24. See William J. Rothwell, *The Self-Directed On-the-Job Learning Workshop* (Amherst, MA: Human Resource Development Press, 1996). See also William J. Rothwell, *The Workplace Learner: How to Align Training Initiatives with Individual Learning Competencies* (New York: Amacom, 2002).

25. Joe Harless, "Performance Technology and Other Popular Myths," *Performance and Instruction 24,* no. 6 (1985): 4.

26. Victor Vroom, *Work and Motivation* (New York: Wiley, 1967).

27. Bob Nelson, *1001 Ways to Reward Employees* (New York: Workman Publishing, 1994). See also Bob Nelson and Dean R. Spitzer, *The 1001 Rewards & Recognition Fieldbook: The Complete Guide* (New York: Workman Publishing, 2003).

Chapter 13

1. David Dubois, *Competency-Based Performance Improvement: A Strategy for Organizational Change* (Amherst, MA: Human Resource Development Press, 1993).

2. David Dubois and William Rothwell, *The Competency Toolkit*, 2 vols. (Amherst, MA: HRD Press, 2000).

3. David Dubois and William Rothwell, *Competency-Based Human Resource Management* (Palo Alto, CA: Davies-Black Publishing, 2004).

4. See, for instance, David McClelland, "Testing for Competence Rather Than for 'Intelligence'," *American Psychologist, 28,* no. 1 (1973): 1–14; David McClelland, *A Guide to Job Competency Assessment* (Boston: McBer and Co., 1976).

5. For a more complete description of Rapid Results Assessment, see William J. Rothwell, *Effective Succession Planning: Ensuring Leadership Continuity and Building Talent from Within,* 2nd ed. (New York: AMACOM, 2004).

6. A classic book on employee selection is Richard D. Arvey and Robert H. Faley, *Fairness in Selecting Employees,* 2nd ed. (Reading, MA: Addison-Wesley, 1988). Also see Robert Wood and Tim Payne, *Competency-Based Recruitment and Selection* (New York: John Wiley & Sons, 1998) and Robert D. Gatewood and Hubert S. Feild *Human Resource Selection* (Cincinnati, OH: South-Western College Publishing, 2000).

Chapter 14

1. So much has been written on training evaluation that it is nearly impossible to capture it all. But several key sources are worth consulting first: Donald L. Kirkpatrick, *Evaluating Training Programs: The Four Levels*, 2nd ed. (San Francisco: Berrett-Koehler, 1998); Jack J. Phillips, *Return on Investment in Training and Performance Improvement Programs*, 2nd ed. (Burlington, MA: Butterworth-Heinemann, 2003); Jack Phillips and Ron Stone, *How to Measure Training Results: A Practical Guide to Tracking the Six Key Indicators* (New York: McGraw-Hill, 2002). For more, see: Judith Hale, *Performance Based Evaluation: Tools and Techniques to Measure the Impact of Training* (San Francisco: Jossey-Bass/Pfeiffer, 2002), Judith Hale, *The Performance Consultant's Fieldbook: Tools and Techniques for Improving Organizations and People* (San Francisco: Jossey-Bass/Pfeiffer, 1998). See also Mel Silberman (Ed.), *The Consultant's Toolkit: High-Impact Questionnaires, Activities and How-To Guides for Diagnosing and Solving Client Problems* (New York: McGraw-Hill, 2000).
2. See William J. Rothwell and H. C. Kazanas, *Developing In-House Leadership and Management Development Programs: Their Creation, Management, and Continuous Improvement* (Westport, CT: Greenwood Publishing, 1999).
3. Dave Francis and Mike Woodcock, *Unblocking Organizational Values* (Glenview, IL: Scott, Foresman & Co., 1990), p. 3.
4. Ibid., pp. 3–4.
5. For more ideas on forecasting the financial benefits of HPE, see Richard A. Swanson, *Assessing the Financial Benefits of Human Resource Development* (Reading, MA: Perseus Press, 2001).
6. See, for instance, the classic book on the subject: B. Bloom, J. Hastings, and G. Madaus, *Handbook on Formative and Summative Evaluation of Student Learning* (New York: McGraw-Hill, 1971).
7. Ibid.
8. William J. Rothwell and H. C. Kazanas, *Developing In-House Leadership and Management Development Programs.*
9. Donald Kirkpatrick, "Techniques for Evaluating Training Programs," *Journal of the American Society for Training and Development* [now *Training and Development*] *14,* no. 1 (1960): 13–18. While old, the article remains a classic.

10. The classic article on this topic is Robert O. Brinkerhoff, "The Success Case: A Low-Cost High-Yield Evaluation," *Training and Development Journal 37,* no. 8 (1983): 58–61.

11. See Sharon Korth, "Consolidating Needs Assessment and Evaluation," *Performance Improvement 40,* no. 1 (2001): 38–43; Adele Sommers, "When Performance Improvement Efforts Fizzle, Stumble, or Stall," *Performance Improvement 39,* no. 9 (2000): 20–26; Debra Sieloff, "The Bridge Evaluation Model," *Performance Improvement 38,* no. 10 (1999): 14–18; Judith Hale, "Eleven Techniques to Jump-Start Performance Dialogue," *Performance Improvement 37,* no. 1 (1998): 24–26.

Epilogue

1. Danny G. Landon, "A Look into the Future of Human Performance Technology," *Performance Improvement 36,* no. 6 (1997): 6–9 and Marc Luoma, "The Future of Performance Improvement in International Health," *Performance Improvement 42,* no. 8 (2003): 29–32. See also: Roger Kaufman and Mariano L. Bernardez, "Human Performance Technology and Its Future," *Performance Improvement Quarterly 25,* no. 1 (2012): 5–11.

Index

Made in the USA
Middletown, DE
12 January 2016